# Sea War

# Sea War

## Great Naval Battles
## of World War II

FRANK PEARCE

ROBERT HALE · LONDON

Robert Hale Limited
Clerkenwell House
Clerkenwell Green
London EC1R 0HT

**British Library Cataloguing in Publication Data**

Pearce, Frank, *1909–*
Sea war 1939–45
1. World War   2. Naval operations by Great Britain.
Royal Navy
I. Title
940.54′5941

ISBN 0–7090–4013–X

Photoset in North Wales by
Derek Doyle & Associates, Mold, Clwyd.
Printed in Great Britain by
St Edmundsbury Press Ltd, Bury St Edmunds, Suffolk.
Bound by WBC Bookbinders Limited.

# Contents

# *Maps*

# *Illustrations*

*Between pages 64 and 65*

*Between pages 128 and 129*

PICTURE CREDITS

Peter Gibbings: 2. All other pictures were supplied courtesy of the Imperial War Museum.

# *Acknowledgements*

The author acknowledges with gratitude the contributions provided by those who served in the ships mentioned and to others closely associated with the events, among whom are:

Vice-Admiral Sir Arthur Fitzroy-Talbot KBE, CB, DSO and Bar, RN (Retd)
Vice-Admiral Sir George Raper KCB, CB, RN (Retd)
Rear-Admiral G.H. Collett CB, DSC, RN (Retd)
Captain L.S. Saunders DSO, RN (Retd)
Captain H.R. Harold OBE, RN (Retd)
Captain J.W. Daniels RM (Retd)
Captain G. Roberts CBE, RD (Retd)
Lieutenant-Colonel R.F.V. Griffiths OBE, RM (Retd)
Commander P. Rees RN (Retd)
Commander J. Johnson RN (Retd)
Commander A.J. Bailey OBE, RN (Retd)
Commander J.B. Herapath DSC, RN (Retd)
Commander P.R. House OBE, RN (Retd)
Commander G. Mann RN (Retd)
Commander F. Bradley DSC, RN (Retd)
Lieutenant-Commander C. Broadway RN (Retd)
Paymaster Lieutenant-Commander B.C. McLean RN (Retd)
Flight-Colonel Ernst August Roth, German Air Force (Retd)

The HMS *Gloucester* Association
The HMS *Orion* Association

F. Moulder                              P. Gibbings
W. Crocker                              R. Wainwright
J. Rowntree                             I. Easterbrook (Mrs)

F.C. Hunter
I. Davis
E. Le Tissier
R. Robinson
F. Pick
M. Flynn
J. Oddynorman (Mrs)
W. James
M. Finn
R. Riggs
P. Palmer
I. Biddington
R. Apps
J. Hartnell (Mrs)
J. Edmonds
R. Cole
C. Pearson
G. McKay
C. Beggs
C. Ashman
R. Mullaney
E. Rickard
C. Churchward
N. Butler
J. Tithecott

H. Isaac
P. Milborrow (Mrs)
B. Miller
W. Miller
V. Theobald
L. Bounty (Mrs)
A. Start
L. Bradley
M. Pascoe
W. Fiddick
H. Cook
R. Phillips
W. Jones
R. Bennett
C. Long
F. Woodley
W. Amitham
F. Hodges
R. Levick
P. Jefford
J. Doyle
J. Harper
G. Stripe
Ritter von Berger (Mrs)

Special thanks are due to Lieutenant-Commander J.R. Smith, RN (Retd) Chief Librarian at the Plymouth Naval History Library, for much assistance in research.

Also to my son, Derek Pearce, for diagram contribution, to the staff of the Paignton Library and to Plymouth Sound Radio Station.

To Mr Peter Gibbings for permission to publish photographs.

The Battle of Britain is about to begin. Let us therefore
brace ourselves to our duties, so bear ourselves
that men will say ... 'This was their finest hour.'

The Rt. Hon. Winston Spencer Churchill

Prime Minister of Great Britain
and First Lord of the Admiralty, 1940–45

# Introduction:
# The Price of Appeasement

When at the close of the First World War, the Germans sailed their High Seas Fleet into Scapa Flow on 21 November 1918 under the terms of surrender, it was assumed that this, along with other transactions of reparation, would bring about a situation whereby that nation would never again be able to launch war as she had done three times in the preceding hundred years – 1814, 1870 and 1914. The war-weary people of Great Britain and France who thought that the firing of the last shot on 11 November 1918 heralded future peace were soon to be sadly disillusioned. Hardly had the anchors of the Kaiser's defeated fleet settled on the sea bed at Scapa, than moves were afoot in Germany to re-arm and to regain her former power as a warring nation. Although at the end of 1918 Britain had the most powerful navy in the world, many of its ships were out of date and nearing the end of their useful lives. This created a difficult situation, for Britain needed a large navy to protect her Empire and honour her global commitments.

However, under the terms of the Washington Treaty of 1921 she found herself handicapped by an inadequate and belated programme of new construction governed by self-imposed limitations. At that time, in a political climate favourable to economics and disarmament, international attempts had been made to reduce the size of warships and navies. At the London Naval Conference in 1930, the leading powers drew up a set of conditions which, though favourable to the Americans who dictated them, was conceded by Great Britain to her loss.

It was in this climate of military stagnation that Adolf Hitler vowed his revenge and proclaimed his hatred of the enemies of the so-called glorious Fatherland. Although the Allies, triumphant but

13

crippled under the cost of the war, had asserted they would squeeze Germany dry for her cruel aggression – this to pacify the people – the clauses were never enforced. In fact, while Germany was repaying demands of £1,000 million mainly by surrender of capital assets, the United States and Britain were loaning her a total of £1,500 million, which allowed the ruin of war in that country to be repaired, the factories to be restarted and a re-armament programme to begin.

Undaunted by restrictive treaties conceived by the Allies which she failed to recognize, Germany set about secretly building 12,000-ton pocket battleships and the production of submarines which the Treaty of Versailles directly forbade her to do. By 1934, the Germans had laid down two battle-cruisers each of 32,000 tons, the *Scharnhorst* and *Gneisenau*; between then and 1937, two fast battleships of 43,000 tons, *Bismarck* and *Tirpitz*; five cruisers, *Lützow, Seydlitz, Prinz Eugen, Blücher* and *Admiral Hipper* each of 14,000 tons; and an advanced programme of 200 submarines. Such was Germany's construction capability that by the end of World War II she had built or was in the act of building 4,000 submarines. The Italians also, in direct defiance of treaty obligations had laid down two battleships of 42,000 tons, *Littorio* and *Vittorio Veneto* and a powerful force of heavy cruisers. Japan too, renouncing naval treaties, launched a massive building programme comprising nine big capital ships and a fleet of heavy cruisers to support their grandiose plans for conquests in the Far East. So the re-armament race began, with the obvious threat of another war.

In 1933 – the ingredients for such a calamity already in place – Britain had sunk to be the fifth air power. Worse still, the ten-year programme for gradual re-armament was delayed for another year – this despite the march of events in Germany. Even at this early stage, German military forces amounted to over a million men partially equipped. Incredibly, it was at this time that the former Labour leader Ramsey MacDonald with the agreement of the then Prime Minister Stanley Baldwin proposed that Britain and France should reduce their air forces to 500 planes apiece. As 1933 drew to a close, the news from Germany was even more alarming and Churchill in the Commons was forced to say:

Not one of the lessons of the past has been learned, not one of them has been applied and the situation is incomparably more dangerous. Then we had the navy and no air menace. We cannot say that now. This cursed hellish invention and development of war from the air has revolutionised our position. We are not the same country we used to be when we were an island only twenty years ago.

But the speech did little good. At this time, the Labour and Liberal parties remained impassive to the grave events unfolding. Both urged further disarmament. Those who differed with them were called 'warmongers'.

In July 1934, the Government made a token proposal to strengthen the Royal Air Force by 820 planes but this was only to be completed over the *next five years*. In the meantime, Germany was rapidly building up her existing air force. The response to this proposal was beyond belief. The Labour and Liberal parties moved a vote of censure: 'We regret that His Majesty's Government should enter upon a policy of re-armament ... certain to jeopardize the prospects for international agreement.'

In May of the following year 1935, Baldwin made the shocking confession that he was wrong about the German re-armament figures. No single minister was responsible he said – the whole Government was to blame. Despite this, again nothing was done to redress the situation and Britain drifted on in its apathy and to the disaster which would erupt within four years. There now came another setback, as Italy, under the dictatorship of Mussolini, transferred its support to Hitler complete with a considerable army, navy and air force. It was a move which was to cost Britain dearly in its fight to maintain a hold on the Mediterranean.

By this time, Hitler felt himself in a position of such power and authority that on 7 March 1936, he ordered his army to march into and occupy the Rhineland which under the Treaty of Versailles had been demilitarized.

On the retirement of Stanley Baldwin in 1937, Neville Chamberlain took over the reins of Prime Minister. In contrast to Baldwin's *laissez-faire* attitude to European affairs, Chamberlain, self-confident and opinionated, professed to understand the whole range of European policy and indeed that of the whole world. With a narrow, sharp efficiency, he tightly controlled all military expenditure and as a result became the undisputed opponent of all emergency measures. Unfortunately, his decisive judgements on affairs at home and abroad were partnered with a conviction that his name would go down in history as the twentieth-century peacemaker. To achieve this, he was prepared to place the country and himself at great risk in a policy of appeasement – a course of action that was to bring Great Britain to the brink of disaster. Towards the end of the year, it was revealed from reliable sources that Hitler was spending the equivalent of £1,000 million per annum on re-armament. It certainly wasn't for defence, for no country threatened him and indeed no country was in a position to threaten him.

Early in the New Year January 1938, there came a ray of hope which might well have brought a satisfactory conclusion to what appeared to be the certainty of war. Franklin D. Roosevelt, the then US President, sent a confidential letter to Chamberlain offering to use his influence to bring together the governments of Britain, France, Germany and Italy to discuss the chances of a general settlement. This offer Chamberlain refused on the grounds that it might offend the dictators! And so the last frail chance to deliver the world from the impending holocaust was lost, by the attitude of one man who spurned the outstretched hand from across the Atlantic.

Hitler now revealed himself in his true colours, for having proclaimed to the world that Germany had no further territorial demands in Europe, his troops entered Austria on 12 March and possessed it. Two months later he was ready to swallow Czechoslovakia.

Chamberlain had already remonstrated with the German Chancellor on two previous occasions, and on 29 September 1938, he again flew to Germany to meet Hitler. On his return to London, he waved a piece of paper signed by the Chancellor and himself in which it had been agreed that Czechoslovakia would be ceded to Germany without resistance by that nation and without interference from England or France. As he addressed the delighted crowd from the windows of Downing Street later that day, he declared, 'I believe it is peace in our time.' The following day the Czechs bowed to the Munich decision and registered their protest against an imposed course of action in which they had no choice.

At this time, Germany's forces were immensely strong. Her army was estimated to number 3 million with twelve armoured divisions. Her output of aircraft for 1939 alone amounted to 5,000 with an industry so organized it was producing 1,000 planes per month and increasing. However, as far as the navy was concerned, Britain was superior. At the outbreak of war the comparative strengths were as follows:

*Germany*
2 battleships, 2 battle-cruisers, 3 pocket battleships, 5 heavy cruisers, 6 light cruisers, 56 destroyers and a possible 100 submarines.

*British Commonwealth including the Dominions*
12 battleships, 3 battle-cruisers, 7 aircraft-carriers, 15 cruisers, 116 destroyers and 56 submarines.

But this seeming advantage was narrowed by Britain's global commitments. Whereas Germany had no overseas territories to defend, Britain had an Empire covering over 13 million square miles and responsible for 450 million people. Her sea-lanes and ocean routes had to be kept open. As will be seen in the events described, she was committed to fighting the menace of the pocket battleships and submarines raiding our lifeline of convoys in the North Atlantic, the South Atlantic, the Arctic Ocean, the Far East and the Mediterranean, where Mussolini's fleet comprised 4 battleships, 19 cruisers, 59 destroyers, 68 torpedo boats and 108 submarines.

On 1 September 1939, Hitler, despite all his solemn assurances that he had no further territorial claims, launched a full-scale military attack on Poland. When the news was received at Downing Street, Chamberlain was devastated. All his beliefs in the integrity of the German Chancellor, all his assertions there would be no war, all his resistance to re-armament, all his dreams of 'peace in our time', were shattered. In the depths of despair, Chamberlain issued his famous ultimatum.

Having gambled all on his policy of conciliation and lost, Chamberlain could now only contemplate the ruin that lay around him; a broken man staring into a future for which he was neither ready nor equipped. Great Britain was an island with its bulwark and first line of defence the Royal Navy. Who should now lead it and hopefully assure its survival? Only one man could fill that post: Winston Churchill as First Lord of the Admiralty, a position he had successfully occupied twenty-five years earlier in the First World War. Later that day of 3 September, Chamberlain sent for him and offered him the post of First Lord and a seat on the War Cabinet. Having been denied any ministerial position for several years because of his unpopular and constant warnings of impending war, he accepted readily. Such was the urgency of the situation that he

declined to wait formally to receive his office from the King, and by
six o'clock that evening arrived at the Admiralty to take charge.
Immediately a signal was flashed around the fleet: 'Winston is
back.'

And so Britain went to war, naked, vulnerable and facing with
resolute urgency the impossible task of trying to repair in a few
weeks, months, the damage caused by neglect, indifference and the
placatory posture of its leaders of the time.

# 1    *The Loss of* HMS **Courageous**

*At the outbreak of hostilities in World War II, the Royal Navy commissioned every available ship, but because of Britain's state of unreadiness they were rushed to sea, many carrying crews of untrained young conscripts and grey-haired Royal Naval Reserve pensioners.*

*Unwisely deployed on anti-submarine patrol in the Western Approaches, the aircraft-carrier* Courageous *was torpedoed and sunk with heavy loss of life, caused mainly by the inefficiency of life-saving equipment.*

Following Hitler's invasion of Poland, there was world-wide amazement when his expected attack on the West failed to materialize. Fully occupied with his eastward advance, he held back his attack on the West for a while. This pause of war activity against Britain and France by land and air forces during the autumn and winter of 1939 led to the period's being referred to as 'the phoney war'.

At sea, however, things were far different. On that first day, the Atlantic liner *Athenia*, outward-bound from Liverpool, was torpedoed by submarine *U-30* and sunk 250 miles north-west of Ireland. The rule, unconditionally accepted by Germany, that no passenger ship should be sunk without warning and without giving the passengers and crew the opportunity to take to the boats was ignored. Worse still, Goebbels, the official German propagandist, asserted that the ship had been sunk by Britain to arouse the sympathy of the United States, some of whose citizens were on board. (On different occasions, his propaganda machine stated that the ship had been sunk in four different ways, by submarine, destroyers, a mine and sabotage. He did not even take the trouble

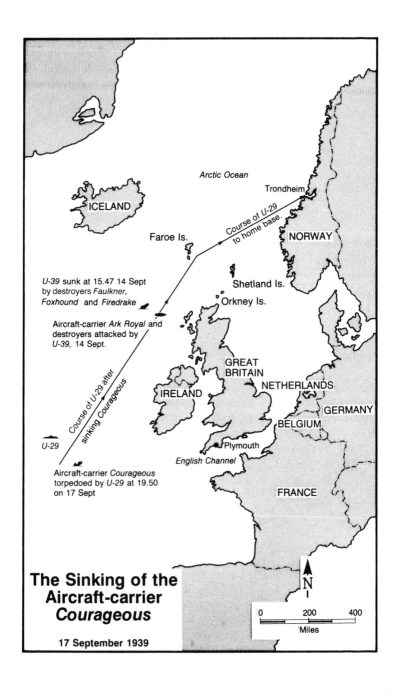

Arctic Ocean

Trondheim

*Course of U-29 to home base.*

ICELAND

Faroe Is.

NORWAY

*U-39* sunk at 15.47 14 Sept
by destroyers *Faulkner*,
*Foxhound* and *Firedrake*

Shetland Is.

Orkney Is.

Aircraft-carrier *Ark Royal* and
destroyers attacked by
*U-39*, 14 Sept.

GREAT
BRITAIN

*Course of U-29 after
sinking Courageous*

NETHERLANDS

IRELAND

GERMANY

BELGIUM

*U-29*

Plymouth

*English Channel*

FRANCE

Aircraft-carrier *Courageous*
torpedoed by *U-29* at 19.50
on 17 Sept

N

# The Sinking of the
# Aircraft-carrier
# *Courageous*

### 17 September 1939

0    200    400
Miles

to stick to the same lie.) Of the 862 people aboard, 112 were killed, the remainder being rescued by British warships, a Norwegian cargo boat, an American freighter and a Swedish yacht. This was the first of forty merchant ships sunk that month.

Two weeks later, on the 17th, the Royal Navy suffered its first loss of a major ship when the aircraft-carrier *Courageous* was torpedoed in the Western Approaches by the submarine *U-29*. This 22,500-ton Devonport ship was originally a large cruiser built between the two wars and had been converted into a carrier in the 1930s.

The sinking of *Courageous*, an old ship by fleet standards, was a tragic saga of events attending a capital ship that was sent to sea unprepared, with a crew of recalled, ageing naval pensioners and a few youngsters, untrained for the task assigned to them, many joining the ship in civilian clothes. Against this, one has to consider the fact that the war was then only fourteen days old.

The result, when war did come, was chaos, with Britain's forces, especially the Navy, unready for the horrendous conflict in which they would be engaged for the next five or six years.

It seems incredible, for instance, that the ship's company of *Courageous*, over 1,200 men, were sent to sea without lifebelts being issued; that the large Carley floats attached to the sides of the ship, which in the event of sinking, in theory at least, could be released at the tug of a rope and dropped into the sea, enabling a considerable number of men to be supported, were so stuck to the ship's sides with generations of paint that they were immovable. In fact, the ropes securing them had been painted twice a year for some twenty years, and no amount of effort or even knife hacking could release them. No effort had been made to check if they were operational. In the Swordfish aircraft section, the story was equally lamentable: no spares of any sort for the engines, no manuals for training, and few tools to make repairs or adjustments. Only four pans of ammunition could be allotted to each plane, and there were no sights for the Lewis guns they carried.

The story of the sinking of *Courageous* remained somewhat of a mystery for years. Despite extensive enquiries, relatives of those who perished gained little information as to the whereabouts or the circumstances of her sinking. Very few details emerged and even today the Public Record Office has a closure on some documents relating to *Courageous* extending to the year 2015. However, through interviews with the few still living, a much clearer picture emerges. The author also, by the permission and courtesy of Mr Peter Gibbings of Devon, whose father was sadly lost in the sinking, has been able to examine the log-book of the German commander of the U-boat which sank *Courageous*, details of which are here recorded.

On 17 September the carrier, positioned 350 miles west of Ireland with its four escorting destroyers, *Inglefield, Intrepid, Impulsive* and *Ivanhoe*, investigating a report that German U-boats were operating out of southern Ireland, received a signal that the merchant ship SS *Kafiristan* was being shelled by an enemy submarine on the Atlantic edge of the Bay of Biscay. Two of the escorts, *Inglefield* and *Intrepid*, raced off to pick up her passengers and crew, while the carrier's Swordfish flew off to find and attack the U-boat. The submarine was eventually sighted by one of the aircraft, which began its attack. However, owing to an error in the bomb connections, the leads had been plugged into the wrong sockets, and when the Swordfish dived over the target, and the firing button was pressed, it released only smoke floats instead of bombs, and the U-boat escaped.

At 16.30 the patrolling aircraft returned to land on the carrier's flight deck.

The Admiralty's Board of Inquiry report states that at this time none of the carrier's patrol planes was up, as, owing to the incompleteness of training, the captain did not wish to have too many aircraft in the air at one time. He was now heading in the direction of *Kafiristan*'s position to lessen the distance of his returning striking force. Speed was increased and by 18.40 the ship was racing along at 26½ knots to meet the returning aircraft. At 19.00 the first Swordfish returned, with the ship's speed reduced to 18 knots, and by 19.45 all planes were safely aboard. The report states that during the 26½ knot acceleration the accompanying destroyers *Impulsive* and *Ivanhoe* had their Asdic (anti-submarine detection) domes housed, a necessary move to lessen drag and improve speed. But there is no mention that when the speed was reduced to 18 knots, the domes were lowered and re-activated to detect loitering submarines. While the last of the striking force was landing on the carrier, the slender periscope of a trailing U-boat went unobserved and undetected by the escorting destroyers.

This was *U-29*, commanded by Kapitän-Leutnant Otto Schuhart. His boat had been in position some days before in a waiting position on the American steamer route and wasn't even looking for *Courageous*. The commander's log-book takes up the story from here:

Date and time. 17.9 Position East 2. Sea state 2–3.
Long slow swell, clear, sunny, very good visibility.

**16.05** Steamer approaching from the west. Seen late because he comes directly out of the sun. The boat is apparently on his general track.
Submerged.
Steamer zigzags – English. Freighter with passenger-carrying capability. What is it being used for? Size about 10,000 tons.
Manchester Line? Steamer does not zigzag long, therefore the passing distance will be quite large, about 5,000 m.
Now I see he is flying a reddish flag and I am getting suspicious about the nationality, perhaps American?
Suddenly I see an aircraft approaching from astern at low altitude next to the steamer – war materials then or troop transport?
Decision to fire a torpedo.
Steamer zigzags away before torpedo can be fired. Angle is getting too wide.
Intention: After it is out of sight, to surface, keep in contact and carry out a surprise attack at night. Because of air cover, down to 20 m.

When Schuhart saw the aircraft astern of the steamer, he at once realized that it couldn't be land-based, for the British Isles were a round-distance trip of some 900 miles, and therefore the plane must have come from an aircraft-carrier not too far distant. He decided to investigate. The time was 18.00.

**18.00** At 13 m look around. Ahead to port a square-shaped cloud on the horizon; not a smoke cloud but an aircraft-carrier, assume *Ark Royal*. Range more than 10,000 m.
I can recognize the masts of an escort destroyer ahead of the carrier. I realize immediately that the aircraft observed by the steamer belongs not to him but to *Ark Royal*.
Moving *U-29* at slow speed toward the ships. I estimate

half-ahead. I can't see the air cover. I'm looking for more escorts in the distance without success.

His 'looking for more escorts' is understandable, for at this time the aircraft-carriers *Ark Royal, Hermes* and *Courageous* were also operating in areas west of Ireland looking for U-boats. Standard intelligence information would have told him that *Ark Royal* would normally have a six-destroyer escort, *Hermes* four and *Courageous* four. Schuhart had, of course, made a mistake in his identification of the ship. He had assumed this was *Ark Royal,* so where were the rest of the escorts? No carrier would roam around the Western Approaches with just one or two destroyers, surely. What he didn't know, of course, was that the carrier he observed (*Courageous*) had detached two destroyers to go to the aid of *Kafiristan.* Apprehensive, he slowly approached. He continues:

As to the close escort I find one destroyer ahead, one astern. The boats ahead are stationed about 1,000 m from the carrier. The carrier turns onto a westerly heading.
Decision. To fire three [Etos torpedoes] as a fan with a narrow spread in order to achieve possibly two hits. Depth setting 6 m. The reason I don't trust magnetic torpedoes is because of the experience with *Neptunia.*

His experience with the sinking of *Neptunia* on 11 September had been rather alarming. He had lined up the vessel and fired two of their new magnetic torpedoes, one of which exploded soon after leaving the tube, producing frightening shock waves on the hull of the submarine, while the other exploded before hitting the ship. He eventually finished her off with a conventional Etos torpedo. He then radioed the other U-boats in the vicinity: 'Don't use your magnetic torpedoes. They will probably give away your position.' This warning was ignored by the commander of *U-39* when, only three days later the carrier *Ark Royal,* with destroyer escort, while carrying out anti-submarine operations off the west of Scotland was sighted by *U-39.*

At 14.25 on that day, 14 September, *Ark Royal* was positioned about 150 miles west of the Hebrides, with *Faulkner, Foxhound* and *Firedrake* acting as a screen for her. Three other destroyers, *Tartar, Bedouin* and *Punjabi,* had been detached to go on ahead towards the position where SS *Fanadhead* had been attacked by a

U-boat about 180 miles to the south-westward. At 14.32 *Ark Royal* turned into the wind to fly off three Skua aircraft, whilst the destroyers maintained their course and speed. These Skuas were the Royal Navy's first operational monoplanes, used as a dual-purpose fighter and dive-bomber. *Ark Royal* turned back after the aircraft had flown off and was then about four miles astern of the screen.

Despite the warning from Schuhart, *U-39* fired two magnetic torpedoes at her, both of which missed the stern and blew up in the wake. The carrier was then doing 26 knots. *U-39* had passed about 3,000 yards from the nearest destroyer and, hearing the explosions, assumed she had scored a hit. The destroyers immediately turned back, spread 2,000 yards apart and started a search.

*Faulkner* and *Foxhound* got a contact at 15.25. *Foxhound* attacked and dropped two depth-charges. Although *U-39* dived deep when she saw the destroyers approaching, the attack put out the lights and damaged the main battery. The main electric motors were also put out of action, due to flooding. *Faulkner* dropped another full pattern of depth-charges, and this caused further leaks in the submarine. At 15.46 *Firedrake* carried out another attack with depth-charges. This did the most damage, and water started pouring into the boat, sending it out of control and filling it with chlorine gas. At 15.47 *U-39* broke surface, and all three destroyers opened fire. As the 4-inch shells hit the black conning-tower causing bright flashes, German sailors came pouring out of the hatch with their hands up and wearing lifebelts. When it was seen that they were surrendering, fire was checked and all three destroyers launched lifeboats, *Firedrake* picking up eight men, while *Faulkner* and *Foxhound*'s boat collected forty-five. All the crew were saved. The U-boat was settling fast, and in minutes she moved forward and downward to sink bows first, followed by a sharp explosion as her scuttling-charges blew up.

It is reasonable to assume that, if Schuhart had not had this experience with the magnetic torpedoes, he would have fired them at *Courageous*. The premature explosions would have warned the two destroyers, and *Courageous* could have accelerated away at full speed and escaped. Despite her great bulk, she could reach 32 knots with all her eighteen boilers going.

The log continues:

**19.00** Concerning the convoy, I can see two aircraft occasionally circling over the other two ships.

I am running at periscope depth constantly watching the

carrier zigzagging.

The carrier has increased his range from me when he suddenly turns onto a southerly heading.

From now on everything develops quickly. I estimate that the passing distance for angle on the bow will be 3,000 m but I am also ready to fire at a greater range; I can expect the Etos to run for 4,000 to 5,000 m.

I have nothing to use as a reference for distance because of the enormous height of freeboard of the carrier, plus I have to look into the sun.

The periscope is from time to time just beneath the surface as I am running at right angles to the swell. Because of the risk of detection speed slow or dead slow.

Attack depth 14 m.

**19.50** In the turn hard starboard, three torpedoes fired.

Aiming points about 20 m ahead of the bow, midships and 20 m astern.

On firing I see the port side destroyer 500 m ahead of the ship. Hard starboard to 360, both engines full ahead and quickly down to 50 m. The boat climbed very little after the launch of the three torpedoes and the chief engineer has all well in hand.

**19.53** In the whole boat we can clearly hear the explosions from two torpedo hits. Immediately after the second hit an enormous detonation followed by a few smaller ones. The noise is so loud that I have the impression that we ourselves have been damaged.

Jubilation in the boat, although everyone is apprehensive about what will happen next.

The boat is meanwhile down to 60 m and because we have no ill effects from this depth we can go down to 80 m. Because of water in the boat, the limited use of engines and because of the danger of detection, the boat gets so heavy that we go further down to 105 m. The boat is behaving magnificently.

**19.59** Loud propeller noises quickly approaching and passing overhead. Four depth-charges falling – exploding directly overhead but far too high. Strong vibrations in the boat.

I am standing in the conning-tower which shakes

completely. No apparent changes in depth. A few minutes later another six depth-charges with the same result.

More destroyer propeller noises – starboard astern to starboard ahead. Boat passed over by two destroyers. Four loud depth-charge detonations overhead from astern to ahead. Simultaneous weaker detonations on each side – destroyers obviously running in line abreast.

**20.01** Destroyers moving away. Continuous detonations in close proximity to the boat and then further away.

**20.03** Two destroyers coming nearer – one running over the boat between conning-tower and bow – six loud explosions – destroyers apparently again in line abreast.

**20.08** Destroyers coming closer – detonations in close proximity to the boat and some on top but much shallower setting.

**20.41** Destroyers have stopped and are launching depth-charges in a larger radius.

**21.56** Destroyers apparently forming search formation. Numerous explosions – it sounds as if they are dropping 40 to 50 depth-charges in one position – each time further away from the boat.

**23.21** Propeller noises moving astern.

**23.40** Propeller noises getting stronger and moving astern. Boat turns to starboard. Noise getting quieter – only a few detonations.

**23.56** Propeller noises getting weaker and no longer measurable.

**01.35** Surfaced.

At 22.00 the boat was approximately 4 nautical miles away from attack position, however by midnight we are reasonably certain we have escaped detection.

**01.35**  Hatch open. Course 340. Speed 13 knots.

Intention:

To move as far away as possible from the attack position until dawn and then investigate the state of the boat.

The result is that the boat is completely intact apart from the attack periscope. No traces of depth-charges or pressure effects on the upper deck. The attack periscope is full of water which had got in through the neck. The attack periscope is U/S [unserviceable].

The question is: how successful was *U-29*'s attack? I cannot decide to return and attack again should the ship have been only badly damaged as I have run low on attack weapons. Only one Eto in the bow tubes and fuel enough only for a direct course back to base.

The conviction is that the ship was destroyed. The explosions were so loud that the ship either must have disintegrated or exploded.

**10.00**  Returning to base.

At 12.00 I received information from British radio confirming the success of *U-29*. We did not sink *Ark Royal* but *Courageous* and they say that we were also destroyed.

Tremendous pleasure in the boat.

We must now take up the story from the time *Courageous* was hit. It was a glorious sunny Sunday evening, and about half an hour before sunset the last of the strike aircraft returned and stopped on the flight-deck. Only minutes later, torpedoes ploughed into the port side of the ship, and she immediately listed to starboard, with smoke pouring from her funnel. To make matters worse, all the lights below decks went out and electrical short-circuiting set off her siren, which made it impossible for orders to be heard.

One survivor described how he was in the hangar at the time of the explosion and realized they had been torpedoed as the ship began to list. The place was suddenly plunged into darkness, and he had difficulty in finding the door leading out onto the deck. When he arrived there, he saw some of the older members of the crew jumping into the sea and then finding it colder than they thought, shouting for help and being dragged back again. It took only eighteen minutes from the time the ship was torpedoed until she sank.

The noise of the siren was such that 'Abandon ship!' was passed by word of mouth, and when he arrived at his 'abandon ship' station, frantic efforts were being made to release the Carley float rafts fixed onto structures on the ship's side and secured with ropes, so that in theory all that needed to be done was to pull a rope and the float would fall into the sea. But the rafts refused to move being stuck to the ship's side with thick layers of paint built up over many years. As far as he remembers, only one raft got away and this had so many men on it that it was four feet under water. Realizing it was every man for himself, he dived into the sea and swam towards a destroyer about a mile away.

After swimming a hundred yards from the ship, he turned on his back in time to see *Courageous* take her final plunge. Very slowly at first, the bow went down, and hundreds of men began scrambling from the decks, some even jumping from the flight-deck. As she slowly rolled over onto her starboard, scores of the crew slid and slipped down the canting side. On the bridge, one man remained at his post to the last, the commanding officer, Captain Makeig-Jones, watching the mostly grey-haired members of his crew drop into the cold sea where so many would perish. The enormous bulk of the stern rose high into the air, exposing the great propellers.

As she took her last dive, two figures scrambled across the quarter-deck and on to the stern. One slipped over the edge and fell across the massive blades of the screws, the other squatted on the stern as the ship vanished into the boiling surf. Immediately after the ship disappeared, huge baulks of timber and planking shot out of the sea and fell back, hitting some of those swimming. Very few boats got away. He saw only two, one of which capsized, with the number of men clambering to get aboard.

He continued swimming towards the destroyer and was eventually hauled aboard. Very soon more survivors began to arrive, and before long the mess decks and upper decks were crowded. The search for survivors continued well into the night, and when no more could be found, the destroyer got under way. By midday the following day they arrived at Devonport.

A few remarkable stories emerged from survivors. There were good swimmers who perished, whilst some who couldn't swim survived. A photographer was in a compartment playing cards with three of his friends with the door locked when the torpedoes struck. The lights went out and a heavy steel rack fell across the door. After a struggle they managed to move it out of the way but in the dark failed to find the key, which had fallen out of the door. Unscrewing the deadlight over the porthole, they dropped into the sea one by one, the water all the while slowly creeping up the side of the ship. The photographer was the last man out and unfortunately his hips stuck in the porthole. Suddenly the force of trapped air blew him out like a cork out of a bottle, and he burst to the surface. Here he managed to grasp a piece of timber and clung to it until he was picked up some time later – he was a non-swimmer.

This description of the sinking comes from another survivor:

We were due on watch at 8 p.m. as part of the crew of the gun on the fo'c'sle. With another of the crew we went there early to enjoy a smoke while it was still daylight. We were in time to see the last of our aircraft land, while the ship, which had turned into the wind for this, altered course to proceed to our area of patrol. Minutes later the ship was struck by torpedoes just forward of midships. The ship very quickly took a heavy list to starboard and all the lights in the ship went out which added to the very heavy loss of life. Several of us on the fo'c'sle attempted to release a raft which had been well secured and periodically painted for years. We found this impossible to move. It was then we realized that the starboard side was almost under water. We took off our shoes and most of our clothes and walked into the water. I saw only one boat get away and that was very crowded. I obtained a piece of wood which probably saved my life. The destroyers which had been well ahead of us did not appear to turn to come back. Sometime later I was picked up by a merchant ship bound for Liverpool which supplied us with clothing and warm food.

RAF fitter Jack Rowntree recalls that, as he was swimming away from the ship, there was a long, heavy swell rising six to ten feet, which at times lifted him so that he had a clear view of all that was happening. He remembers seeing the sea littered with bodies floating face down, and watching *Courageous*, in her last moments, straightening up onto an even keel before plunging forward and downward bows first.

A letter of tribute to the commanding officer, Captain Makeig-Jones, from another survivor states:

We had so little time to get to know our shipmates and we were just shaking down to the ship's routine. I remember the captain, a great sailor and gentleman, sitting on his bridge stool puffing his pipe with his cap slightly tilted and his fine westcountry face looking pink and bluff.

Occasionally it fell to me to take signals to him in his cabin and he always smiled and said 'thank you'. I remember the ship's company being called to general assembly on the flight deck just on the outbreak of war to hear a short address from him. He spoke of the necessity of stopping this fellow Hitler and expressed the hope that if we all did our best, the war would soon be over. He was a fine man and was I believe at one time Navy boxing champion. As you know already, many of the ship's company were RNVR pensioners.

And finally a letter from the chief gunner's mate of *Courageous* sums up the impact of the tragedy of war on those who were widowed:

Many years after the war I had a poignant reminder of the tragedy of war. I was introduced to Mrs Harry Shore, wife of Harry Shore of *Courageous*. I remember her as a young wife in 1939 and now could not recognize the elderly-looking lady before me. Very recently she died. She had kept all the clothes and belongings of her husband who had died in the ship. I was told she would not believe that her husband had gone down in *Courageous* but always believed that he had been picked up by a passing ship and that some day he would return when he would need his clothes. The years passed but he never came back.

The former commander of *U-29*, Kapitän-Leutnant, Otto Schuhart, is still living and recently wrote a letter to Mr Gibbings, a part of which is here recorded: 'You ask for my sentiments. To say it briefly – I was a soldier and had to do my duty. I felt no enthusiasm for war nor had I sentiments of hate towards my adversary. It was war. I loved my country and had to do my duty.'

Of the crew of 1,260 of *Courageous*, the captain and 500 men were lost in the sinking. The effect on the city of Plymouth was one of numbed shock, partly for its strong local connection and partly because many of those lost were ageing naval pensioners. It was one of the first examples of Adolf Hitler's policy that 'Terrorism is absolutely indispensable in every case of founding a new power.'

The official Admiralty report was swift to explain that, to bridge the gap of two or more weeks between the outbreak of war and the completion of auxiliary anti-U-boat flotillas, it had been decided to use aircraft-carriers with an amount of freedom to assist in bringing in the unarmed, unorganized and unescorted convoy traffic which was then nearing British shores in large numbers. It was a risk that had to be run. While that was, of course, necessary, it still begs the question – why were not preparations advanced to meet the unconcealed threat of war?

With the sinking of *Courageous*, the war at sea had begun in earnest. It was one of the first down-payments in the terrible cost of lives that would have to be paid for the years of apathy and neglect.

As was only to be expected in Britain's state of unreadiness, disasters at sea came swift and sure, with the enemy holding the initiative and their ships already at sea well before Britain's declaration of war.

On 14 October a German submarine, *U-47*, commanded by Lieutenant Günther Prien, daringly and skilfully penetrated the defences of the reputedly safe harbour at Scapa Flow in the Orkneys and successfully torpedoed the 30,000-ton battleship *Royal Oak*, with the loss of over 800 men. Guarded by patrols, booms and minefields, the anchorage was supposed to be invulnerable. Twenty-four hours later, a blockship arrived to close the gap in the defences – too late.

Again, had the lessons of World War I been learned and had action been substituted for apathy and preparations advanced for the defence of the Home Fleet in World War II, this calamity need never have happened.

# 2 *The Pocket Battleship* Graf Spee

*On that sunny day in July 1929 when the new cruiser* HMS
Exeter *was launched at Devonport dockyard amid much
celebration, little did the dockyard constructors and
well-wishers who cheered her entry into the River Tamar
know that ten years later, in December 1939, in the horror of
World War II, the 8,000-ton warship would become the
focus of world-wide attention and admiration for her
courage and indomitable resolve in her memorable
engagement with the German battleship* Graf Spee, *off
Montevideo, which was to become known as 'The Battle of
the River Plate'. The two-funnel cruiser with armament of six
8-inch and four 4-inch guns and six torpedo tubes, and
carrying two aircraft, was commissioned into the Second
Cruiser Squadron in 1931 and rendered invaluable service in
the West Indies and South Atlantic until 13 December 1939.*

*Even before Britain and France had declared war on
Germany on 3 September 1939, the German High Command
had secretly sailed two pocket battleships –* Graf Spee *and*
Deutschland – *into the South and North Atlantic respectively
to operate as raiders against the rich convoy routes bringing
vital supplies to the Allied war effort. The pocket battleship*
Graf Spee, *of 13,000 tons, was specifically designed as a
raider, with her 11-inch guns, and had an operational range
of 15,000 miles. Once within the vast area of the South
Atlantic, she proceeded to sink merchant shipping at will.*

*This is the epic story of one of the greatest naval sea
engagements of the war, in which the British cruiser* HMS
Exeter *with her consorts* Ajax *and* Achilles, *fought with such*

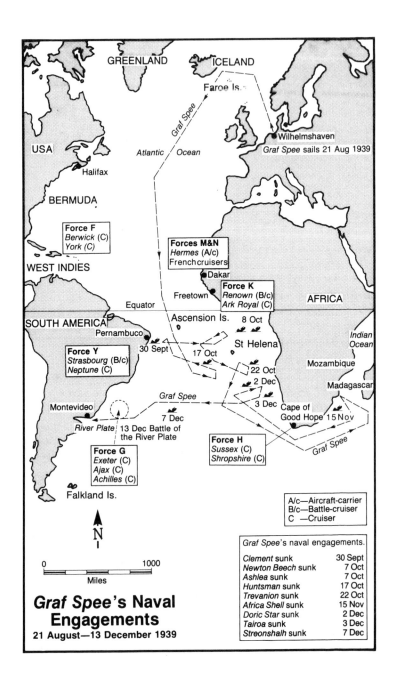

GREENLAND

ICELAND

Faroe Is.

*Graf Spee*

Wilhelmshaven

USA

Atlantic / Ocean

*Graf Spee* sails 21 Aug 1939

Halifax

BERMUDA

**Force F**
*Berwick* (C)
*York* (C)

WEST INDIES

**Forces M&N**
*Hermes* (A/c)
French cruisers

Dakar

**Force K**
*Renown* (B/c)
*Ark Royal* (C)

Freetown

AFRICA

Equator

SOUTH AMERICA

Ascension Is.      8 Oct

Pernambuco

**Force Y**
*Strasbourg* (B/c)
*Neptune* (C)

30 Sept

17 Oct

St Helena

*Indian Ocean*

22 Oct

2 Dec

Mozambique

Madagascar

*Graf Spee*

Montevideo

3 Dec    Cape of
Good Hope  15 Nov

7 Dec

River Plate  13 Dec Battle of
the River Plate

*Graf Spee*

**Force G**
*Exeter* (C)
*Ajax* (C)
*Achilles* (C)

**Force H**
*Sussex* (C)
*Shropshire* (C)

Falkland Is.

A/c—Aircraft-carrier
B/c—Battle-cruiser
C —Cruiser

N

0                    1000
Miles

*Graf Spee*'s naval engagements.

| | |
|---|---|
| *Clement* sunk | 30 Sept |
| *Newton Beech* sunk | 7 Oct |
| *Ashlea* sunk | 7 Oct |
| *Huntsman* sunk | 17 Oct |
| *Trevanion* sunk | 22 Oct |
| *Africa Shell* sunk | 15 Nov |
| *Doric Star* sunk | 2 Dec |
| *Tairoa* sunk | 3 Dec |
| *Streonshalh* sunk | 7 Dec |

# *Graf Spee*'s Naval Engagements
**21 August—13 December 1939**

*valour and fortitude that even the defeated German commanding officer of the* Graf Spee, *Captain Hans Langsdorff, was forced to say, 'When you fight brave men like that, you cannot feel enmity, you only want to shake hands with them....* Exeter *was beaten but would not know it.'*

In terms of outright naval combat between warships, the declaration of war on Germany was followed by a brief period of uneasy inertia. However, on 30 September Hitler began his opening phase of the war at sea by sinking the British liner *Clement* off the coast of Pernambuco, Brazil. A very simple achievement for the new German pocket battleship *Graf Spee*, roaming the South Atlantic. It was the prelude to a long, hard-fought battle between ships of the Royal Navy and the elusive raider. All three of Germany's notorious pocket battleships – *Graf Spee, Deutschland* (to be renamed *Lützow*) and *Scheer* – had a mandate from Grand Admiral Raeder, Commander-in-Chief of the German Navy, to sweep the North and South Atlantic to destroy Allied commercial shipping. As long as the raiders could avoid direct battle with Allied warships, keep out of trouble, pounce on shipping where it was least expected, and keep switching areas of action, it would have the by-product of forcing the Allies to provide heavy surface forces to protect every convoy. By this means, the attacking power of the Royal Navy would be weakened, thus making it more convenient for Germany to mount further strikes.

Even under the conditions of the Versailles Treaty, the Germans had designed and built their three pocket battleships with the deliberate objective of destroying sea commerce. After the experiences of the First World War, the treaty limited the German building programme in capital ships to 10,000 tons. Shrewd revolutionary thinking in production, however, produced a warship that within its displacement carried six 11-inch, eight 6-inch and six 4-inch guns and 4-inch side-armour protection and had a speed of 26 knots. Despite the terms of the treaty, Germany cheated on the displacement programme, so that by the time the 'pockets' were ready, they were nearer 13,000 tons. The six 11-inch powerful guns were contained in two triple turrets fore and aft, with the quarter-deck fully occupied by two quadruple 21-inch torpedo mounts. Their designed operational range of 15,000 miles at a cruising speed of 19 knots gave the lie to their propaganda that they were simply to be used as troop convoy escorts in the protection of the Fatherland. At the Admiralty it was accepted that no single British cruiser could match them.

Even before the outbreak of war, reports arrived that one or two of these pocket battleships had sailed from Germany. Taking full advantage of the initiative, *Graf Spee* and *Deutschland* sailed for the Atlantic nearly a fortnight before the outbreak of war. They were already through and loose in the oceans well in advance of defence patrols being organized. By 3 September *Graf Spee* had reached as far south as the Azores, while *Deutschland* swept the North Atlantic.

By early November, *Graf Spee* had sunk *Ashlea, Newton Beech* and *Trevanion*, all south of St Helena. Then, switching her operations to the Indian Ocean, she disposed of the tanker *Africa Shell* off the coast of Mozambique and by early December was back to her old hunting-ground off St Helena to sink *Tairoa* and *Doric Star*. Such losses called for desperate measures. As a result, the Admiralty formed hunting groups. One comprised the battle-cruiser *Renown* and the aircraft-carrier *Ark Royal* working from Freetown in conjunction with a French group of two heavy cruisers and the British aircraft-carrier *Hermes* from Dakar. Based at the Cape of Good Hope were the two heavy cruisers *Sussex* and *Shropshire*. Across the South Atlantic, the east coast of South America was covered by Commodore Harwood's group, consisting of the 8-inch gun cruisers *Cumberland* and *Exeter* and the lighter, 6-inch gun cruisers *Ajax* and *Achilles*.

While these groups were searching and patrolling, *Graf Spee* made her last rendezvous with *Altmark* and, heading west towards the richer trade routes operating out of the River Plate estuary, sank the *Streonshalh* almost midway between the two continents.

Ever since Commodore Harwood had been assigned the special duty of protecting British shipping off the eastern coast of South America between the River Plate and Rio de Janeiro, a patrol area of something like 3,000 square miles, he had been convinced that sooner or later *Graf Spee* would head for the Plate estuary. By 7 December that conviction had developed into certainty.

His calculation that the pocket battleship would arrive off the estuary by the 13th proved absolutely correct, and by 12 December Harwood was flying his flag in the cruiser *Ajax*, in company with *Exeter* and *Achilles*, patrolling the line between 100 and 200 miles to seaward.

Just after 06.00 on 13 December, the three British cruisers sighted *Graf Spee* heading in their direction. Whether Langsdorff interpreted the far-distant masts, spotted by lookouts, as a small merchant convoy or as one light cruiser and two destroyers is uncertain, but whatever the explanation he headed on at full speed to engage. Moments later he realized his mistake, when the clear outline of the 8-inch gun cruiser *Exeter* materialized, followed by two other cruisers. At a closing speed of over fifty miles an hour he had but seconds to make a decision. In retrospect he should have carried out the orders given to him four months earlier: 'Enemy forces, even if inferior, are only to be engaged if it should further the principal task.' If he had turned and retreated immediately, he would have been able to keep his pursuers for some time under the superior range and power of his 11-inch guns, to which the British ships would have had no answer until perhaps their extra speed allowed them to catch up. By this means there would have been every possibility of destroying his assailants before they could inflict damage. But on the contrary, he committed himself, held his course and made straight for *Exeter*.

Harwood's battle-orders in the event of engaging such opposition had always been clear: to attack at once and engage on both flanks. Accordingly *Exeter* (Captain F. Bell) turned to the west, steering to attack from a southerly direction, while *Ajax* (Captain C. Woodhouse) and *Achilles* (Captain W. Parry) swung north-eastward across the line of the approaching enemy. By this means, *Graf Spee*'s forward turret had to be divided between the two opposing forces.

At 06.17 the battleship opened fire on *Exeter* at a range of twelve miles. Barely over the horizon, her shells straddled the British cruiser. Simultaneously *Exeter* opened fire, with her 8-inch finding their target on the *Spee*. Almost at once the shells of the *Spee* whined over the wilderness of water and smashed into the British cruiser. That first direct hit amidships killed the torpedo crew in the starboard waist. Another hit, on the forecastle, lay bare a mass of tortured metal and burning debris. Despite these wounds, *Exeter* ran on and on, her own shells scoring hits on the enemy. But now came more trouble as a shell scored a direct hit on *Exeter*'s B turret, manned by Royal Marines, killing most of the turret crew. Seconds later a further hit on the rear of the turret scattered hot splinters and jagged shrapnel over the bridge and superstructure, killing most of the bridge staff but miraculously leaving Captain Bell with only a head wound. As the ship reeled under a further hail of shells, the wheelhouse was destroyed and the main steering-gear put out of action. Running the gauntlet of shrapnel and exploding shells, fires and twisted steel, Captain Bell eventually reached the after steering position, and from then on until the end of the engagement the ship was conned from this point, with orders being passed along a chain of sailors to the men at the wheel.

Meanwhile, in other parts of the ship, so many heroic actions were being played out that they became almost commonplace: damage-control parties fighting raging fires threatening to engulf them; other units throwing overboard smouldering cordite charges; men trying to flood compartments swamping in aircraft petrol while the area below grew hot with blazing fire.

All this while, men were being struck down by flying shrapnel as shells burst through the ship from one side to the other. By 06.30, five 11-inch and many 6-inch shells had penetrated the cruiser, with thousands of pieces of shrapnel turning the superstructure and funnels into a virtual pepperpot. In an attempt to torpedo *Graf Spee*, the surviving tubes fired six torpedoes, but they failed to register a hit. More shells destroyed *Exeter*'s A turret, putting both forward turrets out of action. This now left only the after Y turret firing, compelling the ship to swing hard to port or starboard to allow the remaining guns to bear. But still she came on, guns blazing.

By 06.45 *Exeter* had taken as much punishment as any ship could take, but in the final moments of her great and gallant fight one of the shells from Y turret scored a direct hit in the middle of the giant bridge control of *Graf Spee*, producing a bright yellow flash. However, *Exeter* was now virtually a helpless wreck, for even Y turret became useless owing to flooding. At 07.30, with her dead and dying and her many wounded, listing to starboard, her forward turrets a mass of flame and her superstructure a devil's scrapyard, HMS *Exeter* turned away from the battle, heading south on the long 1,200-mile haul to the safety of Port Stanley in the Falklands.

One of the unsung heroes of this famous action was Lieutenant Lewin,* pilot of HMS *Ajax*'s tiny Seafox aircraft who, with his

* Lieutenant Lewin, later to become Captain E.D.G. Lewin CB, CBE, DSO, DSC, RN, having served in the aircraft-carriers *Glorious* and *Eagle*, joined the *Ajax* in 1938. This was followed by service in the *Ark Royal* and a term at the Admiralty. Given command of the *Glory* in the Korean War, he was awarded the CBE and became a Director of Plans at the Admiralty prior to his retirement in 1957.

observer Lieutenant Kearney, catapulted off the ship within feet of the blasts from the belching muzzles of the 6-inch guns of X and Y turrets to climb to 3,000 feet above *Graf Spee*. Despite being rocked by the fury of the pocket battleship's forty-two anti-aircraft guns, he maintained a visual observation of the action as a spotter, giving information to the command ship on the fall of shells from the British cruisers. Later he was to be awarded the DSC for his part in the battle.

In the meantime, *Ajax* and *Achilles*, cramming on speed, had been pounding away on *Graf Spee*'s port flank, while *Exeter* was straddling the battleship. The combination of this firing was taking its toll of the German's ability to maintain the offensive. In fact, *Spee*, plastered from three directions at the same time, soon found the engagement too hot. She was repeatedly hit by the lighter shells, three of which penetrated the control tower, damaging the range and firing-apparatus. From this point it could be said that *Spee*'s gunnery accuracy deteriorated in some degree.

Nevertheless, she was still a dangerous opponent. Shells from *Graf Spee* put four guns of *Ajax* out of action and brought down her topmast. *Achilles* also received some damage, with a direct hit on the director tower killing three and wounding two more. It was just at this moment, when Commodore Harwood was realizing that his ships were no match for the heavy guns of the battleship and was about to break off the action to conserve his ammunition until nightfall, that *Graf Spee* effected a smoke-screen, attempting to escape. Harwood's decision was based on the premise that by nightfall his chances of closing to a range at which his lighter armament and torpedoes would have a decisive result would improve.

Now began the long chase, with *Ajax* and *Achilles* rigidly hanging on to the retreating ship, despite the enemy's repeatedly lashing out with her big guns to deter them. For Captain Langsdorff, it was now decision time. Below decks, thirty-six of his men had been killed and sixty wounded, gunnery control had been impaired and, more important, he was running short of fuel-oil. Ahead, to the west, in the port of Montevideo, the German supply ship SS *Tacoma*, with a full cargo of oil fuel, lay at anchor. Behind him were two British cruisers, stubbornly refusing to withdraw to allow him freedom of movement to head back into the South Atlantic. And there was always the reasonable assumption that, closing in to support the two British cruisers, there could be units of a British battle squadron not far distant. In the event, he opted for the safety of Montevideo, and just after midnight of the 14th *Spee* anchored in the roads, while the two British cruisers took up station off the mouth of the estuary.

That night the big cruiser *Cumberland* arrived from the Falklands, joining *Ajax* and *Achilles* to replace the crippled *Exeter*. Meanwhile to the east, from the Cape of Good Hope, the cruisers *Dorsetshire* and *Shropshire* headed west to give further support if the pocket battleship should attempt to break out. The trap was shut.

Below decks in *Graf Spee*, wedged between an 11-inch gun turret and a bulkhead, sixty-two masters and officers of merchant ships captured by *Spee* in previous encounters waited and listened to the roar of guns and the impact of exploding shells. (Captain Patrick Dove, master of *Africa Shell*, who had been captured on 15 November, gives a splendid graphic account of the tense situation in his book *I Was Graf Spee's Prisoner*.) Locked in below decks, they listened with bated breath to the gun battle raging above them. The attacking ships must obviously be British, intent on blowing *Graf Spee* to pieces but in so doing hastening their own destruction. They all hoped and prayed for a British victory, yet surely for them the destruction of the ship would mean their own deaths.

After a long lull, the engines suddenly stopped, and sometime later the door was opened to admit the German lieutenant who had been their guardian, followed by sentries.

'Gentlemen,' he said, 'for you the war is over. We are now anchored in Montevideo harbour, and the captain has told me to say that you will be freed tomorrow.'

Barely able to comprehend the wonderful news, the prisoners cheered and clapped and even shook hands with the guards who had come to release them.

Captain Dove, who had been a guest of Captain Langsdorff for the first two weeks, was asked to follow one of the sentries as the captain wished to speak to him, in his cabin. When Captain Dove arrived, he was shocked at the change in the man. In the last few hours the earlier humour and confidence had been replaced by sadness and care. Langsdorff had been wounded in the face, and his right arm was in a sling, yet his kindness and chivalry remained. He had nothing but praise for the men of *Exeter*.

'When you fight brave men like that,' he said, 'you cannot feel enmity, you only want to shake hands with them. You English are hard. You do not know when you are beaten. The *Exeter* was beaten but would not know it.'

Then, holding out his injured hand, he shook hands with Captain Dove. The rest of the conversation offered some hint as to the course of action he was about to follow, for he seemed convinced that British capital ships were approaching the Uruguayan coast. 'Why else,' he said, 'would the cruisers try to cut me off from shore and drive me out to sea?'

Twelve hours later Captain Dove and his colleagues were mustered on the quarter-deck close to the thirty-six coffins of *Graf Spee*'s dead. After turning and saluting the coffins, they walked quickly down the gangway and into the tug waiting to take them ashore.

Now began a diplomatic row. International law demanded that no warship belonging to a belligerent power should stay in a neutral port for more than twenty-four hours without being interned. For Captain Langsdorff, however, twenty-four hours would in no way be sufficient to allow him to have the necessary repairs completed. Investigation of the damage by the port authorities showed that *Graf Spee* had received considerable damage but not sufficient to deem her unseaworthy, although there were fifteen holes on the starboard side and twelve on the port. Her fire-fighting efficiency had been impaired, and all the kitchens and stores shot away. The German minister at Montevideo, Otto Langmann, argued that a fifteen-day stay would be required to complete the necessary repairs. However, the British minister, E. Millington-Drake, protested that under the ruling of the Twelfth Hague Convention of 1907 *Graf Spee* was entitled to a respite of only twenty-four hours. After considerable argument between the factions, the Uruguayan government granted Captain Langsdorff seventy-two hours in which to carry out the necessary recovery. But it was made clear that, should that time-limit be exceeded, *Graf Spee* would be interned. As the hours passed, apprehension grew as to the eventual outcome, not only in Montevideo but also at the Admiralty in London.

The Uruguayans were convinced that the pocket battleship would make a break for it. In a letter to Neville Chamberlain, the Prime Minister, dated 17 December, Winston Churchill wrote, 'We should prefer that she [*Graf Spee*] should be interned, as this will be less creditable to the German Navy than being sunk in action. Moreover, a battle of this kind is full of hazard, and needless bloodshed must never be sought.'

In the meantime, to lend weight to a possible internment, the BBC transmitted a wily propaganda net reporting that a preponderance of British capital ships, including the battleship *Renown* and the aircraft-carrier *Ark Royal*, were speeding towards the River Plate to destroy *Graf Spee* if she should break out. It appeared to have the desired effect, for it confirmed Langsdorff's earlier prediction that his pocket battleship would stand no chance against the over-whelming odds that would face him outside the mouth of the Plate.

One of Captain Langsdorff's first actions was to make arrangements for the burial of his dead with full military honours and to land some 300 men for the purpose. Five thousand people saw the funeral, but while their attitude was respectful, it was distant. Alongside the many wreaths presented by the colony of Germans in Montevideo was one from the British merchant navy captains who had been prisoners below decks during the battle. It bore the inscription 'To the memory of the brave men of the sea from their comrades of the British merchant service.' The Nazi propaganda machine in the meantime sank to its usual despicable depths when it issued a report that, 'The British seamen prisoners had spat upon the graves of the buried German sailors.'

The Uruguayan government, by its steadfast refusal to break the neutrality act and allow more time for the battleship to be repaired, brought upon itself the threat of all sorts of penalties and impositions from the Nazis. Despite Adolf Hitler's screaming long-distance telephone demands, the game of bluff and sabre-rattling was up.

During the afternoon of Sunday 16 December, the crew of the anchored battleship refused to take their ship to sea. They were mustered on deck at least eight times and harangued by one officer after another. The final appeal was made by Captain Langsdorff himself, but still the men refused to return to duty. During these musters, the crew broke ranks, shouted and behaved in a disorderly manner verging on the mutinous. Eventually the captain dismissed his men and went ashore to consult with the German minister.

This bitter news must have been conveyed to Hitler just before Langsdorff telegraphed his official report, which read as follows: 'Strategic position off Montevideo. Besides the cruisers and destroyers, *Ark Royal* and *Renown*. Close blockade at night. Escape into open sea and break-through to home waters hopeless ... Request decision on whether the ship should be scuttled in spite of insufficient depth in the estuary of the Plate or whether internment is preferred.'

Immediately upon receiving this report a conference was called at which Hitler, Grand Admiral Raeder and General Jodl were present, and the following answer was sent: 'Attempt by all means to extend the time in neutral waters. Fight your way through to Buenos Aires if possible. No internment in Uruguay. Attempt effective destruction if ship is scuttled.'

But the authorities were adamant. No extension of the time-limit would be granted. During that afternoon of the 17th, *Graf Spee* transferred more than 700 men, with their provisions and baggage, to the German merchant ship *Tacoma*. In the meantime Commodore Harwood in the cruiser *Ajax* ordered his cruisers to head inshore, knowing that in the next hour or two *Graf Spee* would either scuttle herself or accept internment.

At 18.15 the pocket battleship weighed anchor and headed slowly seawards with just a demolition crew on board, followed by *Tacoma*. It was estimated that a crowd of three-quarters of a million people watched as the ship moved slowly out into the estuary. Minutes later the demolition crew were transferred to the supply ship, and at 20.54, just as the sun sank below the distant hills, the great ship was rocked and torn by violent explosions as the bottom was ripped out of her. Quickly she sank into the mud fringing the main channel, almost blocking the fairway, as though in protest against her treatment by the Uruguayans.

Langsdorff himself was shattered by the loss of his ship and the manner in which she was destroyed. Three days later, on Wednesday the 19th, he wrote a final letter: 'I can now only prove by my death that the fighting services of the Third Reich are ready to die for the honour of the flag. I alone bear the responsibility for scuttling the pocket battleship *Admiral Graf Spee*. I am happy to pay with my life for any possible reflection on the honour of the flag. I shall face my fate with firm faith in the cause and future of the nation and of my Führer.'

That night Captain Hans Langsdorff wrapped himself in the flag of the Imperial German Navy under which he had fought in the First World War and shot himself. He was indeed a brave man who would not readily accept the Nazi regime but who was dedicated to the Fatherland. He was never seen to give a Nazi salute.

While Lord Haw-Haw, the notorious propagandist, was steadily broadcasting that the British cruiser *Exeter* was at the bottom of the sea, that ship was safely in harbour at Port Stanley, licking her wounds but preparing to go home to a grateful nation.

Some days later, the cruisers *Dorsetshire* (Captain D. Martin) and *Shropshire* (Captain A. Bisset) arrived at Port Stanley, and during the afternoon Captain Bisset stood at the top of the gangway leading to *Exeter*'s deck, removed his cap, stood to attention and said to the quartermaster and the lieutenant, 'Gentlemen, may I have the honour to come aboard your gallant ship?'

On 14 February *Exeter* arrived at Plymouth. The grassy slopes of the Hoe were covered with thousands of people shouting, cheering and frantically waving to the blackened, charred, tangled scrapyard of steel that moved slowly along into the Hamoaze followed by a group of important people in the Commander-in-Chief's barge. As they moved into the area of the dockyard, sirens hooted, cranes dipped in salute and workmen banged their hammers in an hysterical welcome. As the gangway dropped to the dock wall at Devonport, a smiling, chubby-faced, bowler-hatted figure, cigar-armed, hauled himself aboard.

Mr Winston Churchill, First Lord of the Admiralty, had arrived to present his congratulations to the captain and crew of *Exeter*.

# 3   *HMS* Glowworm:
# *The Supreme Sacrifice*

Not once or twice in our rough island story,
The path of duty was the way to Glory.

> By Tennyson – from the
> Ode on the death of the Duke of Wellington

*This could well be said of the little destroyer* Glowworm, *which, with only her four 4.7-inch guns, turned and fought against the overpowering armament of three enemy ships carrying a total of eight 8-inch, ten 5-inch and twelve 4-inch guns.*

The old year died quietly enough but by April 1940 it was clear that the so-called 'phoney war' had ended.

On Sunday the 7th, air reconnaissance revealed that several groups of the German fleet had sailed north, with the apparent intention of seizing Norwegian ports, including the important port of Narvik. To delay this operation, the British organized a mine-laying operation covered by the battle-cruiser *Renown*, the cruiser *Birmingham* and eight destroyers; this to give the mine-laying force some re-assurance that help was at hand if needed.

During this operation, the 1,350-ton destroyer *Glowworm*, commanded by Lieutenant-Commander G.B. Roope, lost a man overboard and had to turn back in atrocious weather conditions to make a search. After some difficulty she at last succeeded in recovering the seaman but in so doing found herself miles behind the main British force and completely out of touch. It has to be remembered that destroyers at that time had no radar and no electronic navigational aids. All this was accomplished by the sun, the stars and a vigilant look-out. But in this case the sky was storm-laden, with extremely poor visibility, and the main force, unaware of the lagging destroyer's track-back, zigzagged away at the best speed possible in the rough conditions. Wireless silence was all-important. Following the recovery of the man washed overboard, *Glowworm* put on speed in an endeavour to try to locate and rejoin *Renown* and her consorts.

In the meantime, German Group 1, comprising the heavy cruiser *Hipper* of 13,900 tons and four destroyers carrying 1,700 troops to occupy Trondheim, were in the vicinity. Early on the morning of 8 April, *Glowworm* sighted two warships, which, much to her surprise, identified themselves as German. These were von Röder Class destroyers of 2,400 tons, each armed with five 5-inch guns. Already *Glowworm* was outgunned, with only her four 4.7-inch guns, to defend herself, but without hesitation she fearlessly engaged the enemy, and a running fight ensued in the heavy sea. It was at this point that *Hipper* appeared and opened fire. *Glowworm* had little chance of survival in the overpowering encounter. Her puny guns were now matched not only against the combined fire of the ten 5-inch guns of the two enemy destroyers but against the heavy cruiser's massive armament of eight 8-inch and twelve 4-inch guns. Manoeuvring into a position to fire her torpedoes at *Hipper* and after receiving several direct hits of 8-inch shells from the pursuing enemy, *Glowworm* in desperation retired behind her own smoke-screen. The German cruiser adroitly avoided the torpedoes and charged into the murk and smoke to annihilate the British ship.

There could be only one outcome to such a one-sided engagement, and *Glowworm* promptly signalled Admiralty of her encounter with the enemy and of her intention to attack, which she promptly did. Turning about, she steered directly for the oncoming cruiser at her full speed of 38 knots, firing her pitiful little guns at the giant ship. In some respects, it was not unlike the gallant action of 1591 when Sir Richard Grenville in his small flagship *Revenge* tore into the big Spanish galleons at Flores in the Azores.

*Hipper*, storming on through the smoke-screen, suddenly found the British destroyer very close, dead ahead and speeding straight for her. Unable to take avoiding action, *Hipper* could only wait for the impact as the little ship rammed her bow-on, tearing away part of her armoured hull to leave a gaping hole 150 feet wide in her side.

Mortally wounded, *Glowworm* fell away crippled, a sorry sight indeed. From the decks of the three German ships surrounding her, the crews watched in wonderment. Her bows were torn away almost back to her forward turret, she was ablaze from stem to stern, and most of her crew were dead or dying.

For a few minutes she lay there in her agony, her ensign fluttering in the wind, then, as though committing herself to the deep, she heeled over and blew up close to her adversary.

To their credit, the Germans made strenuous efforts to rescue survivors from the sea in difficult conditions. They eventually managed to pull some forty men aboard, and these were treated with great respect by the German crew, so impressed were they by *Glowworm*'s action.

The commanding officer, Lieutenant-Commander Gerard B. Roope was a great naval cricketer of his time and, while struggling in the water at the end and trying to get aboard the enemy ship, he fell back exhausted, saying he had played his last innings. *Glowworm* had been sunk with the loss of over a hundred of her crew, but her commander was awarded the Victoria Cross posthumously, not only for himself but also on behalf of all those who perished. It was the highest award the British sovereign could bestow.

Although *Hipper* was able eventually to arrive at Trondheim, this powerful vessel of the German fleet was out of action for some weeks.

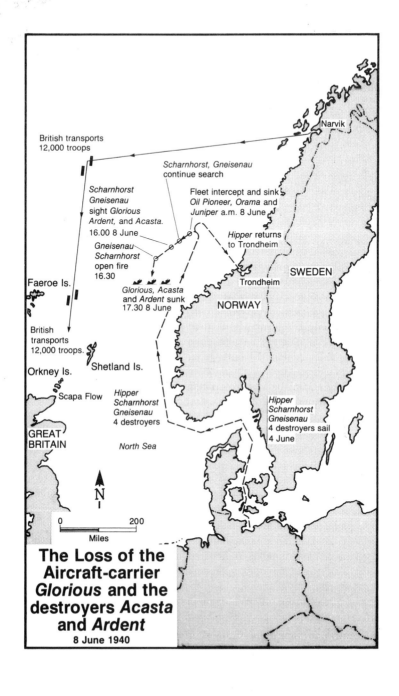

British transports
12,000 troops

Narvik

*Scharnhorst, Gneisenau*
continue search

*Scharnhorst
Gneisenau*
sight *Glorious
Ardent*, and *Acasta*.
16.00 8 June

Fleet intercept and sink
*Oil Pioneer, Orama* and
*Juniper* a.m. 8 June

*Gneisenau
Scharnhorst*
open fire
16.30

*Hipper* returns
to Trondheim

SWEDEN

Faeroe Is.

*Glorious, Acasta*
and *Ardent* sunk
17.30 8 June

Trondheim

NORWAY

British
transports
12,000 troops.

Shetland Is.

Orkney Is.

Scapa Flow

*Hipper
Scharnhorst
Gneisenau*
4 destroyers

*Hipper
Scharnhorst
Gneisenau*
4 destroyers sail
4 June

GREAT
BRITAIN

*North Sea*

N

0                    200

Miles

# The Loss of the
# Aircraft-carrier
# *Glorious* and the
# destroyers *Acasta*
# and *Ardent*
**8 June 1940**

# 4  The Defence of the Aircraft-carrier Glorious

*The 22,500-ton carrier* Glorious, *like her sister-ship* Courageous, *which had been sunk on 17 September 1939 in the Western Approaches, had been converted in 1924 from a heavily armed cruiser into an aircraft-carrier, armed with only 4.7-inch guns. This seemingly light armoury was apparently justified to save weight, and the Admiralty considered that such carriers would have to rely on their screening ships to protect them. In the naval engagement off the coast of Norway on 8 June 1940* Glorious *found herself facing the two German battle-cruisers* Gneisenau *and* Scharnhorst, *with only the two little destroyers* Acasta *and* Ardent *to defend her.*

The threat from Hitler's campaign in Europe had provoked Britain into making an attempt to occupy Norway, but this had not achieved the success hoped for, and by the beginning of June 1940 a situation had developed whereby it was necessary, indeed imperative, to withdraw the forces already landed. In fact, Britain now had to relinquish all that she had won after much painful exertion.

So it was that on 4 June a convoy of troopships and supply transports was organized. But by a necessary dispersal of heavy ships for other emergencies, only a close escort of anti-submarine ships and an aircraft-carrier could be provided. The evacuation at Narvik made good progress, and by 8 June all the troops, amounting to 24,000, were embarked and sailed in four convoys without being attacked by the enemy.

In the final withdrawal, valuable protection was given against the German Air Force not only by naval aircraft but by a squadron of shore-based Hurricanes. They had been ordered to remain in action until the end, destroying their aircraft if necessary. By their skill and courage, however, they performed the unprecedented feat of flying their Hurricanes on board the carrier *Glorious*. None of these pilots had ever landed on the deck of a moving ship before, but this was performed with great skill and without loss.

At this time a certain complacency, bred by the absence of any German surface threat was also responsible for the lack of adequate heavy supporting force. In fact, despite reconnaissance, no activity by German heavy ships had hitherto been detected.

Unknown to the British, however, the battle-cruisers *Scharnhorst* and *Gneisenau*, both of 32,000 tons and each armed with nine 11-inch and twelve 5.9-inch guns, and the heavy cruiser *Hipper*, of 13,900 tons, with four destroyers, all under the command of Admiral Wilhelm Marschall, sailed from Kiel on 4 June with orders to bombard the British base at Harstad, near Narvik. No hint of the British withdrawal reached them until 7 June. On the news that British troop-carrying convoys were at sea and in two groups, one to the north and another to the south, the German admiral on his own initiative decided to attack the southernmost one. With thousands of troops aboard the transports at sea, there were all the elements of an impending tragedy of the first magnitude. But here fate intervened in the most unusual circumstances.

Early on the morning of the 8th, the German force intercepted four British ships, the oil-tanker *Oil Pioneer*, the empty troopship *Orama*, the escort trawler *Juniper* and the hospital ship *Atlantis*. Only *Atlantis* was spared; the rest were shelled and sent to the bottom. This relatively minor engagement had, however, cost the Germans time and an expenditure of fuel. As a result, *Hipper*, with her four escorting destroyers, was ordered to return to Trondheim to refuel, while the two battle-cruisers continued their search for a British troop convoy carrying 10,000 men.

Instead, at 16.00 they sighted the smoke of the aircraft-carrier *Glorious* with her two escorting destroyers, *Acasta* and *Ardent*. The carrier, short of fuel and hampered by the extra aircraft which had flown aboard and thereby unable to operate her own scouting planes, was caught by surprise. The engagement began at 16.30, with *Gneisenau* and *Scharnhorst* hitting *Glorious* with their 11-inch shells at a distance of fifteen miles. *Glorious*, with only her

4-inch guns, was helpless. Frantic efforts were made to get her torpedo-bombers into the air, but this was made impossible by the accurate shooting of the enemy.

In *Gneisenau*, Admiral Marschall, Commander-in-Chief of Group Fleet 1, watched through binoculars the vigorous attempts of the aircrews to get the planes airborne. The first 11-inch shell from *Scharnhorst* was a direct hit on the carrier, tearing up the flight-deck like the lid of a box. It went on to explode inside the hangar and set the petrol afire, causing incredible damage and chaos. Both enemy ships were now firing their main armament with great accuracy and at will. There was one horrifying hit on the bridge superstructure which killed everyone there and in adjacent compartments. Any assistance from British covering forces was out of the question. The cruiser *Devonshire* was 100 miles away, the aircraft-carrier *Ark Royal* and her destroyers were 200 miles away, and the cruisers *Southampton* and *Coventry* 470 miles away.

At 17.20 the *Devonshire* alone picked up an obscure and puzzling message, barely intelligible, but as it did not seem relevant, she did not break wireless silence to pass it on. On board she had embarked the King of Norway and his ministers to take them to Britain. To have broken radio silence at this stage would have involved serious risk of revealing her position. None of the other ships received *Glorious*'s signal, nor any shore station. The cryptic whisper received by *Devonshire* therefore remained untransmitted.

By now *Glorious* was being hit repeatedly, but her speed was not impaired and, providing she could maintain a reasonable forward momentum, there was just the possibility she could escape. However, another hit in the boiler uptakes produced a rapid drop in steam pressure, and her speed was reduced, allowing the two German cruisers to close in and position themselves one on each of the carrier's quarters. Later one hit near the centre engine-room brought her to a standstill. The whole side of the ship caved in with a great cloud of smoke and a mighty roar that echoed across the shell-torn water. By this time, *Glorious* was just a pillar of smoke and flame, and the list to starboard was increasing. As she began to heel over amidst a hail of machine-gun bullets, there came the order 'Abandon ship!'

While *Glorious* was being crucified by the great guns of the two cruisers, the two British destroyers *Ardent* and *Acasta*, each of 1,350 tons, carrying only four 4.7-inch guns and a complement of 138 men, sailed out to challenge the enemy.

*Ardent*, under Lieutenant-Commander J.F. Barker, having laid a smoke-screen, raced on to close the enemy ships at full speed while firing her two forward guns, one shell from which hit *Scharnhorst*'s B turret. The two cruisers fought off the oncoming destroyer, raking her continuously, creating havoc on the little ship. But even as she sped towards the enemy amid the roar and scream of exploding shells, her bows angling back sharply, with snow-white bow waves streaming back under her forefoot, and a boiling wake spreading behind her, she fired her last torpedo. She was still doing 35 knots, driving in under the guns of the enemy, when her bows went down, driving deep into the black waters of the Atlantic Ocean.

There now remained only *Acasta*, under Commander C.E. Glasfurd, left facing hopeless odds. The German ships first became aware of *Acasta* when she emerged from the right-hand edge of the smoke-screen, firing her guns and positioning to make a torpedo attack. The story of her gallant action has been told by the sole survivor, Leading Seaman C. Carter. He takes up the story preceding the moment when *Gneisenau* and *Scharnhorst* first sighted the destroyer:

On board our ship, what a deadly calm, hardly a word spoken, the ship was now steaming full speed away from the enemy, then came a host of orders, prepare all smoke floats. Hose pipes connected up, various other jobs were prepared, we were still stealing away from the enemy and making smoke and all our smoke floats had been set going. The Captain then had this message passed to all positions: 'You may think we are running away from the enemy, we are not, our chummy ship [*Ardent*] has sunk, the *Glorious* is sinking, the least we can do is to make a show, good luck to you all.'

We then altered course into the smoke-screen. I had the order stand by to fire tubes 6 and 7, we then came out of the smoke-screen, altered course to starboard firing our torpedoes from port side. It was then I had my first glimpse of the enemy, to be honest it appeared to me to be a large ship and a small one, and we were very close. I fired my two torpedoes from my tubes (aft), the foremost tubes fired theirs, we were all watching results. I'll never forget that cheer that went up; on the port bow of one of the ships a yellow flash and a great column of smoke and water shot up from her. We knew we had hit, personally I could not see how we could have missed so close as we were. The enemy never fired a shot at us, I feel they must have been very surprised. After we had fired our torpedoes we went back into our own smoke-screen, altered course again to starboard.

'Stand by to fire remaining torpedoes', and this time as soon as we poked our nose out of the smoke-screen, the enemy let us have it. A shell hit the engine-room, killed my tube's crew, I was blown to the after end of the tubes, I must have been knocked out for a while, because when I came to, my arm hurt me; the ship had stopped with a list to port.

Here is something believe it or believe it not, I climbed back into the control seat, I see those two ships, I fired the remaining torpedoes, no one told me to, I guess I was raving mad. God alone knows why I fired them, but I did. The *Acasta*'s guns were firing the whole time, even firing with a list on the ship. The enemy then hit us several times but one big explosion took place right aft. I have often wondered whether the enemy hit us with a torpedo, in any case it seemed to lift the ship out of the water.

At last the Captain gave orders to abandon ship. I will always remember Surgeon Lieutenant H.J. Stammers RNVR, his first ship, his first action. Before I jumped over the side, I saw him still attending to the wounded, a hopeless task, and when I was in the water I saw the Captain leaning over the bridge, take a cigarette from a case and light it. We shouted to him to come on our raft, he waved 'Good-bye and good luck' – the end of a gallant man.

The torpedo from *Acasta* struck *Scharnhorst* abreast the after gun turret. Two officers and forty-six ratings were killed, with considerable damage to the after turret and flooding of the shell- and magazine-rooms. Some 2,500 tons of water flooded into the ship to reach the two main engine-rooms. This reduced her speed to 20 knots.

Even as *Acasta*, with 137 men aboard, went down, the end of *Glorious* was near. The carrier took on a heavy list and was sinking fast before she took her final plunge. As she poised for the long dive, hundreds of survivors were still clinging to her sides, men in fear shouting for a help which would not come. And then she heeled over amid a rush of turbulent water and the evil stench of fuel-oil. Within minutes she began to descend, burrowing deeper and deeper into the dark water, and then almost startlingly the massive bulk of the 23,000-ton aircraft-carrier *Glorious* had disappeared.

Many must have perished in the enormous suction created by her final plunge. The sea was now covered with hundreds of men swimming in life-jackets or clinging to timbers or struggling to climb aboard Carley floats. The last bitter blow from the enemy came when the two cruisers passed the survivors and machine-gunned them in the water. Disdainfully the German ships sailed on, ignoring the cries for help, later to return to Trondheim. In this engagement *Gneisenau* and *Scharnhorst* had fired nearly 400 rounds of 11-inch shells and 1,100 rounds of 5.9-inch.

As the ships disappeared, the surface of the sea resumed its long, steady swell, and in the place of the sound of battle there was now only one strong, lone voice. It was that of the chaplain of *Glorious*, the Reverend John Bernard King, leading his fellow survivors on one of the rafts in a hymn in which he had led so many congregations on the ship in the past. As one survivor said, 'It was a magnificent effort from one of the most miserable choirs I have ever heard.' But how appropriate the words:

Lead us, Heavenly Father, lead us, o'er the world's tempestuous sea.
Guard us, guide us, keep us, feed us, for we have no help but Thee.

As the hours passed, exposure and exhaustion took their toll. One by one, men numbed by the cold drifted into unconsciousness and slipped off the rafts to join the hundreds of corpses floating in the swell. In time the chaplain's voice fell silent too, and later he lapsed into a deep coma from which there was no awakening.

A German broadcast on 9 June informed the world that German units had sunk the British aircraft-carrier *Glorious*, with other ships, and that many prisoners had been taken. This concerning the prisoners was, of course, a lie in an attempt to cover their pitiless disregard of survivors in the water. The statement naturally gave rise to many a British widow's hope that her husband might have been saved. A cruel hoax indeed. There *were* prisoners, but only six, and these from the first action when *Orama* and *Oil Pioneer* were sunk. There were no prisoners from *Glorious*.

The Admiralty at this time knew nothing of the calamity, and it was only on the following morning, when the 30,000 ton battleship *Valiant* met the hospital ship *Atlantis*, which had been spared destruction, that the Commander-in-Chief, Admiral Forbes, received information that enemy capital ships were at sea. Immediately operations were put in hand to make a search, and the carrier *Ark Royal*'s aircraft swept the sea for several hundred miles, but without result. In fact, the men in the water from *Glorious* had seen the aircraft and tried to attract attention but failed. By now their numbers were dwindling, and a second day had to be faced on the floats.

Although nearly a thousand men had abandoned ship, only a relatively small proportion survived their wounds and the shock of the cold water, many dying before they even reached the floats. Of the thirty on one raft, only ten survived; on another only five out of sixty. By the evening of 10 June, two full days later, the floats were dispersed over a large area, but on many of these no one was left alive.

Eventually, by a stroke of good luck, a rescue was made – not by the searching aircraft nor by British warships but by the Norwegian motor vessel *Borgund*. She picked up all those who were left alive and brought them to the Faroes on the evening of 13 June. From the three warships, *Glorious, Acasta* and *Ardent*, there were only thirty-nine survivors. Thus perished 1,474 officers and men of the Royal Navy and forty-one of the Royal Air Force.

It was a highly sensitive and embarrassing time for the Admiralty, and some hard questions were asked in Parliament by the Labour candidate Richard Stokes on behalf of the widows of those who died. Among the questions he raised with the First Lord of the Admiralty was whether Admiral Forbes, who was then within 800 miles of the sinking, really knew of the movements of HMS *Glorious* and whether, if he did not know, he could still have given assistance if the carrier met with some misfortune. He went on to ask if the Admiralty had thought at the time that two small destroyers were really enough to escort a valuable carrier, and if two destroyers were *not* enough, why were not extra defence measures taken to protect her.

Stokes' strongest criticism was reserved for the reason for the tragedy of those who had died in the water after abandoning ship. He asked whether it was true, as stated in the newspapers, that over a thousand men were drifting on floats for three nights and two days before being rescued by chance and why were the stories of the few survivors being suppressed by the Admiralty.

However, it was war time, and the government could not and dare not release any information that might be of use to the enemy.

In the country as a whole there was a widely held view that the Admiralty had blundered. The general impression was that *Glorious* had been employed and sunk too distant from any help, proceeding without proper escort and with no one in authority really certain where she was or what she was supposed to be doing. It was a most damaging indictment of the Admiralty, and one to which history has found no answer.

In the meantime, German forces had broken through the Netherlands and Belgium, smashed French military resistance and driven the British Expeditionary Force back to the sea. Then came the miracle of Dunkirk, on 26 May–4 June 1940. Trapped on the beaches, strafed by bombs and shells, it seemed they were doomed. But the Navy, using 230 warships of all kinds and supported by over 700 private motor boats and small and large fishing trawlers, sailed in under intense fire and carried 335,000 men out of the jaws of death back to the coast of Britain. It was a miracle of deliverance achieved by discipline, by skill and by valour.

# 5   The Taranto Raid

*The Battle of Taranto is marked in history as one of the great shock-tactics employed by the Royal Naval Fleet Air Arm which through the courage of its aircrews succeeded in severely mauling the Italian fleet in the safety of its anchorage.*

*It kept the Mediterranean Sea clear for some time and made possible General Wavell's attack against the Italian army in Libya.*

In 1940 the significance of the strategic value of the Mediterranean was not lost on the new British Prime Minister, Winston Churchill, and despite the apparent threat of invasion from across the Channel he did not hesitate to send some of Britain's most powerful ships to maintain control over this vital sea. Hitler, fully absorbed with his plans for the invasion of the Soviet Union, seemed reluctant to switch any weight of forces in that direction.

The entrance of Italy into the war in June meant that Britain's convoys were under constant threat of attack from the forays of the Italian fleet, which the Italians could deploy under the protection of their coastal air-power at their convenience. But this was not all: they also had deep central bases near their operational routes which could be relied upon to provide rapid repairs and refits, short sea routes and surprise initiative. Against this, the British fleet was not only inferior in numbers but had to operate thousands of miles from its bases.

With Italy's entry into the war, the British Mediterranean Fleet was augmented and its main base at Malta transferred to Alexandria, but this simply weakened the Home Fleet's strength. There was at this time the very real threat of an invasion of Great

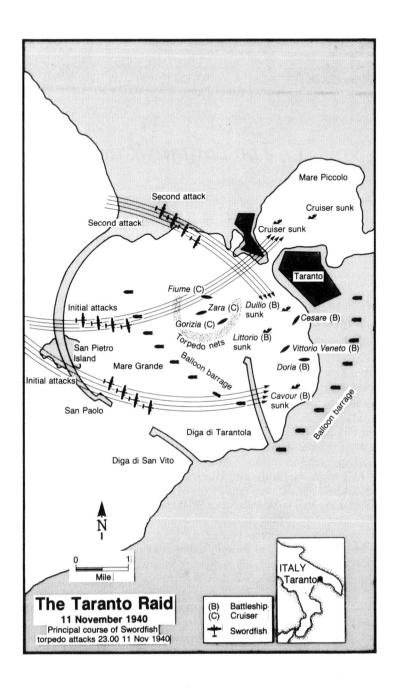

Mare Piccolo

Cruiser sunk

Second attack

Second attack

Cruiser sunk

Cruiser sunk

Taranto

*Fiume* (C)

Initial attacks

*Zara* (C)

*Duilio* (B)
sunk

*Cesare* (B)

*Gorizia* (C)

*Littorio* (B)
sunk

*Vittorio Veneto* (B)

Torpedo nets

San Pietro
Island

*Doria* (B)

Mare Grande

Balloon barrage

Initial attacks

San Paolo

*Cavour* (B)
sunk

Balloon barrage

Diga di Tarantola

Diga di San Vito

N

0        1

Mile

**The Taranto Raid**
**11 November 1940**
Principal course of Swordfish
torpedo attacks 23.00 11 Nov 1940

ITALY
Taranto

(B)   Battleship
(C)   Cruiser
✈   Swordfish

Britain, and so the fleet build-up in the Mediterranean had to be severely limited. But the defence of this important sea was urgent if Britain was to retain her hold on the Suez Canal.

The British naval presence was divided into two groups. One was based at Gibraltar under Admiral Sir James Somerville, and the other at Alexandria under the command of Sir Andrew Cunningham. Among the ships transferred to this theatre of war was the battleship *Warspite*, to become the flagship of Admiral Cunningham, who was destined to be recognized as the most distinguished and courageous admiral since Nelson. Cunningham's vigorous command was, however, not enough to outweigh the advantage of Italian naval superiority, and a forcible request was made to the First Sea Lord, Admiral Sir Dudley Pound, for another battleship, in addition to the modernized old *Warspite*, with a gun range that was similar to the two new Italian 35,000-ton, 15-inch battleships *Littorio* and *Vittorio Veneto*.

Cunningham also realized that, with the disparity in speed between his existing battleships and those of the Italian fleet, the only way to balance the inequality was to acquire torpedo-carrying aircraft. He therefore stressed the urgent need for one of the new armoured aircraft-carriers and for suitable fighter protection for the fleet and its convoys when within range of enemy territory. The Admiralty responded, and the modernized old battleship *Valiant* and the new armoured aircraft-carrier *Illustrious*, together with the two anti-aircraft cruisers *Calcutta* and *Coventry*, sailed into the Mediterranean escorted by Admiral Somerville's fleet and, after negotiating the Sicilian narrows at night unescorted, joined Admiral Cunningham's fleet at Alexandria. Apart from the advantage of their presence, there were also two bonuses: *Valiant* and *Illustrious* were both fitted with radar and could provide warning of approaching enemy aircraft and surface ships forty miles away and, more important, the carrier had brought numbers of fighters which could reduce the effect of enemy bombers and permit Cunningham's ships more freedom of action and initiative.

With the arrival of these forces the material advantage previously held by the Italians was diminished. Two tasks were assigned to the British naval forces; to search for and destroy the Italian fleet and to keep the Mediterranean clear for British troops and arms traffic in the Libya campaign.

The first of the tasks proved quite difficult, for on most occasions the Italians, when sighted by Cunningham's forces, turned and sped swiftly back to home ports, principally the safety of the harbour at Taranto, sited at the heel of the Italian mainland. In spite of the trap Cunningham set in October by escorting a convoy through the Mediterranean with the express purpose of luring the Italian fleet out into the open, the battleships stayed safely in port. This was in line with the policy laid down by the Italian naval chief of staff, Don Amico Cavagnari, that, whenever possible, confrontation with the British fleet was to be avoided. Cavagnari was well informed by his sources of intelligence of the constitution of British naval forces and was determined that his battleships and heavy cruisers should not be caught at sea in attacks from British aircraft-carriers. To this end he retained his powerful fleet in the harbour at Taranto.

As the year moved into October, Cunningham became increasingly aware that, if ever the time was right for a shock offensive at the Italian fleet, it was now, and if their ships would not come out, the only way to accomplish this was to go in after them – not by deploying his battle fleet in a shoot-out on the Italian coast but by attacking the Taranto base with aircraft. The architect of the plan was Rear-Admiral Lumley-Lyster who had brought the aircraft-carrier *Illustrious* from Britain to Alexandria to join Cunningham's force. His plan was daring and highly dangerous; some called it rash.

Torpedo-carrying planes from *Illustrious* would reach Taranto's main anchorage undetected and, skimming low across the outer harbour, release their torpedoes at point-blank range just a few hundred yards from the big capital ships. There would, of course, be massive anti-aircraft fire but with luck and precipitate evasive action they could speed away into the darkness and escape. While there were many circumstances governing the success of the operation, one factor was paramount: the efficiency of the aircraft to be used. At this time *Illustrious* carried the torpedo-carrying Swordfish, and with such limitations it greatly increased the dangers in attack.

Various criticisms were levelled at the Swordfish: 'ungainly dinosaur', 'antiquated stringbag', certain game for defensive fighters. It was a fabric-covered open-cockpit biplane and looked so crude and ineffective that an American airman, seeing it for the first time, was reputed to have said, 'My God, you don't mean to say you fly those things?' Its good points were excellent manoeuvrability, easy maintenance and the ability to operate in the most deplorable weather conditions despite heaving decks that prevented other craft from taking off. However, its main drawback was its limited speed of 139 m.p.h., reduced to about 100 m.p.h. when fully loaded, making it a vulnerable target. This called for the Taranto operation to be carried out under cover of darkness, with all its attendant perils.

The plan necessitated a period of concentrated training using the fleet's most experienced crews on night-time drills, under the expert supervision of Admiral Lumley-Lyster himself. It envisaged two waves of aircraft an hour apart. *Illustrious* would reach a spot for the fly-off some 170 miles from Taranto, and when each wave arrived, they would split up and dive towards their targets from different angles.

Following weeks of intensive practice, Admiral Cunningham was informed that thirty air crews and planes were ready. After a careful study of the calendar, Cunningham and Lumley-Lyster chose the night of 21 October, when a full moon would aid navigation in finding Taranto and help survivors to return to the carrier. As 21 October was Trafalgar Day, celebrating Nelson's victory, the two admirals considered it a most suitable date to launch the attack on Mussolini's battle-fleet. But 'the best laid plans of mice and men ...': an accidental fire in the hangar of *Illustrious* destroyed two of the aircraft and, with others having contaminated petrol in their tanks, the date had to be postponed, with only twenty-one planes taking part instead of the original thirty.

The attack, code-named 'Operation Judgment', was given a new date, 11 November. Meanwhile, reconnaissance flights over Taranto had gone ahead with unfailing regularity, and by 10 November 1940 Lumley-Lyster had detailed and accurate pictures of the numbers and positions of the Italian warships anchored in Taranto harbour. These photographs were to have an important bearing on the operation. Earlier in the month, No. 431 Flight of the RAF had arrived in Malta with three of the new fast American planes, the Martin Marylands. Apart from their fighter/bomber capacity, they were ideally suitable for speedy reconnaissance flights. At speeds nearing 300 m.p.h., they were far faster than the Sunderland flying-boats and were able to attain better heights and could keep a regular watch on the Taranto base with ease. As a result, Cunningham no longer had to wait to locate the enemy at sea to know where he was or what he was doing.

The naval base at Taranto, lying within the Gulf of Taranto and strategically positioned deep within the arch of the Italian mainland boot, has two harbours, an outer and an inner, named respectively the Mare Grande and the Mare Piccolo. The circular harbour of Mare Grande has an area of over ten square miles, its outlet to the west protected by partly submerged breakwaters connecting the larger island, San Pietro, and the smaller, San Paulo. These, contiguous with the natural southern and northern claws of the land, Cape San Vito and Cape Rondinella, form the spacious anchorage.

The latest photographs provided by the Marylands showed six battleships and three cruisers all at anchor. Of the former, four were the Cavour class, each with ten 12-inch guns, namely the *Conte di Cavour, Caio Duilio, Cesare* and *Andrea Dorea*, while some distance away lay the two new giants, *Vittorio Veneto* and *Littorio* with their 15-inch guns. On the northern side of the anchorage were the three 8-inch gun cruisers *Fiume, Zara* and *Gorizia*.

In Cairo, where the RAF photo intelligence HQ was stationed, the Maryland photos were carefully studied. At first, everything seemed straightforward, but a close examination showed up some odd markings on each photograph, small white spots strung out across the target area that were far too regularly spaced to be interpreted as camera-lens blemishes. It was soon realized that these were, in fact, barrage balloons floating over the anchorage held captive by strong steel cables, deadly enough to tear the wings off a low-flying aircraft. Because of this, the whole plan had to be re-assessed. It would be suicidal to try to fly between the cables with only the aid of moonlight. Extra luminosity would therefore have to be provided by dropping a line of flares to show up the whole target area and reveal the balloon cables to the attackers. As a result, some of the torpedo planes were re-assigned to carry magnesium flares and bombs.

During that day of the 11th, *Illustrious* moved steadily towards the point at which she would fly off her aircraft. Italian reconnaissance planes sent to search for British naval forces were immediately attacked and promptly shot down by fighter pilots from the carrier. The Italian High Command were therefore completely in the dark as to the whereabouts of Cunningham's force. Just before 20.00, *Illustrious*, escorted by four cruisers and four destroyers, reached the launching-point 170 miles from Taranto and forty miles south-west of the island of Cephalonia.

Meanwhile, in the hangars, last-minute preparations were being completed, final instructions given. The twenty-one Swordfish would fly off in two waves. The first, of twelve, would be led by Lieutenant-Commander K. Williamson, with Lieutenant N. Scarlett as observer. The second, of nine, would be led by Lieutenant-Commander J. Hale, with his observer, Lieutenant G. Carline. But not all these aircraft would carry torpedoes. Only six in the first wave and five in the second would be so armed; the rest would carry bombs or flares and bombs.

Apart from the balloon defences, the Italian ships were also protected by steel anti-torpedo nets. These were steel mesh curtains several feet deep surrounding the ship and suspended from floating buoys. To hit a ship so protected, the torpedo fired would have to be set deep enough to pass under the nets but not too deep otherwise it would also pass under the keel of the targeted ship. But if the latter happened, the then new device, the fitted Duplex pistol, would trigger the explosive mechanism in the torpedo by the magnetic attraction of the steel ship above it.

Despite the courage of the forty-two airmen, the imminent raid inevitably brought its dread and apprehension. They were not unaware of the prospects that faced them. Apart from the concentration of gunfire from battleships, cruisers, destroyers and other vessels in the anchorage, they would also have to fly through a curtain of flak from harbour defences. These comprised twenty-one batteries of 4-inch guns, in addition to 200 smaller guns, including pom-poms. At 20.35, the first wave of twelve Swordfish, led by Williamson in L4A, lumbered off the deck of the carrier, heading north-west towards Taranto, followed by the five other torpedo bomber pilots, Maund in E4F, Swayne in L4M, Kemp in L4K, Macauley in L4R and Patch in E5A. The remainder of the planes were the bombers and flare-droppers. Swayne had unfortunately become detached from the rest of the squadron in the dark and arrived over the Italian base some twenty minutes early. The sound of his approaching engine alerted the defences, giving the Taranto garrison their first introduction to a Brtish air raid. Almost at once, anti-aircraft gunfire began to fill the night sky with exploding shells. Wisely, Swayne flew back and forth at a safe distance, waiting.

By the time Williamson arrived in L4A to begin his run-in, small parachute flares were slowly floating down, to send an eerie golden light over the anchorage, clearly illuminating the Italian battleships and cruisers in the outer harbour of Mare Grande. Plunging into a steep dive from 7,000 feet to 700, he straightened out, then dipped

again to water-level to see a steel cable flash by. Now he was inside
the balloon barrier, with the roar and flash of guns almost numbing
the senses. Now the breakwater and then nothing but the big grey
shape of a giant battleship directly ahead. Springing suddenly out of
the inert superstructure came the blinding flashes of its guns. To
right and left other guns centred their fire on him. Swerving and
lurching in a macabre dance of survival, Williamson raced on
towards his target, throttle wide open. Then, when a crash seemed
inevitable, he released the torpedo.

Shed of its weight, the Swordfish suddenly leaped upwards and
away to the right – but unluckily into a blast of gunfire. It was a
direct shell hit. The plane shook under the impact, dived out of
control and plunged into the harbour. Under water, Williamson
had time to unclip his harness and swim to the surface, gasping for
air, to find his observer, Scarlett, alive and clinging to the sinking
aircraft. Reaching shore, they were taken prisoner and ironically
treated as honoured guests by the Italians until Italy later
capitulated.

Williamson's courage in the face of such devastating fire had
brought remarkable results, for the battleship *Conte di Cavour* had
suffered a mortal hit and, though beached, was never again to take
part in the war.

While Williamson was making his run-in, Kemp in *L4K* made his
approach over the western breakwater past Cape Rondinella to the
north, then, diving steeply, whistled through the gap of barrage
balloons between the anchored cruiser *Fiume* and Taranto Island.
A wall of ack-ack fire blazed at him from every direction. Apart
from the guns of the harbour defence batteries, the anchored
warships and even merchant ships opened up with everything they
had. Streaking low just above water-level, Kemp targeted on the
northernmost battleship of the six. Rocked by exploding shells,
almost blinded by the tracers and gun flashes, he released his
torpedo at less than 1,000 yards, then, banking steeply to the right
and climbing over the masts of the remaining battleships, the mole
and the long span of balloons, he raced away southwards, scarce
believing that he had escaped the blazing inferno of Taranto
harbour. Although his plane was riddled with bullets and shrapnel
holes, he and his observer were untouched, and breathing a sigh of
thankfulness they sped away into the darkness towards the waiting,
welcoming *Illustrious*.

And what of *L4K*'s homing torpedo? That had been dead·on

The aircraft-carrier HMS *Courageous* shortly before sinking

Kapitän-Leutnant Otto Schuhart being congratulated by Grand Admiral
Karl Dönitz after the sinking of HMS *Courageous*

The pocket-battleship *Graf Spee* on fire and sinking after being scuttled at Montevideo
*Bismarck* survivors being lifted aboard a British ship ⇨

The little shell-torn destroyer HMS *Glowworm* races on to ram the German battle-cruiser *Hipper*. Grand Admiral Erich Raeder, Commander-in-Chief, German Navy (*inset*)

Ships of the Italian battle-fleet on fire and sinking following the Fleet Air Arm raid at Taranto

The Italian warship *Colleoni* sinking during the Battle of Matapan

The cruiser HMS *Gloucester* turning turtle after being hit by German dive-bombers

The cruiser HMS *Kent* being dive-bombed in the Arctic, May 1942

After the third torpedo hit, HMS *Edinburgh* is listing and sinking

HMS *Trinidad* on fire and sinking due to attack by German dive-bombers; and torpedo damage to the same vessel after being hit by her own torpedo (*inset*)

The German destroyer *Hermann-Schömann* on fire and sinking after shell-hits from HMS *Edinburgh*

Survivors from the German destroyer *Z-26* receiving medals from their commanding officer, Commander Ritter von Berger

HMS *Trinidad* survivors having landed at Greenock

target, plunging into the hull of the 25,000-ton *Duilio* with an armament of ten 13-inch, twelve 5-inch and ten 4-inch guns. Despite its 10-inch side armour plating, the torpedo, its warhead filled with 750 pounds of Amatol, tore a huge hole in the *Duilio*'s side, putting the prize battleship out of service for over six months.

Only seconds after Kemp released his torpedo and banked sharply to escape, Swayne in *L4M* roared in over the western San Pietro island, across the Mare Grande water, through the central balloon gap and into port, targeting on *Littorio*. With shell blasts rocking the plane, Swayne released his deadly steel fish at only 400 yards range and lifted *L4K* over the masts of the battleship, heading south over the Taranto Gulf. In quick succession the other three Swordfish, piloted by Maund, Macauley and Patch, roared in over the anchorage, selecting their targets amid a Dante's inferno of fire and eruption. Out of the total of six torpedoes, four were bull's eyes, causing devastating destruction. And while the torpedo bombers were busy at water-level, the remaining Swordfish of the first flight, each carrying eight 60-pound bombs, hit their assigned targets on inner harbour ships and shore installations. As the pilots looked back at the Mare Grande and the Mare Piccolo, all they could see was a huge cloud of orange-coloured billowing smoke, while through it and above shone the brilliance of bursting anti-aircraft shells and reflective flame.

Just an hour after the first, the second wave of Swordfish of 819 Squadron, led by Lieutenant-Commander J.W. Hale, took off from *Illustrious*. An accident on the flight-deck scrapped one plane, leaving only eight aircraft to make the attack. These were piloted by Hale in *L5A*, Lea in *L5H*, Torrens-Spence in *L5K*, Bayley in *E4H* and Wellham in *E5H* with torpedoes and the other three with bombs and flares.

At 23.10, as the flight neared Taranto, they could see the target sixty miles away. The cloud ceiling for miles around reflected an orange-red glow and below it a crucible of erupting fires. As they closed, the whole saucered anchorage vibrated and twinkled with a curtain of bursting shells and stabbing roots of flame. In fact, adding the guns of the harbour defences to those of the anchored ships, they were looking at a cannonade saturation of nearly a thousand guns, seeming to cover every part of the sky. And that was the terrifying inferno into which they had to fly.

Approaching from the west, Hale led the 'stringbags' over the breakwater close to the Rondinella Cape and made for the gap in the defences, with Taranto Island on his port side and the big cruisers to starboard. Already they were being enveloped in a curtain of fire from every angle, and the drifting smoke from the havoc wrought by the first flight made it difficult to identify the main target of their attack. But suddenly, through the screen of smoke, Hale saw the giant silhouette of the prize they sought, the battleship *Littorio*. Bucking and rearing, shaken by exploding shells all around the plane, he realized he was too high. He dropped to fifty feet, forty, then thirty and, flattening out, rushed on, throttle wide open. The wheels were almost touching the water now and the ship looming up as a frightening wall of steel. At only 700 yards he released the torpedo, aware of the blinding stabs of flame from the battleship's multiple guns. Then, with the torpedo gone, the plane leapt up and over the masts of *Littorio* and onward over the southern claw of the harbour. They were through.

One by one the tailing planes followed, selecting their targets but concentrating on the biggest ships. Moments later, however, tragedy struck, when Pilot Torrens-Spence, diving towards his selected ship, suddenly saw another Swordfish across his path. To avoid a collision he dived steeply, to pass below, only to see the plane above him hit in a flash of flame and catch a glimpse of it plunging away out of control. This proved to be Pilot Bayley and his observer Slaughter in *E4H*, which had apparently received a direct hit. Neither of them was ever seen again. This was the only Swordfish lost in the second flight.

The Fleet Air Arm attack on Taranto was over, and as the pilots headed for *Illustrious*, they looked back to see Taranto's safe basin a scene of chaos and devastation, with ships aflame, clouds of black rolling smoke and a confined sea of burning oil.

One by one, the 'stringbags' returned safely and their pilots thankfully to the carrier's deck, planes shot up and riddled with holes.

For the loss of two aircraft, of which the crew of one were rescued, the result of the attack was beyond anyone's imagination. Three battleships, *Littorio, Duilio* and *Conte di Cavour*, two cruisers, including *Trento*, and a few destroyers had been either sunk or so badly damaged that they took little or no further part in the war. In addition, harbour installations, a seaplane base and some oil storage-tanks had received severe damage. All this had been accomplished by a few old-fashioned planes in sixty-five minutes.

The raid had also brought another bonus. The possibility of further attacks prompted an immediate order from the Italian High Command that all major warships that could move were to leave harbour and retire to Naples, 500 miles away. It was a position so far north that their effect on British convoys in the Mediterranean became minimal.

The success of the attack was a revelation in strategic sea power, for it was now realized that control of the sea depended largely on naval air-strength.

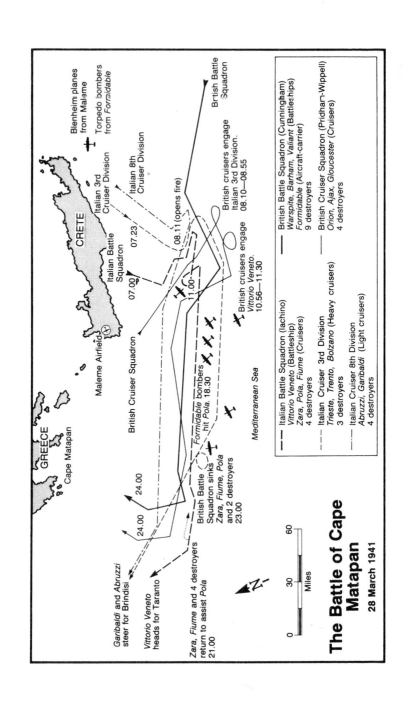

# The Battle of Cape Matapan

## 28 March 1941

GREECE

Cape Matapan

CRETE

Maleme Airfield

Mediterranean Sea

Blenheim planes from Maleme

Torpedo bombers from *Formidable*

British Battle Squadron

Italian 3rd Cruiser Division

Italian 8th Cruiser Division

08.11 (opens fire)

British cruisers engage Italian 3rd Division. 08.10—08.55

07.23

Italian Battle Squadron

07.00

07.00

British Cruiser Squadron

11.00

British cruisers engage *Vittorio Veneto*. 10.56—11.30

*Formidable* bombers hit *Pola.* 18.30

24.00

24.00

*Garibaldi* and *Abruzzi* steer for Brindisi

*Vittorio Veneto* heads for Taranto

*Zara, Fiume* and 4 destroyers return to assist *Pola*
21.00

British Battle Squadron sinks *Zara, Fiume, Pola* and 2 destroyers
23.00

N

0        30        60

Miles

—————  Italian Battle Squadron (Iachino)
*Vittorio Veneto* (Battleship)
*Zara, Pola, Fiume* (Cruisers)
4 destroyers

- - - - -  Italian Cruiser 3rd Division
*Trieste, Trento, Bolzano* (Heavy cruisers)
3 destroyers

—·—·—  Italian Cruiser 8th Division
*Abruzzi, Garibaldi* (Light cruisers)
4 destroyers

—————  British Battle Squadron (Cunningham)
*Warspite, Barham, Valiant* (Battleships)
*Formidable* (Aircraft-carrier)
9 destroyers

—————  British Cruiser Squadron (Pridham–Wippell)
*Orion, Ajax, Gloucester* (Cruisers)
4 destroyers

# 6  The Battle of Cape Matapan

*The Battle of Cape Matapan occupies a special place in naval history, not only for the resoluteness of its action but for the success of the engagement, which clearly demonstrated the superiority of British naval strategy.*

Following the humiliation of the Italian fleet at the hands of the British naval squadron off the coast of Calabria and more so by the crushing defeat inflicted by Admiral Cunningham's Naval Air Arm strike at Taranto in the autumn of 1940, extensive repairs and salvaging were somehow affected, and by late March 1941 a limited Italian fleet was more or less prepared to sail again to attack British convoys operating in the Mediterranean, always assuming that the escorting force was minimal. During this period, in January 1941, the British fleet received a setback, for while escorting a small convoy through the narrows north-west of Malta, the aircraft-carrier *Illustrious* was subjected to such concentrated bombing by the Luftwaffe that she was severely damaged. Limping into Malta, she was again attacked, suffering further damage, and although later she succeeded in reaching Alexandria, she could no longer launch aircraft.

Despite the perilous Atlantic situation, the Admiralty diverted the aircraft-carrier *Formidable* from that theatre of war to round Africa and enter the Mediterranean through the Suez Canal, to take the place of the damaged carrier. Although the loss of *Illustrious* was grievous, Admiral Cunningham was determined to sustain British convoy traffic, and convoys were operated with renewed vigour from Alexandria to supply Malta and to lend support to the Greeks fighting a desperate battle with their invaders. With the presence of the carrier *Formidable* bringing fighter squadrons of

Fulmars and torpedo-carrying Albacores, Cunningham was well satisfied with his replacement.

The Fairey Albacore was a successor to the Fairey Swordfish. Although of the same configuration, that of a single-engined biplane with fixed landing-gear, it had nearly twice the range and could carry the same size torpedo and an increased bomb load. It was to prove itself a supreme aircraft in the Battle of Cape Matapan.

*Formidable* entered Alexandria harbour on the morning of 10 March and the next day, following his promotion to Rear-Admiral Mediterranean Carriers, Denis Boyd transferred his flag from *Illustrious* to *Formidable*.

During February and early March 1941, the British were sending a stream of supply ships and troop reinforcements to Greece, and this action so displeased the German High Command that they brought excessive political pressure to prod the Italian naval staff into action. By 15 March the commander-in-chief of the Italian Navy, Admiral Angelo Iachino had been informed that a naval strike had to be mounted. As a counter to the navy's fears that the British forces would be stronger than their own, the German Luftwaffe gave firm assurances that they would provide ample air reconnaissance over the eastern Mediterranean and Alexandria, and fighter cover for the Italian ships during daylight hours as far as Cape Matapan on the southern tip of Morea in the Peloponnese. Furthermore, the German naval staff in Rome persuaded the Italians that the only British battleship ready for action was HMS *Valiant*. This was, of course, entirely false, but nevertheless it was a bait which lured their ally to sea.

Still suspicious of the reliability of these assurances, Iachino sailed from Naples in the powerful new battleship *Vittorio Veneto* on 26 March. With him he had the 8-inch gun cruisers *Bolzana, Fiume, Trieste, Pola* and *Zara*, the 6-inch gun cruisers *Abruzzi* and *Garibaldi* and thirteen destroyers, *Alpino, Gioberti, Pessagno, Bersagliere, Alfiere, Carazziere, Fuciliere, Oriani, Ascari, Granatiere, Carducci, Carabiniere* and *da Recco*. The *Vittorio Veneto* was very fast for a battleship, capable of over 30 knots, and her nine 15-inch guns were superior to the guns of the old British battleships.

Iachino's doubts as to the credibility of the Luftwaffe's promises were confirmed when the proposed air support failed to materialize. But, worse still, hardly had they set out on their foray when a British Sunderland flying-boat on reconnaissance found them and reported back to Alexandria. In the extremely poor visibility, however, all that could be sighted was three Italian cruisers and a destroyer south-east of Sicily, heading in the direction of Crete. From that moment, Iachino knew that the element of surprise had disappeared.

A day earlier, Cunningham had received special intelligence reports that units of the Italian fleet were preparing for sea, and he therefore took the precaution of clearing the eastern area of convoys to allow him to mount an attack on the Italians rather than be occupied in a defence of his merchant ships. Exercising a brilliant piece of subterfuge to deceive the ever-watchful Axis spies in Alexandria, he sailed his fleet under cover of darkness, flying his flag in the battleship *Warspite*, accompanied by *Barham*, *Valiant* and the carrier *Formidable*. Escorting the battle squadron were the destroyers, *Jervis*, *Janus*, *Nubian*, *Mohawk*, *Stuart*, *Greyhound*, *Griffin*, *Hotspur* and *Havock*. Preceding them was a cruiser squadron under Vice-Admiral Pridham-Wippell, flying his flag in *Orion*. In company were the cruisers *Ajax*, *Perth* and *Gloucester* and the destroyers *Ilex*, *Hasty*, *Hereward* and *Vendetta*.

Anticipating that the enemy might be making for the south of Crete near Gavdo Island to attack the convoy route to Greece, Pridham-Wippell's cruiser squadron headed on a course in roughly the same direction. As a result, throughout the night of the 27th–28th Iachino's fleet and the British cruiser squadron were speeding towards a head-on clash which on the following day would develop into the Battle of Cape Matapan.

By dawn the Italian fleet was in three groups, on a course steering south-east, with the 8-inch gun cruisers in the middle, the 6-inch cruisers to port and the battleship *Vittorio Veneto* to starboard. By now Iachino was deeply frustrated by the lack of air support so glibly promised by the Germans. He hoped he would have been able to count on at least a long-range air reconnaissance effort.

At 06.00 that morning, *Vittorio Veneto* launched her own reconnaissance plane, which an hour later reported four cruisers and four destroyers heading south-east and only about sixty miles away. The approaching British force, matched against his own fleet of one battleship, eight cruisers and thirteen destroyers, would be easy prey and one that admirably suited Iachino's assessment of the balance of power. Assuming there must be a British convoy also in the offing, he pressed on at 30 knots. At 08.12 the British and

Italian forces sighted one another, and action was opened at a range of about twelve miles.

*Orion*'s speed was 6 knots less than the Italians' and realizing that he was being outgunned and outpaced, Pridham-Wippell wisely turned away from the enemy and steered south-east in the hope of luring the pursuing fleet into the guns of the oncoming British battle squadron. Soon he was being hard-pressed.

The lagging *Gloucester* at the rear of the retreating British cruisers was receiving the full, concentrated fire of the Italian ships. Adopting a violent zigzag course, she managed to avoid being hit and was soon able to bring her own rear turrets to bear on the pursuers. Although her salvoes were falling short, it was enough to subdue the sudden enthusiasm of the cruiser admiral, Sansonnetti, and at 08.55 he broke off the action, reversed his course and steered north-west. This was in response to a direct order from the sensitive and suspicious Iachino in the rear of the cruiser force. He still had no idea that Cunningham's battle fleet was some distance to the south-east, speeding to Pridham-Wippell's relief, and even after he received a report from the base at Rhodes that a lone reconnaissance plane had sighted a carrier, two battleships, nine cruisers and fourteen destroyers, he refused to believe it, convinced that this sighting referred to his own force.

By now Pridham-Wippell had again reversed his course and, turning to the north-west, followed the Italian cruisers at a discreet distance to keep in touch and report to Admiral Cunningham, who was well aware that the Italians might have adopted the same idea as Pridham-Wippell and was luring the cruiser squadron towards a heavier force.

Iachino had indeed developed a plan to trap the shadowing British ships by taking his own vessel around to the north-east to come up behind them. When this position was established, he would order Sansonnetti to double back on his pursuers and ambush them between the *Vittorio Veneto* and his cruisers.

In the meantime, however, Admiral Cunningham had made a momentous and what proved to be providential decision. Increasing the speed of his own ships, he signalled *Formidable* to launch a strike and at 10.00 six Albacores and two Fulmars armed with torpedoes took off with an accompanying Swordfish for observation. Also in response to the C-in-C's request, the naval air station at Maleme at the western end of Crete flew off three Swordfish armed with torpedoes.

While this move was in progress, Pridham-Wippell was fully absorbed in keeping as close as he dared to the withdrawing Italian cruisers, unaware of the trap waiting to be sprung. Then, at 11.00, the look-outs in *Orion* suddenly spotted a large ship to the north, and moments later, to Pridham-Wippell's dismay, she was identified as the big Italian battleship *Vittorio Veneto* of 35,000 tons. Within seconds she opened fire. Pridham-Wippell now found himself in a perilous position, with *Vittorio Veneto* on his port quarter and the enemy cruisers to starboard. Once again the British cruisers reversed their course, leading the Italians to the south-east, to Cunningham's forces closing from astern, which Iachino thought were still at Alexandria. But now Pridham-Wippell came under intense and accurate fire from the battleship's 15-inch and the cruiser's 8-inch guns at a closing range of under twelve miles. *Orion* became the target for the battleship's guns, and to avoid annihilation the British cruisers set up a smoke-screen. Despite this, *Orion* was subjected to such intensive fire that she sustained some damage. As the smoke became more effective, however, the pressure on the British force was reduced and the enemy's fire then shifted to *Gloucester*, whose reduced speed, due to an engine fault, made her terribly exposed. Although constantly straddled by the enemy's 15-inch shells, she managed to survive mainly by the aid of the destroyer *Hasty*'s effective smoke-screen.

It was at this critical stage, when disaster seemed inevitable, that out of the sky *Formidable*'s torpedo-carrying aircraft attacked. It appears that Iachino was greatly pleased when his mast-head look-outs reported that supporting Italian planes had arrived, but this turned to anguish when it proved that the planes were British. The Albacores and Fulmars pressed home their attacks, and although the Italian battleship received no actual hits, she only narrowly escaped. Despite the misses, the aircraft attack had saved the British cruisers from possible decimation, for Iachino broke off the engagement and steered north-west towards the Italian mainland, now fully aware that the attacking aircraft could have come from an aircraft-carrier.

About noon the Italian battleship received further attacks from the Maleme-based Swordfish but again without positive result. However, it seemed to strengthen Iachino's determination to reach port as quickly as possible.

In the meantime Pridham-Wippell's force was racing south at top speed under a smoke-screen, unaware of the timely arrival of

*Formidable*'s planes or that *Vittorio Veneto* had reversed course for home at 28 knots.

While the British air attack had saved the British cruisers, it also had the effect of turning the enemy away while still some fifty miles from Cunningham's battle squadron. It was clear there was no chance of engaging the enemy until nightfall at least, and only then if he could be slowed by *Formidable*'s torpedo-bombers.

At 12.30 that day Pridham-Wippell's ships met Cunningham's battle fleet and joined forces with them to pursue the retiring Italians, but speed had to be reduced to 22 knots to allow the labouring *Barham* to keep up.

Following a reconnaissance report that *Vittorio Veneto* was now sixty-five miles ahead, a second striking force was flown off from *Formidable*, comprising high-level bombers, torpedo-bombers and fast fighter aircraft. At 15.20, while the fighters raced in, strafing the bridge and gun positions, and the high-level bombers occupied their full attention, three Albacores swept in low over the water and dropped their torpedoes. The pilot of the leading plane in particular showed great courage and skill by closing to within a thousand yards before dropping his torpedo. But by now every gun that could be brought to bear concentrated on the aircraft, and although taking desperate measures to escape the withering fire, it received many hits and, barely missing *Vittorio*'s bows, crashed into the sea some distance ahead. With the pilot died the observer and the air gunner, all three not knowing that their courageous attack had been successful.

The torpedo sped on its way towards the battleship, and seconds later it struck below the water-line near the port propeller. After the explosion, tons of water poured into the ship, and the engines stopped. As the vessel listed to port and settled by the stern, damage-control parties quickly went into action, and temporary repairs were swiftly carried out. By 17.00, the starboard engines were restarted, and soon the battleship was pushing through the water at nearly 15 knots, still unaware that the British battle squadron, although some miles away, was closing on them at 22 knots. But *Vittorio* was still over 400 miles away from its home port, Taranto.

Fearing further attacks, Iachino summoned his 8-inch cruiser squadron around him to form a close screen. These were the heavy cruisers *Trieste, Trento* and *Bolzano* on one flank and *Fiume, Zara* and *Pola* on the other. The 6-inch gun cruisers *Abruzzi* and

*Garibaldi* with destroyer escort he dispatched to Brindisi.

For Cunningham, with the onset of evening and diminishing light, it was necessary to provide visual contact with the enemy in the shortest possible time. His cruisers were sent on ahead, with a couple of destroyers providing a link between the battle squadron and the advanced Pridham-Wippell. At 17.45, while another strike was being prepared in *Formidable*, Cunningham's own observer, Lieutenant-Commander Bolt, was catapulted from *Warspite* to clarify the uncertain and rather confused reports of the movements of the retreating Italian fleet. Within an hour his accurate assessment of the situation had been received by *Warspite*: *Vittorio Veneto* was 45 miles from the Commander-in-Chief's flagships and heading north-west. The report intercepted by Iachino was so correct and defined that it brought unstinting admiration from him. Even at this time he was still unaware that the British battle squadron was at sea, let alone pursuing him from the south-east.

At 19.00 the last torpedo-striking force from *Formidable* was launched and by 19.15, at sunset, it was over the target. As the torpedo bombers went in to attack, Bolt in his Swordfish overhead watched and reported every move made by the Italians. As dusk deepened into semi-darkness, the Italian ships formed themselves into a more compact mass and waited for the hovering torpedo planes to make their run in. At 19.30 *Formidable*'s Albacores and Fulmars began their attack, choosing independent targets. As a defence, the Italian fleet put up a deafening barrage of anti-aircraft fire, accompanied by vast quantities of coloured tracer from their close-range guns. As additional protection, each ship made a smoke-screen and switched on its searchlights. The result had all the appearance of a Hades inferno, with the rolling, floodlit blankets of smoke reflecting flame and fire.

As the tumult and fire increased, it became impossible to see just what was happening. *Formidable*'s aircraft were met by a withering curtain of fire, but with the Italian ships bunched together, it was almost impossible not to hit something. That something was the 8-inch gun cruiser *Pola* on the starboard wing. The attack on *Pola* was pressed home by an Albacore, piloted by Sub-Lieutenant Williams, who closed to within suicidal range and fired his torpedo just above sea-level. The big cruiser was hit amidships, flooding several compartments and closing down the engines.

While *Vittorio Veneto* and the remaining cruisers sped away, Iachino was unaware that *Pola* had been hit and was stopped. It was not until thirty minutes later, when an assessment was made of the situation, that the loss was discovered. Distressed by the news, Iachino ordered Vice-Admiral Cattaneo, with the two other 8-inch cruisers *Zara* and *Fiume* and four destroyers, to turn back and go to the aid of the stopped *Pola*, while he himself, with the remainder of his fleet, increased speed to 19 knots and altered course to almost due north towards Taranto. By making this decision, Iachino had unwittingly committed Cattaneo's force to destruction, for he still had not the slightest idea that the British squadron was approaching. Obeying the order, Cattaneo reversed his course and steered directly south-east towards the last known position of *Pola* but unknowingly straight towards the oncoming British ships.

Cunningham, urging his fleet on to contact the enemy, was convinced that he would be able to engage the damaged *Vittorio Veneto* during the night. Accordingly he ordered eight of his destroyers to steam ahead, take up positions and await the executive signal to attack. This was a calculated risk, for it left only four destroyers to protect the battle squadron if the enemy should decide to turn about and attack. It was also a crucial decision, for it provided the likelihood of night action with all its risks and the possibility of damage to his own forces. Cunningham went through the formality of inviting the opinion of his staff officers, who were not slow in expressing their doubts on the wisdom of such action, but he himself had no hesitation. His destroyers would go in against the enemy fleet with torpedoes, and if this failed, he would follow in with his battle squadron. At 08.30 he made the executive signal for his destroyers to attack.

The eight ships therefore pressed ahead at 30 knots, and soon after 21.30 Pridham-Wippell reported that his accompanying cruiser *Ajax*, a radar ship, had picked up three unknown ships on her screen, five miles away. These were, of course, part of Cattaneo's force returning to aid *Pola*. On receipt of these reports, Cunningham's hopes ran high that one of the vessels might be *Vittorio*, but in fact the Italian battleship was thirty miles to the north and steaming fast for home.

At 22.00 *Valiant*'s radar-operator reported an echo on the screen of a stopped ship about eight miles distant on the port bow. Ten minutes later the range was down to six miles. At a given signal, *Warspite, Valiant, Formidable* and *Barham* turned together, steering 240 degrees. Twenty minutes later, with the range at only 4½ miles, it was seen that the destroyer *Griffin*, on the port bow, was directly in the line of fire; she was curtly told, 'Get to hell out of it!' *Formidable* was also ordered, for her own safety, to haul out of line.

With all guns loaded and fingers on triggers, the battle squadron cautiously moved nearer, waiting to sight the enemy on the port bow.

Suddenly the destroyer *Stuart* on the starboard side gave the night alarm. With his staff officers, Cunningham could now see the large shapes of darkened ships in a different direction from the pin-pointed stopped ship, steering a course from right to left across the bows of the British ships. These were Cattaneo's cruisers escorted by destroyers. Leading the line was the destroyer *Alfieri*, followed by the large cruisers *Zara* and *Fiume*, with the destroyers *Gioberti*, *Carducci* and *Oriani* bringing up the rear. To quote Cunningham's words,

> I shall never forget the next few minutes. In the dead silence, a silence that could be almost felt, one heard only the voice of the gun control personnel putting the guns on to the new target. One heard the orders repeated in the director tower behind and above the bridge. Looking forward, one saw the turrets swing and steady when the 15 inch guns pointed at the enemy cruisers. Never in my whole life have I experienced a more thrilling moment than when I heard a calm voice from the director tower – 'Director layer sees the target'; sure sign that the guns were ready and that his finger was itching on the trigger. The enemy was at a range of no more than 3,800 yards – point blank.

Suddenly one of the destroyers, slightly ahead, opened her searchlight. The whole formation of enemy ships was now clear. The powerful beam of light fell upon *Fiume* and beyond onto the *Zara*, led by the destroyer *Alfieri*, their guns trained for and aft, quite unprepared. The time was 22.27. Then, in a thunderous barrage of gunfire, the 15-inch broadsides of *Warspite*, *Valiant* and, minutes later, *Barham* hammered into the Italian cruisers. *Fiume* was the first to take the full impact of the bombardment. At an instant her superstructure became a mass of flame, with her after turrets blown clean over the side. Cunningham describes the scene:

One heard the ting-ting-ting of the firing gongs. Then came
the great orange flash and the violent shudder as the six big
guns bearing, were fired simultaneously. At the very same
moment the *Greyhound* switched her searchlight on to one of
the enemy cruisers showing her momentarily as a silver blue
shape in the darkness. Our searchlights shone out with the
first salvo and provided full illumination for what was a
ghastly sight.

Full in the beam I saw our six great projectiles flying
through the air. Five out of the six hit her a few feet below the
level of the cruiser's upper deck and burst with splashes of
brilliant flame. They were hopelessly shattered before they
could put up any resistance. In the midst of all this there was
one milder diversion. Captain Douglas Fisher, the captain of
*Warspite* who was a gunnery officer of note, when he saw the
first salvo hit, was heard to say in a voice of wondering
surprise, 'Good Lord we've hit her!'

Seconds later, *Valiant* shifted fire and engaged the second cruiser,
*Zara*, at a range of under two miles. Meanwhile *Barham*, at the rear
of the line, trained her guns on the leading ship, the destroyer
*Alfieri*, and in moments the latter was a mass of flame from end to
end. *Warspite, Valiant* and *Barham* now concentrated their
combined fire on the two cruisers, which soon became nothing
more than blazing hulks. The three Italian destroyers astern of the
cruisers attempted a desperate retaliatory attack on the British ships
and fired torpedoes. This was seen in time, and Cunningham
immediately ordered an emergency turn to starboard to present the
minimum target, and fire was then directed onto the destroyers,
which, in an attempt to escape, raced off to the west, pursued by the
destroyers *Griffin* and *Greyhound*, keeping up a steady barrage on
the fleeing ships. While this was in progress, the destroyers *Stuart*
and *Havock* returned to the scene of the action to torpedo and
finally sink the Italian cruisers. To give the destroyers a free hand in
the final elimination of the Italian ships, Cunningham ordered that
all forces not so engaged should retire to the north-east.

Ironically, the stopped *Pola*, although hit and badly damaged,
had managed to drift away without further mauling into the
darkness. This was, however, only a temporary reprieve, for she
was soon found by the destroyer *Jervis* commanded by Captain
(later Rear-Admiral) Philip Mack. The cruiser was indeed in a sorry

state, and as *Jervis* approached, hundreds of the panic-stricken crew were seen jumping overboard. For a while Captain Mack considered the idea of trying to tow *Pola* back to Alexandria, but he soon dismissed the thought. In the event he decided to sink her after taking off what remained of her crew. Rather like the old pirates, he decided to board her. As the fenders went out and the heaving lines were thrown across to secure, the forward gun's crews, armed with cutlasses, leapt onto *Pola*'s decks, uttering blood-curling cries, but there was no resistance, for out of the whole ship's company of a thousand only 250 remained. These were a sorry crowd indeed, utterly cowed, huddling fearfully on the forecastle. A thorough search of the ship gave ample evidence of complete chaos, with officers' cabins looted and empty wine bottles scattered everywhere. (This was substantiated when many of the prisoners were found to be drunk.) With the Italian prisoners aboard, Mack gave the order to the destroyer *Nubian* to close in on *Pola* and sink her with torpedoes. At 04.00 *Pola* blew up and sank.

A few hours earlier, just before midnight, *Havock* had also chased and caught one of the three remaining destroyers, *Carducci*, which she quickly sank with torpedoes. Out of the three cruisers and four destroyers which had been involved in the action, only the destroyers *Gioberti* and *Oriani* managed to escape. With these five ships of the Italian Navy had perished 2,400 officers and ratings, including Vice-Admiral Cattaneo.

It had been a crushing defeat for the Italian fleet, and a great victory for the British. Never again in the remaining years of the war did the Italians effectively interfere with Britain's control of this sea route to the East.

The following is the original signal to the fleet despatched by Admiral Sir Andrew Cunningham following the Battle of Matapan.

ESTIMATED DAMAGE TO ENEMY.
VITTORIO HEAVILY DAMAGED
ZARA, POLA, FIUME SUNK
ONE ITALIAN CRUISER (CONDOTTIERI CLASS) PROBABLY SUNK
900 PRISONERS
3 AIRCRAFT SHOT DOWN

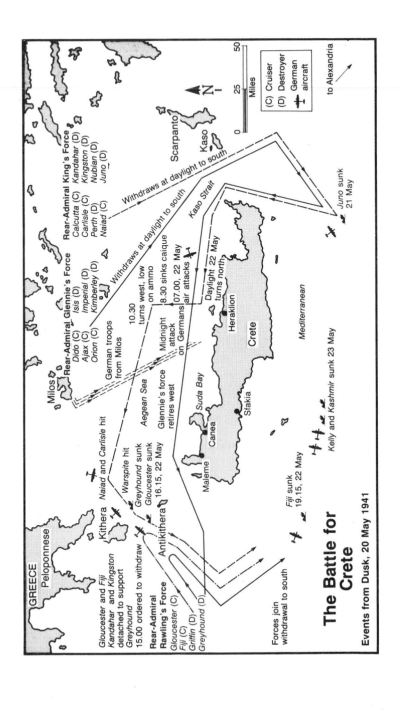

# The Battle for Crete

## Events from Dusk, 20 May 1941

GREECE

Peloponnese

Milos

Kithera

Antikithera

Aegean Sea

German troops
from Milos

**Rear-Admiral Glennie's Force**
Dido (C)
Ajax (C)
Orion (C)
Isis (D)
Imperial (D)
Kimberley (D)

**Rear-Admiral King's Force**
Calcutta (C)
Carlisle (C)
Perth (D)
Naiad (C)
Kandahar (D)
Kingston (D)
Nubian (D)
Juno (D)

Scarpanto

Kaso

Withdraws at daylight to south

Withdraws at daylight to south

10.30
turns west,
low on ammo

8.30 sinks caique

07.00, 22 May
air attacks

Kaso Strait

Juno sunk
21 May

Midnight
attack
on Germans

Daylight 22 May
turns north

Glennie's force
retires west

Heraklion

Crete

Mediterranean

Suda Bay

Canea

Stakia

Maleme

*Naiad and Carlisle hit*

*Warspite hit*

*Greyhound sunk*

*Gloucester sunk*

16.15, 22 May

Gloucester and Fiji
Kandahar and Kingston
detached to support
Greyhound
15.00 ordered to withdraw

**Rear-Admiral
Rawling's Force**
Gloucester (C)
Fiji (C)
Griffin (D)
Greyhound (D)

Forces join
withdrawal to south

*Fiji sunk
19.15, 22 May*

*Kelly and Kashmir sunk 23 May*

N

Miles
0    25    50

(C) Cruiser
(D) Destroyer
✈ German aircraft

to Alexandria

# 7   The Battle for Crete

*Following the evacuation from Greece in May 1941, the British found themselves in heavy conflict with the enemy trying to defend the island of Crete, which they had occupied. To prevent the Germans from landing re-inforcements on the island, the Royal Navy was committed to attacking sea-borne troops from the mainland. To offset this, the Germans launched a massive airborne strike against the Royal Navy which cost them dearly in ships and men. In this action the cruisers* Gloucester *and* Fiji *paid the ultimate price.*

The old saying that the British always win the last battle presupposes that they always lose the first. It was certainly true of World War II, when in the early stages Britain's few successes were far outweighed by her failures. Never more so than in the Mediterranean, where, although the Royal Navy fought with all the resources at its command and with a courage and gallantry far beyond the call of duty, it was soon recognized that sea power in that area without adequate defensive cover from the air was a recipe for disaster.

This was poignantly demonstrated in the Battle for Crete in May 1941, when the German Luftwaffe, under the overall command of General Lohr, launched a massive attack to capture the island with forces from airfields in Greece and the Aegean Islands. He had at his disposal over 700 dive-bombers and fighter bombers to support 600 transport planes of the Fliegerkorps XI parachute and airborne division, with 23,000 men. Additional to this and only thirty minutes flying-time away, the Italians could muster 2,000 aircraft if called upon.

In the period leading up to 20 May, it was clear that the Germans were preparing for an invasion of the island on which Britain had a precarious hold. Although there were some 30,000 British troops there, they were lamentably short of guns, ammunition, vehicles and an assortment of equipment. When General B.C. Freyberg VC, DSO arrived on Crete, he discovered gross deficiencies in the preparation for attack: weak links in the chain of defence, a lack of organization, and the frightening revelation that the air-strength to resist the expected airborne invasion amounted to about seven aircraft. If the airborne invasion were to succeed, however, it would be necessary to support it with a seaborne landing of transports carrying troops, tanks, heavy guns and supplies.

The responsibility for preventing this fell upon the Commander-in-Chief of the Allied Mediterranean Fleet based in Alexandria, Admiral Sir Andrew Cunningham. He had no illusions about the difficulties of the task ahead. The government at home were under the mistaken impression that the fleet could operate without any air support in its defence of Crete, in waters dominated by a mighty enemy air force. Despite Cunningham's appeals for fighter aircraft, his cry went unanswered. The one aircraft-carrier at his disposal was *Formidable*, and she could muster only four serviceable fighter planes. The admiral knew that to send his fleet to sea against such overwhelming numbers of enemy aircraft dominating the skies, and without any defensive air cover, would amount virtually to suicide. Nevertheless, these were his orders, and in duty bound he disposed his ships to meet whatever contingencies might arise, knowing full well that heavy losses in ships and men had to be expected.

On the morning of 20 May the assault on Crete began with several hours of merciless bombing, followed by an air invasion of gliders carrying thousands of German paratroopers. Despite the well-organized attack, the enemy met an opposition far more stubborn than they had expected, and very heavy losses were sustained on both sides but particularly by the enemy.

As soon as Cunningham heard of the assault, he ordered all his forces to move closer to Crete, with the intention of intercepting the sailing of heavy transports and re-inforcement of troops. By that evening two cruiser groups, with their attendant destroyers, were sweeping the sea to the north of Crete in the hope of meeting up with the enemy ships. The cruisers *Dido, Ajax* and *Orion*, in company with three destroyers, *Isis, Kimberley* and *Imperial*, patrolled under the command of Rear-Admiral I.G. Glennie, and to the eastward of these the cruisers *Naiad, Perth, Calcutta* and *Carlisle*, with the destroyers *Kandahar, Nubian, Kingston* and *Juno* under Rear-Admiral E.L.S. King. To avoid heavy losses to his ships from the inevitable air strikes by the Luftwaffe over the island by day, Cunningham ordered the groups to patrol only by night and withdraw to the south of Crete at daylight, when it was known that no enemy forces were at sea. During that night no enemy convoys were discovered, and with the first dawning light they again retired to the southward of the island. But by now, aware of the British ships' day and night manoeuvres, the enemy's long-distance bombers tracked down Cunningham's ships and relentlessly strafed them with high-level bombing and dive-bombing.

These attacks, now assisted by squadrons of the Italian Air Force, resulted in the tragic loss of the destroyer *Juno*. She was hit by three bombs, two of which destroyed her boiler- and engine-rooms; the third, ploughing down into the magazine, blew the ship apart in a mighty explosion. Following this, she broke in half, leaving both parts floating away as flaming pyres. Nearly a hundred of her crew of 183 were lost in this tragedy.

By this time the paratroopers had gained a foothold on the island, and they assumed that now would be the opportunity to launch the main body of their invasion forces by sea. A judgement which was to cost them dearly. A lone British reconnaissance aircraft sighted the troop-carrying force from the island of Milos, already at sea, just before nightfall, heading for Canea Bay, west of Suda Bay. That information, signalled to the British fleet, brought Glennie, flying his flag in the cruiser *Dido*, racing to the area accompanied by his cruisers and destroyers. By midnight they came upon the convoy of twenty-five caiques (wooden schooners) crammed with German soldiers fully equipped and ready for battle, accompanied by Italian destroyers and steamers.

The token defence put up by the escorts was brushed aside, leaving one of their number rapidly sinking. The transports, now without any defence, became sitting targets, and as Glennie's force moved in with torpedoes and gunfire, they were quickly disposed of, with the troops leaping overboard. It became a rout, as the British ships raced in, sinking many by the old-fashioned method of ramming. It was an engagement which lasted nearly three hours, with the loss to the Germans of nearly 2,500 troops.

But dawn was imminent, and at 03.30 on the 21st Glennie called off the attack and ordered his fleet to withdraw and rendezvous with him to the west of Crete. It was a wise move, for his cruisers had used up much of their anti-aircraft ammunition on the previous day. In fact, his own ship, *Dido*, had only twenty-five per cent of her stock left. It would be an act of folly in the circumstances to delay withdrawal, for in the coming daylight they would be a target for the fury of enemy bombers.

Some miles to the east, during that night, Admiral King, flying his flag in *Naiad*, with his cruiser and destroyer consorts, had been patrolling north of the island, off Heraklion, without encountering the enemy. When daylight came, in accordance with the last order, he proceeded northward to search for German transports. Following a reconnaissance report that a convoy was south of Milos and heading for Crete, he raced on to intercept, well aware that his ships would be subjected to heavy bombing attacks. At 07.00 that morning the raids started. This time the Luftwaffe was waiting, and in the ensuing battle nearly 200 bombs were dropped around *Naiad* alone, but by her skilful weaving and dodging none hit the ship. About two hours later King's force encountered a part of the convoy they sought, and a steamer and a schooner full of troops were promptly sunk.

At 10.00 they sighted the main part of the escorted convoy carrying re-inforcements intended to be landed at Heraklion. These ships were, in fact, actually withdrawing northwards, having been recalled after Glennie's previous action, and were laying a defensive smoke-screen to escape. It seemed that an overwhelming destruction of the convoy carrying 4,000 troops was within King's grasp, but circumstances ruled otherwise. With bombs raining down upon his ships, and speed determined by the 20-knot limit of the cruiser *Carlisle*, it was time to reconsider his position.

Overhead, the sky was filled with the incessant drone of enemy dive-bombers screaming down through the concentrated flak of his anti-aircraft guns, accompanied by the crashing boom of the heavier armament, the reverberating thud of bombs bursting in the sea, missing the ship by only a few feet, and amid the smoke and flame of battle the admiral realized he was in a perilous position. One of the grave aspects of the situation was that he was running dangerously short of ammunition. With no cover of darkness, he still had to fight his way to the west through several hours of remaining daylight. So far his ships had been lucky, but it seemed inevitable that sooner or later damage or destruction would follow. In the event, he decided to abandon the chase and signalled his ships to turn westward to rendezvous with Admiral Rawlings' fleet moving in to the west of Crete. So the German troop-carrying convoy was spared destruction but, although they escaped, the attempt to launch seaborne troop-landings in Crete was abandoned.

All this time, Admiral King's fleet was speeding westwards, courageously trying to fight back at the droves of German aircraft roaring down out of the clouds releasing their bombs at almost mast height. Under such fierce and sustained attacks it could only be a matter of time before hits would be scored on his ships.

At noon that day, the inevitable happened. Two heavy bombs squarely hit *Naiad*, putting two gun turrets out of action, flooding several compartments and reducing speed to a mere 16 knots. There were many casualties. The cruiser was now in trouble, and to the west Admiral Rawlings received an urgent signal calling for support. Minutes later, *Carlisle* also received a direct hit, which smashed her bridge, starting a fire. Among those killed was her commanding officer, Captain T.C. Hampton.

Immediately on receiving King's signal, Rawlings' force, comprising the battleships *Warspite* and *Valiant*, the cruisers *Gloucester* and *Fiji* and eight destroyers increased speed to reach the stricken ships.

At 13.30, just as the two forces were in sight of one another, the dive-bombers transferred their attention to Rawlings' force. *Warspite* received a direct hit from a heavy bomb which destroyed her 4-inch and 6-inch batteries and reduced her speed.

The following report was given by the executive officer of *Warspite*, later Admiral Sir Charles Maddon:

On reaching the upper deck it was apparent that one 4 inch mounting had gone overboard completely … There was a huge hole in the deck … from which smoke and steam were pouring out. I then went down to the port 6 inch battery … to try to get at the seat of the fire through the armoured door that connected the port and starboard 6 inch battery decks … We had great difficulty in opening the door and had to use a sledgehammer. Finally, it gave, to display a gruesome scene. The starboard battery was full of flames and smoke, in among which the cries of burned and wounded men could be heard. This was very unnerving and I remember thinking how accurate were the descriptions in C.S. Forester's books of the carnage on the gun decks in Nelson's day. The flames seemed pretty fierce and I was doubtful if we would make headway against them.

However, my two volunteers came either side of me with their hoses and we walked into the battery ... I was soon joined by more fire parties ... but was hampered by the continued cries of the burned men, which distracted the fire parties who wanted to leave their hoses to assist their comrades. I therefore concentrated on administering morphia.... As it was dark and wounded men were thrown in all directions amidst the piles of ironwork and rubbish this was not easy.... I then went to the starboard mess-decks where a fresh scene of carnage greeted me.... When all was under control I went to the bridge to report. The calm blue afternoon seemed unreal after the dark and smelly carnage below. Sorting the dead out and identifying them occupied most of the dog-watches, and they were then sewn up in hammocks for burial. The stout corporal of marines who served so cheerfully in the wardroom bar volunteered for and personally led this operation throughout the next two days till we returned to harbour.

In total, *Warspite* suffered forty-three killed and sixty-nine wounded.

At this time, a signal from Admiral King, who had assumed overall command, ordered the destroyer *Greyhound* to proceed and sink a large schooner to the north, carrying German troops. Having accomplished this successfully, she returned, but on taking up her station with the main fleet she received a concentrated attack by Stuka dive-bombers and was mortally hit by three bombs. Minutes later her stern sank under and she disappeared, leaving those who had survived the bombing floundering in the water. Only one boat managed to get away.

To effect a rescue, King now ordered the destroyers *Kandahar* and *Kingston* to pick up survivors. Reaching the scene, they lowered their whalers and began the task of rescue. But even while they were performing this deed of mercy, enemy planes roared down to sea-level, machine-gunning those who remained alive. It was a perilous situation for the rescuers, and to avoid certain destruction the destroyers threw overboard some Carley floats and made their departure. Wholesale slaughter now developed as the aircraft mercilessly and continuously machine-gunned those who clung to rafts and floats.

A young ordinary seaman, in the ship's whaler with another eighteen men, spotted a plane roaring in towards them. He immediately dived overboard and swam beneath the boat. On surfacing, he found every man in the whaler dead.

King now ordered the cruisers *Gloucester* and *Fiji*, which had also been under constant dive-bombing attack, to give anti-aircraft support to the two rescuing destroyers. This was an unfortunate mistake – made unwittingly, it is true, for King had not received the information that the two big cruisers were woefully short of ammunition. In fact, *Gloucester* had only eighteen per cent of her normal stock left, and *Fiji* thirty per cent. On receipt of the latest report of ammunition stocks, King ordered *Gloucester* and *Fiji* and the two K destroyers to withdraw to join the main fleet. But now more and more dive-bombers were thrown in, their main target being the two cruisers. *Gloucester*, of 9,400 tons, had a complement of 700 crew and was armed with twelve 6-inch, eight 4-inch and twenty smaller guns. The Colony-class *Fiji*, of 8,000 tons, had similar armament. All these guns now came into action, sending up a curtain of fire in an attempt to thwart the bombing attack. But now, on both ships, especially *Gloucester*, ammunition stocks were almost exhausted, and in a short while only the 4-inch were firing spasmodically, with occasional bursts from the pom-poms.

As the intensity of the cruiser's anti-aircraft fire diminished, so the Stuka bomber pilots became more daring and pressed home their attacks in a suicidal bid to sink the British ships. With nothing left, *Gloucester*, heroically fighting back, could fire only harmless star shells. Defenceless and without air cover, she had to dodge and weave her way among the fall of bombs. The end was near. They came in from the north, wing-tip to wing-tip, flying in waves, with three, four, sometimes five planes in each wave. They were low, frighteningly low, at altitudes of only 400–500 feet, concentrating on the two ships. The bursting of star shells among them was contemptuously ignored, and they came roaring down in near-vertical power-dives. (From personal experience, there is nothing more frightening than the screaming dive of a gull-winged Stuka bomber plunging directly towards you and the awareness that you may have only seconds to live.)

The first bomb hit the after part of the ship, entering straight through X turret, and exploded in the gunroom flat, causing serious damage to many compartments and B boiler-room. The second blew the after tripod mast and the HA director clean over the side, killing every man inside. Another landed on the 4-inch gun deck between Port 1 and Port 2 guns, killing all except a lone marine, who, in shock, was trying to load and fire one of the two remaining guns. Yet another bomb landed on the pom-pom gun platform, killing the crews there, ploughing its way down to explode in the canteen. By a cruel twist of fate, the bomb had triggered the pom-pom gun to fire on automatic, and this swung around inboard, firing a hail of shells across the deck, killing many of the crew who were running from the after end of the ship. Minutes later, three enormous explosions from aerial torpedoes opened up the ship's port side, allowing hundreds of tons of water to flood in, and *Gloucester*, now listing badly and dead in the water, began to drift in a circle. The hangar and the aircraft within it were a mass of flame.

The order now came to abandon ship, as yet another bomb landed near the forecastle deck. Shuddering and groaning in her agony, *Gloucester* began to settle deeper in the water. In a desperate bid for survival, planks of wood formerly used for cinema seats were thrown overboard. The commanding-officer, Captain H.A. Rowley, signalled *Fiji* to come alongside to take off survivors, but *Fiji* replied, 'Sorry, but I've already dropped my Carley floats.' It was an agonizing decision for Captain William-Powlett to make, but the cruiser couldn't take the chance of coming alongside, for she also was being heavily bombed. At that time Captain Rowley was heard to say, 'I won't be taken prisoner.' Four weeks later, his body, recognizable only by his uniform and the signals in his pocket, was washed ashore to the west of Mersa Matruh on the north coast of Africa.

By 17.15, those who remained alive had slipped over the side and taken to the water. Two boats managed to get away, but these were so full of holes that within minutes they sunk. The sea was now covered with small and large groups of swimmers clinging to whatever pieces of floating debris they could find. They watched as the big cruiser, which had survived so many bomb hits in the past and which had the reputation of being the most heavily bombed cruiser in the Mediterranean, slowly turned turtle and sank by the stern. As she did so, a massive explosion took place when her boilers blew up, sending shock waves against the bodies of those in the sea.

After the flame and roar of battle, it seemed very quiet and very lonely for a time, for all the British ships had raced on to avoid damage or destruction. But then, out of the late afternoon sky, came a low whisper, merging into a rhythmic hum, like a swarm of angry bees, the familiar drone of dreaded Stuka planes. Little dots at first, growing larger and larger. Would they pass on, heading south, or ...?

The survivors were not left long in doubt. Peeling off in ones and twos, the planes came screaming down. Before them were hundreds of black dots against the blue sea, exhausted men clinging desperately to floating pieces of drifting wood and furniture. As messengers of death, the Stukas swept in low, just above sea-level, with the Nazi pilots of the so-called glorious Third Reich, indoctrinated by Hitler's ideology that 'terrorism and mercilessness are absolutely essential', pouring a stream of bullets into the helpless groups. Time and again they flew up and down, fingers pressed on the triggers, performing their deed of execution, with the sea rapidly becoming stained with the blood of their victims. Then, as suddenly, they were gone and the sea became quiet again, interrupted only by the moans and cries of the wounded still holding on.

As evening turned into night, survivors became fewer. John Stevens relates how he, with seven others, clung to a Carley float for several hours, but one by one, from either sheer exhaustion or the lack of will to live, they slid beneath the waves and disappeared. As the new dawn lit the sky, only he and one other were left, and the latter gave up in the end.

Bob Wainwright, who with a young signalman was clinging to a piece of wood, recalls his experience:

During the afternoon we paddled gently along heading steadily towards another group of men in the sea and came across two young officers hanging on to the bow of an almost sunken motor boat. Only two or three feet of the craft showed above water. By sunset we joined another group of about twenty around a raft normally used for painting the ship's side. This was just a couple of barrels lashed together. During the night it was overturned several times as men struggled to get on it for a rest.

Each time, young Burley and I swam away until things calmed down and by dawn the numbers had reduced to five. We were now able to get a seat or at least part of our bodies out of water but when we lapped over on an empty gut, by

God it seemed terribly cold. By this time, I must have been mentally drifting, because I was convinced that a body lying on the surface astern of us, with long hair and drifting out on the water, was a Martian trailing us and later I remember shouting at the figure of a Maltese boatman to come alongside and take us off. He was about as real as the Martian. Eventually we managed to transfer to a Carley float with only one man left alive on it. The rest were all dead, with the float waterlogged and the bodies still in it. However, we were at least able to haul ourselves out of water and get a little warmth in the sunshine.

One or two naval officers who survived the ordeal described how some men gave up the struggle for existence and allowed themselves to drown without making any effort. Some were first-class swimmers who simply gave up the ghost. They died most peacefully. Twenty were originally in their group, but through the night the numbers dwindled until by afternoon of the following day only four remained alive. That evening they were picked up by a small Greek vessel manned by Germans and taken to Kithera, an island off the southern tip of Greece, and there, with others, sent to a German camp. Their troubles were not yet over, however for here the German parachute officer in charge told them that prisoners were not his responsibility and, as he couldn't feed them, the only course left open to him was to shoot them. It was only through the intervention of an infantry officer that their lives were spared.

*Gloucester* was another of the great naval tragedies of World War II, for, despite the gallant fight she put up against impossible odds, her loss was grievous. Out of the total complement of over 800 of her crew, only two officers and eighty ratings survived the ordeal.

Meanwhile *Fiji*, commanded by Captain William-Powlett, was racing southward, taking violent evasive action from a massive dive-bombing attack now concentrated on his ship. He had had to take the painful decision to abandon his squadron colleague after dropping life-saving rafts and boats beside her. During the next four hours *Fiji* and her two accompanying destroyers, *Kandahar* (Commander W. Robson) and *Kingston* (Lieutenant-Commander P. Somerville), were subjected to no fewer than twenty Stuka attacks, at the end of which, with all her ammunition exhausted, she was forced into firing practice shells at the enemy.

Ironically, despite the scores of bombs loosed at her from which she had escaped, she fell victim to a lone Messerschmitt aircraft which, at the end of its patrol, sighted the cruiser through a thin cloud cover. The time was 18.45. Diving low over the ship, the pilot released his one 500-pound bomb, which exploded close alongside *Fiji*, blowing a huge hole in her hull, flooding one boiler-room. Heeling over, she came to a stop, wallowing in the sea like a wounded animal. Within the hour she was spotted by another plane, which dropped three bombs on the now defenceless ship. It was the *coup de grâce*, for her list increased to 30 degrees and there was no hope for her. Under heavy attack, the two destroyers dropped boats and rafts and withdrew. At 20.15 *Fiji*, like a tired old lady, rolled over in her agony and quickly sank.

By now there were nearly 600 survivors littering the sea, but rescue was at hand, for under cover of darkness *Kandahar* and *Kingston* quietly returned and in two hours, with the aid of torches, rescued 523 of her crew of 780.

The next day units of the 5th Destroyer Flotilla, with Captain Lord Louis Mountbatten in the *Kelly*, were despatched to the north of Crete to make night patrols.

Early the following morning the destroyers *Kelly* and *Kashmir* were set upon by between twenty and thirty Stuka bombers. They both received direct hits and were sent to the bottom. Later the survivors, including Lord Louis Mountbatten, were picked up by the destroyer *Kipling*.

Apart from earlier and later losses, in the forty-eight hours from the morning of the 21st to the 23rd the fleet had lost two valuable cruisers and four destroyers and suffered severe damage to several other ships. Even more tragic was the loss of over a thousand sailors. Admiral Cunningham's forthright criticism of the lack of air support for his fleet was amply justified in the light of these appalling losses and demonstrated the government's lamentable failure to appreciate the impossibility of fleet operations in the Aegean Sea against the overwhelming power of the Luftwaffe without air protection.

On the credit side, the German paratroop regiment had suffered a casualty list of 6,000; fifty enemy aircraft had been destroyed or badly damaged, and the much-vaunted seaborne invasion had had to be abandoned with the loss of thousands of fighting troops.

Despite this, Crete was lost, and the British finally had to withdraw. Britain was now paying the price for the stubborn resistance of the pre-war government to re-arm. Churchill had repeatedly warned of impending disaster and of the weakness of the nation's defence forces, and constantly highlighted the rapidly ascending power of Germany and her air strength. He had pleaded with the government of the day to throw all their resources into a programme of re-armament to defend the nation, but his was a lone voice crying in the wilderness.

This then was a part of the sea war of 1941, a time when Allied fortunes were at their lowest ebb. For the Royal Navy, the losses in ships and men from 1940 to 1942 were most grievous, and for a time it seemed that Britain's tenuous hold on the Mediterranean was in grave danger of being broken. Yet despite such failures, Britain held on, and by the autumn of 1942 the tide of fortune began to flow in her favour.

# 8 The Crete Evacuation

*Despite valiant attempts by Britain's land forces to maintain a hold on the island of Crete, it was clear by 26 May 1941 that, to avoid the total annihilation of her troops, an evacuation was essential. It fell to the Royal Navy to perform another Dunkirk to save the exhausted army, but unfortunately in this operation the cruisers* Orion *and* Dido *were lost, with tragic consequences.*

It has been described in the previous chapter how the Royal Navy prevented the enemy from effecting seaborne landings on the island of Crete – not, however, without incurring grievous losses in ships and men. Despite this setback to the enemy, the Germans flew in thousands of troops in a determined attempt to dislodge the forces occupying the island, especially around the areas of Maleme, Canea, Suda Bay and Heraklion. Such was the lamentable state of the Royal Air Force at the time that no planes could be spared from other theatres of war in the Mediterranean to repulse the build-up of enemy re-inforcements. The situation was perilous.

By 26 May 1941 General Sir Bernard Freyberg, commanding the defence of Crete, reported to Field Marshal Sir Archibald Wavell that the limit of endurance had been reached by the troops under his command, that the position was hopeless and that, to avoid total surrender or annihilation of British forces, immediate and speedy evacuation was vital.

In the hope that the position could somehow be reversed, the Prime Minister telegraphed the Commander-in-Chief the following day: 'Victory in Crete essential at this turning-point in the war. Keep hurling in all aid you can.' But by that evening the situation had rapidly deteriorated, and General Wavell reported that there was no possibility of hurling in re-inforcements, that the weight and scale of air attack were unprecedented and being augmented unopposed. Furthermore, with the garrisons at Suda, Retimo and Heraklion almost surrounded, the only chance of survival was to withdraw some forces to the beach at Sfakia, in the south of the island, and for the Royal Navy to make what would amount to a suicidal attempt to rescue them.

But first, fighting a rearguard action, the troops to be evacuated to Sfakia had to travel overland, a distance of some twenty miles across 7,000-foot mountains, stumbling and scrambling along narrow mountain goat-tracks in the dark, a physically punishing endeavour even for fit and fresh men. Only four days earlier, these same troops had had to be evacuated from beaches and ports in Greece and transported to Crete to re-inforce the garrisons there. Battle-weary from bombardment and dive-bombing on the mainland, they had tried to make a stand in Crete, only to be faced with an even greater tax upon their diminishing endurance. To escape imprisonment or death, further demands on their strength were now called for in the exhausting retreat to Sfakia.

Due to enemy action, communication between forces in the north and those at or near Sfakia were almost non-existent, causing much confusion. During daylight hours, the troops lay hidden under bushes or concealed in burrows while enemy planes roared overhead seeking them. Only by night, under cover of darkness, could they move, treading warily along the precipitous single track that led across the mountains and down the 600-foot-high bluff to Sfakia and its small beach. Here, patiently and at the limit of their endurance, they waited, with implicit faith that the Royal Navy would reach them. Perhaps it was in this trust that mitigation of all the Navy suffered in its historic rescue of the bulk of the forces from Crete is to be judged.

Responsibility for the evacuation of the whole Crete army now rested on the shoulders of one man, Admiral Sir Andrew Cunningham, who had a prodigious task indeed, with the risks outrageously high. The Admiral was faced with the harrowing prospect of having to accept further losses to his rapidly diminishing fleet with no surety of success.

The cost in ships and men in the battle for Crete had been harsh to bear: two cruisers and four destroyers lost, one aircraft-carrier, two battleships, one cruiser and a destroyer crippled, and five cruisers and four destroyers with minor damage. With no remission from their recent mauling by the enemy, the remnants of the Mediterranean fleet were now asked to face even greater hazards, with fewer ships, far less resources and in conditions and circumstances far more difficult. Wearily and with some dismay but no hesitation, they set their faces to the task ahead and sailed for Crete and the 22,000 exhausted troops awaiting rescue.

So critical had the situation become that the Commander-in-Chief of the Mediterranean Allied Fleet, Admiral Sir Andrew Cunningham, despatched the following signal to his ships.

IMPORTANT. During the past few days the fleet has been having a hard battle against a high proportion of the German Air Force and has kepts its end up by dint of determination. We have sustained some hard knocks in the process of preventing any considerable enemy sea borne landing in Crete, but we have also given some. Some thousands of enemy troops have been trapped and sunk at sea. The battle for Crete is still progressing, to win is essential. The army is just holding its own against constant reinforcements of air borne enemy troops. We must not let them down. At whatever cost we must take reinforcements for them and keep the enemy from using the sea. There are indications that the enemy's resources are stretched to the limit. We can and must out-last them. Stick it out.

Skilful organization by General Freyberg had reduced withdrawal to two main evacuation points, Heraklion in the north and Sfakia in the south. He himself had been under no illusion about the impossibility of holding Crete against a German assault on the island. As early as 1 May he had informed General Wavell that, 'Forces at my disposal are totally inadequate to meet attack envisaged. Unless fighter aircraft are greatly increased and naval forces made available ... I cannot hope to hold out with land forces alone which as a result of campaign in Greece are now devoid of any artillery, have insufficient tools for digging, very little transport, and inadequate war reserves of equipment and ammunition.'

It would not be amiss at this point to say a word about this courageous soldier who had fought with such valour in World War I that he had been awarded the Victoria Cross and the DSO, with two bars, to mark his distinguished service. Winston Churchill once described Freyberg as a 'salamander', a man who thrived in the fire of battle and was literally shot to pieces in his campaigns. Once, pressured into revealing his wounds, twenty-seven separate gashes were counted, but modestly he explained that, 'You always get two wounds for every bullet, because they mostly have to go out as well as go in.'

To cover the two evacuation points at Crete, Cunningham split his rescuing fleet into three groups.

Force B, under the command of Rear-Admiral Rawlings, comprised the cruisers *Orion* (flagship), *Ajax* and *Dido* and the destroyers *Decoy, Jackal, Imperial, Hotspur, Kimberley* and *Hereward*. It was given the task of evacuating the hard-pressed troops at Heraklion.

Force C, part of the 7th Destroyer Flotilla, comprised *Napier* (Captain Arliss), *Nizam, Kelvin* and *Kandahar*. Force D was under the command of Rear-Admiral King, with the cruisers *Phoebe* (flagship), *Perth, Glengyle, Coventry* and *Calcutta*, and the destroyers *Jervis, Janus* and *Hasty*. C and D would be repsonsible for the evacuation at Sfakia.

They left Alexandria very early on the morning of the 28th, and during the next forty-eight hours Forces C and D managed to evacuate some 12,000 troops from the beach at Sfakia, despite being heavily dive-bombed throughout the rescue. Sadly, however, the anti-aircraft cruiser *Calcutta* received two bomb hits and sank early on the morning of 1 June.

Admiral Rawlings' Force B, speeding to Heraklion, met the full fury of the enemy. His ships had to pass through the Kaso Strait to the east of Crete – on the doorstep of the enemy, for the Luftwaffe air base at Scarpanto was barely sixty miles away. From 17.00 until dark his force was under severe attack. The cruiser *Ajax*, of the Battle of the River Plate fame, was damaged and had to return to Alexandria, and the destroyer *Imperial* received a near miss under the stern, weakening her steering.

As darkness fell, the two cruisers waited outside the harbour at Heraklion while the destroyers crept silently in alongside the jetty to receive the exhausted troops, between 700 and 800 to each destroyer, many of whom were transferred to the cruisers. Just after 03.00, much later than had been planned, with 4,000 men embarked, Rawlings' force withdrew and raced for the Kaso Strait, which they had to pass through before daylight.

Misfortune struck at a most untimely point in the operation.

Thirty minutes into the homeward voyage, *Imperial* suddenly swerved violently off course. Her steering had failed, due to the earlier bomb explosion, and in a few frantic moments of near disaster she narrowly missed colliding with *Kimberley* and both cruisers. Quickly she fell behind the main force, and Rawlings detached *Hotspur* to investigate, while he himself reduced speed. The planned evacuation was already 1½ hours behind schedule; soon it would be dawn, and it was imperative that he should be through the strait before daylight, to avoid enemy attention.

*Hotspur*'s signal to Rawlings was alarming: *Imperial* was out of control and quite unable to join the main force. It was a time for rigorous decisions, and Rawlings ordered *Hotspur* to take off the troops and crew of *Imperial* and to sink her. This melancholy business was completed an hour later, and *Hotspur*, wth two ships' companies and 900 troops crowding her decks, sped off in pursuit of the flagship. The thought of trying to get through the Kaso narrows in daylight, being subjected to concentrated dive-bombing with nearly 1,300 men crammed aboard the little ship, was one of despair. It was with great relief therefore that just as dawn broke *Hotspur* sighted Rawlings' force ahead – he had slowed his homeward race to allow the destroyer to catch up.

As *Hotspur* joined, there was some comfort in the thought that, with another six ships in company, their combined anti-aircraft fire might provide a deterrent to the enemy. It was a forlorn hope. For the next nine hours, until the ships were within a hundred miles of Alexandria, they were subjected to one of the most concentrated bombing attacks of the Crete campaign. There was little or no fighter protection, for, although this had been planned, by mischance the planes failed to find the British ships.

Hardly had the dawn lit up the waters of the Kaso Strait than the air was filled with the drone of approaching aircraft. They came in droves, Stukas, Junker 87s and 88s, Messerschmitt 109s and Heinkel 111s, all determined to seek revenge for the British victory in preventing a seaborne landing on Crete, some time earlier, when several thousand German troops perished as their transports were sunk. As Rawlings' force sped through the strait at top speed with bombs raining down upon them, it seemed impossible that any ship could survive such a massive attack.

Ironically, *Hotspur*, the most crowded destroyer of the group received the impact of the first attack, yet, despite being hidden in a hail of bombs that fell all around her, she escaped undamaged. Not so her sister ship, *Hereward*, which received direct hits from Stuka bombers, which made her lose speed, fall out of station and limp towards the coast of Crete barely five miles distant. To detach one or more of Rawlings' fleet to go back to assist *Hereward* would have invited disaster, and rightly he decided to abandon her. Reduced to a mere walking pace, *Hereward* moved slowly towards the land. She later sank; her crew and troops were rescued by Italian patrol boats and taken prisoner.

The fleet now closed ranks to provide more effective anti-aircraft fire.

Barely had this manoeuvre been completed than the destroyer *Decoy* suffered a near miss which reduced her speed, and consequently that of the squadron, to a mere 25 knots. But now a concentrated effort was made to sink the two cruisers *Orion* and *Dido*.

Weatherwise it was a beautiful day, with wisps of thin marching clouds that temporarily hid the bombers before they dived on their targets. They fell out of the sun at blinding speed. *Dido* was the first to be hit. A Junker 87, defying the flak that rocked and riddled it, dropped a 500-pound bomb directly on to B turret, which crashed on down into the marine's mess deck crowded with troops. Casualties and damage were horrific, with immediate help to the wounded and burnt denied because of the raging fires.

The main attack was now centred on the flagship *Orion*, which had little hope of escape. In seconds, a host of bombs fell around her. The surface of the sea rose in huge white spouts, covering the decks and gunners, who sweated at their posts. The explosions were frightening, barely covering the demoralizing stutter of machine-gun fire as the planes pulled out of their dives, aiming at the bridge, where Admiral Rawlings was wounded and the flag-captain, Captain Back, killed. Minutes later the flagship suffered a crippling blow when one of the Stuka pilots made a kamikaze-like attack, dropping his bomb on A turret with devastating effect. It blew away most of the turret and crippled B turret immediately behind, causing severe casualties. Below decks, conditions were appalling, for apart from her own crew of 600 she had 1,100 troops aboard. Packed like sardines in the mess decks, they could only crouch and pray that no bombs would reach them if the cruiser received further hits.

At 10.45 came disaster, as more mass attacks were launched upon *Orion*. The planes came in waves, dropping their bombs within the target area and producing tall columns of water, stately and dreadful. These waterspouts, missing by only a few feet and expanding at their turbulent bases, hung momentarily against the blue sky then, yielding to the force of gravity, collapsed and shrank into a pool of white fury. Suddenly there was no time to take avoiding action, no time to hope or think, as a cluster of jettisoned bombs crashed down upon the ship.

The main damage was created by one that ploughed through the bridge, the canteen flat and the stokers' mess deck, where most of the troop passengers had congregated, there to explode on top of the 4-inch magazine, which blew up in a shattering roar of flame and steel. (This had always been considered the safest part of the ship.) The explosion produced indescribable carnage. From within the darkness and smoke came the screams of the wounded and dying. Had the blast gone downwards, it would have blown out the bottom of the ship, with unthinkable consequences; instead it erupted upwards and outwards through three decks, blowing a yawning pit open to the sky, spewing bodies, steel, fire and thick black smoke. Official figures were put at 260 killed and 280 wounded. Fire-control parties did a magnificent job, fighting their way through the fire and tangled web of mangled steel to rescue and tend those who remained alive.

As for the ship, damage was extensive. Communications, boiler-rooms, oil tanks and steering: all had suffered. For a while the flagship was out of control, drifting back towards the jaws of the Kaso Strait, with clouds of yellow and black smoke pouring from her open wound. Around her, the consorts waited in breathless suspense, wondering if this was the end of the fine cruiser which had served with such distinction in the Mediterranean and other areas of war.

Aboard *Orion*, the crew worked frantically to restore control. By a series of heroic efforts, the ship regained command of the situation, and although listing to starboard, she managed to resume station and head southwards towards Alexandria. Utterly exhausted, *Orion*'s crew managed to bring their ship into port, with only two rounds of 6-inch ammunition and a pitiful ten tons of fuel-oil left.

Despite further bombing attacks, the force gradually withdrew from the range of enemy aircraft and, having reached the naval base, disembarked nearly 4,000 troops. It was estimated that the killed or captured on passage amounted to 600 or more.

As far as the Crete evacuation was concerned, some 18,000 troops had been successfully withdrawn out of 22,000, and German casualties amounting to 6,000 had been inflicted.

When Admiral Cunningham visited his battered ships on their return, the sight filled him with dismay: 500-ton turrets ripped apart as with a giant hand, superstructures shattered into obscene sculptures of twisted steel, and flame-blackened decks crowded with weary and haggard troops. Although the Navy had achieved its set purpose in rescuing the greatest proportion of the Crete forces, it had been achieved at an unacceptable and unnecessary cost. It was a melancholy end to a bloody evacuation operation which might have been avoided had fighter planes been available. The Navy had played its part in preventing enemy seaborne landings, and if aircraft had been present in sufficient numbers, the German paratroop invasion could have been smashed and Crete saved.

So where were the British planes? The simple truth was that the pathetically small number allocated to the Mediterranean theatre of war were already operationally overstretched defending Malta and fighting in the Libyan campaign. As an instance of this, only days before the Crete fiasco only eight British planes could be spared to face the 700 of the Luftwaffe.

The responsibility for this deplorable situation into which Britain had drifted must again be laid at the door of the Neville Chamberlain administration of 1937–40, when the Prime Minister had firmly rejected all pleas for proportional re-armament. His maniac obsession for appeasing the two dictators Hitler and Mussolini overruled all other considerations and sane reasoning. From the outbreak of war in 1939 to the end of hostilities, his pre-war policy of 'peace at any price' was to bring Britain to the brink of defeat and cost millions of lives.

In these bitter engagements covering the evacuation from Crete, in which British ships suffered grievously, emergencies were so commonplace they ceased to be emergencies and acts of heroism so numerous they were looked upon as simply dedication to duty. Some deeds of courage, however, were so outstanding they were recognized by the award of the Conspicuous Gallantry Medal.

In one instance, Ordnance Artificer John Bache's ship was dive-bombed by aircraft and seriously damaged. A mess deck was heavily flooded and water began to enter the magazine beneath it, so the magazine crew were told to leave. As he could not reach the magazine hatch because of the flooded mess deck, Bache climbed down into the magazine through the narrow ammunition-supply trunk and managed to shut the hatch. Then the lights went out. In the darkness and confined space, he climbed back up the trunk, found a torch and again went down to the flooding magazine. Though he knew he was shut in, with the flooded magazine above him, he began to send ammunition to the guns, enabling them to remain in action and at length to drive off the enemy.

In another, Ordinary Seaman Ivor Rhodes of the Royal Australian Naval Volunteer Reserve, whose ship had been hit by bombs and was rapidly sinking, left the port gun of which he was gunlayer and which was going under water and climbed across the deck to the starboard gun. This he turned on an aircraft which was machine-gunning his shipmates and brought it down in flames.

On another ship, Able Seaman Robert Bridge, though terribly wounded in a bombing attack, stood to his gun and went on firing without thought for his injury.

These are but a few examples of the acts of bravery that symbolized the courage of men under extreme pressure.

But, to return to the surviving ships at Alexandria, *Orion* had been saved and had lived to fight again. After refit and from then until the end of hostilities, she powerfully contributed to the success of the war at sea and to supporting Allied landings in Europe. For survivors of those ordeals, and members of the existing HMS *Orion* Association, the ship's battle honours are recorded with pride.

HMS *Orion*
Battle honours 3 September 1939 to 15 August 1945

Denoted in brackets, (), number of 6-inch shells fired.

| | | |
|---|---|---|
| 1939 | *West Indies* (Convoy protection and contraband control) | |
| 1940 | Bardia | 21 June (119) |
| | Cape Matapan | 28 June (591) |
| | Calabria | 9th July (419) |
| | Otranto Convoy | 12 November (280) |
| | Aegean and Malta Convoys | |
| 1941 | Battle of Cape Matapan | 28/29 March |
| | Greece | 11–28 April |
| | Crete | 1–29 May |
| | Malta Convoys | 6 September 1941–25 February 1942 |

1942  Mare Island Navy Yard, USA, for repairs

| 1943 | Pantelleria | 13 May–12 June (1450) |
|------|-------------|----------------------|
|      | Lampedusa | 11/12 June (75) |
|      | Sicily | 10 July–8 August (1045) |
|      | Toe of Italy | 19–31 August (385) |
|      | Salerno | 9–17 September (1160) |
|      | Gaeta | 27 November–19 January 1944 (1548) |

| 1944 | Anzio | 22 January–18 March (1788) |
|------|-------|----------------------------|
|      | Formia | 2/3 February (665) |
|      | Normandy | 6–12 June (3358) |
|      | South of France | 15–17 August (40) |
|      | Relief of Greece | 15 October–18 December |

| 1945 | Italian Riviera | 12–26 April (554) |
|------|-----------------|-------------------|
|      | Trieste | 11 May–5 July |

Another two years of exhausting and bitter fighting were to pass before the naval war in the Mediterranean could be said to have been finally won, when on the 8th September 1943, under the terms of truce, the main body of the Italian Fleet sailed out from their ports of Genoa and Spezia at night to surrender to the British forces at sea, which had so often sought them under different circumstances, and were escorted to Malta.

# 9  *The Mighty* Bismarck

*In 1941 the pursuit and destruction of the mighty German battleship* Bismarck, *sister-ship of the* Tirpitz, *caught the imagination of the world. It was an engagement within the vast track of the Atlantic Ocean, in which chance, outstanding courage and luck all played their part. The pursuit was without precedent in British naval history, and losses on both sides were horrific, yet the bad luck which seemed at first to dog the British forces was more than balanced by miraculous good fortune and ultimate success. At long last, the spectre which might have dominated the sea-lanes of the Atlantic, destroying Britain's supplies, was eliminated.*

Where is the *Bismarck*? For a while in May 1941 that question hung heavily upon the lips of every member of the British War Cabinet. They, more than anyone else, understood the consequences if the mighty German battleship, now reported on the move, should not be found and destroyed. If the powerful and supposedly invincible raider broke out into the Atlantic sea-lanes, she could annihilate British convoys and their escorts, cut off supplies of food and fuel and possibly succeed in starving Great Britain into surrender. At least, that was the hope and purpose of Germany's Naval Command.

The effect that this great modern battleship could have on the conduct of the war had been foreseen as far back as November 1939, when, at a conference with the French naval authorities near Paris, Churchill said, 'The arrival of the *Bismarck* on the oceans ... would be disastrous in the highest degree, as it can neither be caught nor killed.' And again in August 1940, in a letter to the

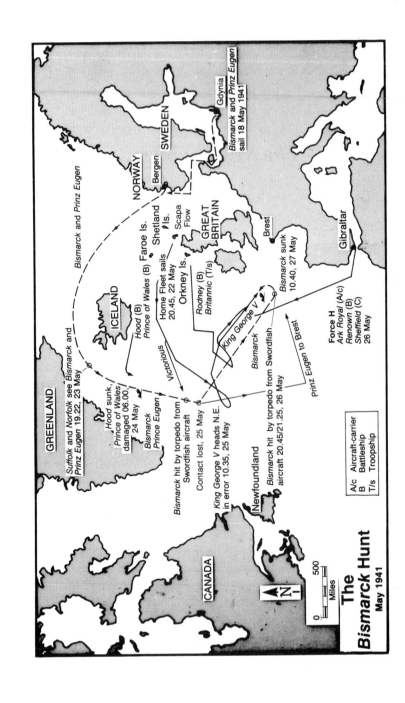

# The Bismarck Hunt
### May 1941

**Bismarck and Prinz Eugen sail 18 May 1941**

Gdynia

SWEDEN

NORWAY

Bergen

*Bismarck and Prinz Eugen*

Faroe Is.

Shetland Is.

Scapa Flow

GREAT BRITAIN

Orkney Is.

Brest

Gibraltar

*Bismarck sunk 10.40, 27 May*

**Force H**
*Ark Royal* (A/c)
*Renown* (B)
*Sheffield* (C)
26 May

*Rodney* (B)
*Britannic* (T/s)

*King George V*

*Bismarck*

*Prinz Eugen to Brest*

*Bismarck hit by torpedo from Swordfish aircraft 20.45/21.25, 26 May*

*King George V heads N.E. in error 10.35, 25 May*

Newfoundland

CANADA

*Contact lost, 25 May*

*Bismarck hit by torpedo from Swordfish aircraft*

*Victorious*

*Home Fleet sails 20.45, 22 May*

*Hood* (B)
*Prince of Wales* (B)

ICELAND

*Hood sunk, Prince of Wales damaged 06.00, 24 May*

*Bismarck Prince Eugen*

*Suffolk and Norfolk see Bismarck and Prinz Eugen 19.22, 23 May*

GREENLAND

| A/c | Aircraft-carrier |
| B | Battleship |
| T/s | Troopship |

N

0    500
Miles

British Air Minister pointing out the overriding need to mount heavy air attacks to delay the construction of the *Bismarck*, he said, 'Even a few months delay in *Bismarck* will affect the whole balance of sea-power to a serious degree.'

The course of action which the Commander-in-Chief of the German Navy, Grand Admiral Erich Raeder, had planned originated in the first few weeks of 1941. The fleet commander, Admiral Günther Lutjens, had brought the battle-cruisers *Scharnhorst* and *Gneisenau*, each of 32,000 tons, into Brest in late March. There they would be ideally placed to break out into the Atlantic at will to attack the British west-east convoys. At the same time the battleship *Bismarck*, of 43,000 tons, and the cruiser *Prinz Eugen*, of 14,000 tons, then in the Baltic completing their exercises, would break loose into the Atlantic from the north to complete the northern claw of a momentous naval pincer-movement. Such a combination of naval forces would compel the British to denude their convoys of battleship protection, for by gathering their heavy units into a sufficiently strong force to compete with the German battle squadron, the merchant ships would be left almost defenceless against German cruisers.

By late March the German Naval War Staff (*Seekriegsleitung*) had distributed an operational memorandum which drew attention to the fact that the main objective in the war with Britain was to destroy her trade. This could be most effectively accomplished in the North Atlantic, where all the convoy supply lines came together. By deploying the *Bismarck* to distract the convoy escorts, other units would be able to engage and destroy the convoys themselves. This operation was given the code name *Rheinübung* (Exercise Rhine). Already in 1941, between January and March, the battle-cruisers *Scharnhorst* and *Gneisenau*, commanded by Admiral Günther Lutjens, had roamed the Atlantic with surprise attacks on British shipping, sinking some 122,000 tons of merchant ships.

The strategy had imposed a tremendous strain on the British fleet. Significant forces now had to be employed in those ocean areas threatened by *Scharnhorst* and *Gneisenau* by providing an escort of at least one battleship to each convoy. The British convoy system was therefore stretched to the limit. Furthermore, Admiral Raeder held the initiative, for by keeping his battle squadron in the Baltic, allowing easy access to the North Sea, and occasionally leaking false information that his ships were about to make a foray into the Atlantic, he forced the Admiralty to maintain a readily available battle squadron at Scapa Flow, the base for the Home Fleet, to the weakening of forces in other theatres of war. There was another factor: Germany would not have to keep her ships at a state of 'instant call'; she could choose her own time for Atlantic or other operation.

That was the *Rheinübung*, but from the start it misfired. *Scharnhorst* needed a complete overhaul of her engines. She would be a compulsory citizen of Brest dockyard and out of commission until June or July. This left *Gneisenau* as the lone raider of the southern claw to break out into the Atlantic when the time came.

As convenient as the Brest port was for the Germans, it was vulnerable to strikes from RAF Bomber Command – not an easy target, however, for the whole port was ringed by a terrifying concentration of anti-aircraft guns and a night defence of hundreds of glaring searchlights. Despite these defences, the RAF pressed home their attacks, and in one of these raids a large unexploded bomb fell dangerously close to *Gneisenau*. Until this could be detonated, the battle-cruiser was moved out into the open harbour and to fresh moorings. Its new positioning offered an opportunity to destroy or at least cripple the ship. As a result, on 6th April Coastal Command made a determined attack by flying directly into the concentration of a thousand anti-aircraft guns. In this attack Flying Officer K. Campbell of 22 Squadron was shot down and killed with his crew, but not before the released torpedo had torn a huge gash in the stern of *Gneisenau*, destroying her propeller shaft and putting her out of action for at least nine months.

Operation *Rheinübung* had received a material setback. With both battle-cruisers non-operational at Brest, the effectiveness of the enterprise was now considerably minimized. Nevertheless, Raeder was not discouraged, and although the task force was reduced to *Bismarck* and *Prinz Eugen*, he accelerated his plans for the overall operation. If Lutjens could break through into the Atlantic with the two ships, the first part of the assignment would be accomplished. *Bismarck* would then act as the bait to draw the British battleship groupings away from the convoys, to allow *Prinz Eugen* to attack at will.

And then came another misfortune for the Germans: on 25 April, on the eve of putting *Rheinübung* into operation, *Prinz Eugen* suffered considerable damage on her way to Kiel, when she hit a mine. It was more than a fortnight before repairs were completed, forcing another postponement. Actually another three weeks passed before the two ships were ready to sail, but in the meantime there had been feverish activity in the preparation.

The fleet staff embarked in *Bismarck* on 12 May, headed by the fleet commander, Admiral Günther Lutjens. Aged fifty-one, he was a man of impassive features, tall and lean, of sober disposition. Throughout his earlier career he had come to be recognized as having outstanding intelligence coupled with inherent courage. The commanding officer, Captain Ernst Lindemann, had a distinguished reputation as a first-rate gunnery officer. Though not physically strong, he had endured the rigours of cadet training and emerged twenty-seven years later in command of the new mighty battleship *Bismarck*.

At last, on 18 May, the two ships sailed from Gdynia for the Atlantic, their mission to destroy the British convoys. At the same time five tankers and three store ships sailed, to act as supply vessels for the task force. *Bismarck* and *Prinz Eugen* had, however, been observed by Swedish intelligence passing through the Great Belt, and this news was quickly transmitted to the Admiralty, London. On 21 May a Coastal Command Spitfire circled above the Skagerrack Channel and photographed the two ships refuelling at Grimstad Fjord at the southern tip of German Occupied Norway.

To Admiral Sir John Tovey, Commander-in-Chief of the Home Fleet based at Scapa Flow, the news of *Bismarck* and *Prinz Eugen* brought no great surprise. Since early May German air reconnaissance over the British naval base had been increased, foreshadowing an enemy surface operation in the Atlantic. But if the enemy's intention was to break out, which course would he take? There were five options.

1  The Denmark Strait between Iceland and Greenland, a route which Lutjens had successfully used before in *Gneisenau* but which at this time of year was reduced by pack-ice to a gap not more than sixty miles wide.

2  The passage between Iceland and the Faroe Islands, 200 miles wide.

3  That between the Faroes and the Shetland Isles, 100 miles wide.

4  Another between the Shetlands and Orkneys.

5  That between the Orkneys and the coast of Scotland.

It was all a matter of putting oneself in the enemy's position and guessing his intention. After careful consideration, Tovey's hunch was that Lutjens would use the favourite Denmark Strait route. He therefore deployed his forces to counter the situation, while at the same time keeping a watch on the Iceland–Faroes passage.

The cruisers *Norfolk* and *Suffolk*, the former flying the flag of Rear-Admiral W. Wake-Walker and commanded by Captain A.J. Phillips, and the latter commanded by Captain R.M. Ellis, were ordered north to patrol the Denmark Strait together, and the cruisers *Manchester, Arethusa* and *Birmingham* to sweep the Iceland–Faroes passage. While awaiting news of the enemy's movements Tovey dispatched the battle-cruiser HMS *Hood*, of 41,000 tons, flying the flag of Vice-Admiral Lancelot Holland, in company with the new battleship *Prince of Wales* (Captain R. Leach) and the destroyers *Achates, Antelope, Anthony, Echo, Electra* and *Icarus* to Hvalfjord in Iceland. The Admiralty were obviously concerned by receipt of the intelligence reports, for they at once placed the new aircraft-carrier *Victorious* and the battleship *Repulse* at the disposal of Admiral Tovey to deploy as he thought best. He himself, in the battleship *King George V*, waited in Scapa Flow, conserving his fuel supply until it was necessary to put to sea.

Then the occurrence he most dreaded happened. The weather shut down. Throughout the period 22/23 May a bitter wind from the east raised a thick mist over the sea, and with it came rain, bringing visibility at times to little more than a few hundred yards. This was Lutjens' opportunity and, accepting it gratefully, he at once put to sea, heading speedily north-west for the Denmark Strait. It was a bonus for Lutjens, a time of tortured anxiety for Tovey, for the bad weather almost completely restricted air reconnaissance. His thoughts must have been centred on two areas: the north, almost 900 miles away, where at that time *Bismarck* with her consort might be trying to break through the Denmark Strait, and an equal distance to the south, where the vital convoys from the USA were steering for Britain, unaware of the threat which could engulf them from the north.

Then, on the evening of 22 May, Tovey received the report he had so anxiously waited for. A Royal Navy reconnaissance plane from the Orkneys had braved the foul weather, flown across the North Sea and over the hills of Norway and brought back the news that *Bismarck* and *Prinz Eugen* had left Grimstad. A little over two hours later Tovey with the Home Fleet put to sea, steering north-west, heading for the southern exit of the Denmark Strait. With his battleship *King George V* were *Victorious* and *Repulse*, the cruisers *Galatea, Hermione, Kenya, Aurora* and *Neptune* and

as escort the destroyers *Intrepid, Inglefield, Active, Punjabi, Nestor*
and *Lance*. The hunt was on. Tovey now had one deadly purpose:
to find the *Bismarck* before *Bismarck* found the convoys. In the
meantime, Admiral Holland, in *Hood* and with *Prince of
Wales*, was ordered to cover the area to the south-west of Iceland,
while in the Denmark Strait itself the cruisers *Norfolk* and *Suffolk*
patrolled north-east and south-west to cover the possible escape
route.

The weather was atrocious, but for Lutjens conditions could not
have been better, for he was now swinging west, around the
northern coast of Iceland, with bad visibility well suited to his
purpose.

Meanwhile to the south the battleship *Rodney*, escorting
*Britannic* to the west, was recalled to join in the hunt, and she at
once turned away from her charge and headed north.

A formidable British force had been mounted but they were
widely dispersed – and therein lay the weakness. The battle
squadron lying across the path of the German advance were *Hood*
and *Prince of Wales*. Ironically, of all the British ships, these two
were the least suited to be matched against *Bismarck*. *Hood* was a
comparatively old ship out of the 1918 mould, and was a
battle-cruiser not a battleship. While in gun-power and side armour
the two ships were equally matched, *Hood*'s weakness lay not so
much in her age as in her deck armoured protection, 3-inch against
*Bismarck*'s 8-inch. By comparison, *Bismarck* was the most
powerful and largest ship afloat in the Atlantic hemisphere. She was
more heavily armed than *Hood*, carrying eight 15-inch guns, twelve
5.9-inch and sixteen 4-inch.

All through that day of the 23rd, the weather showed no sign of
improvement. The thick mist and heavy rain continued to
compound the gravity of the situation. And when Tovey received a
signal from Scotland that, because of weather conditions, nearly all
reconnaissance had had to be suspended, the urgency increased. He
now had no means of knowing just where *Bismarck* was or, if she
intended to break out into the Atlantic, which passage she might
take. He could now rely only on sightings from surface ships.
Further gloom was added when he received a signal from Iceland
reporting that with care a heavy ship might shoulder its way
through patches of open water within the pack-ice edge close to the
Greenland shore without having to use the wider channel of the
strait where the cruisers *Norfolk* and *Suffolk* were patrolling.

This was exactly where *Bismarck was* sailing. At 19.00 Lutjens took his ship through the ice floes close to the Greenland edge in a sea-lane only three miles wide, with visibility ahead and to starboard clear, while to port a convenient fog haze hung over the sea, shielding him from observation. It was the ideal escape route.

Despite all the drawbacks that seemed to be encompassing Tovey, he had one advantage over the enemy – radar. The Germans had set out on their mission presuming that British radar was sub-standard and could in no way match that carried in *Bismarck* and *Prinz Eugen*. How wrong they were. The two British cruisers in the strait both had radar. *Norfolk* carried the older type which was unrotatable and would contact a ship only directly ahead, but *Suffolk* carried the latest, improved type which could cover all angles except directly astern.

Just after 19.00 that evening, *Suffolk*, patrolling where the visibility was suddenly clear, sighted the Germans ships coming up behind her on the same course a little over seven miles distant, point-blank range for the 15-inch *Bismarck* guns. No match for the enemy, Captain Ellis swung his ship to port into the fog banks and signalled *Norfolk*: 'One battleship, one cruiser in sight bearing 20 degrees distant seven miles, course 240 degrees.' Soon *Norfolk* joined her sister-ship, and the two cruisers, keeping well into the fog banks on each quarter of the enemy, followed at a distance of twelve miles, the limit of their radar.

It was not until forty minutes later that Admiral Holland in *Hood* received one of *Suffolk*'s reports of the enemy's presence. Immediately he put on speed to intercept. The situation was encouraging and, always assuming that the cruisers could maintain their shadowing, there was every possibility that the enemy could be brought to battle in the early morning.

At 20.30 a critical situation arose when *Norfolk* suddenly sped out of a fog bank to find the German ships to port and barely six miles away. This time the enemy was ready for her, and immediately *Bismarck*'s guns opened fire, three of her five salvoes accurately straddling the British cruiser. At that instant *Norfolk* swung hard to starboard into the sheltering fog, making smoke and escaping from the murderous fire. Fortunately, although a few splinters landed on board, no direct hits were scored and she again settled down to shadow the enemy. The report of the action now reached Tovey, who was by this time 600 miles south-east of *Bismarck* and *Prinz Eugen*. Obviously *Hood* and *Prince of Wales* were the only two ships that could join battle with the enemy before they might reach the vast Atlantic. In the event, Tovey signalled the accompanying cruiser *Galatea*: 'I am hoping *Hood* may head them off and force them to turn back or to the southward.'

Now fully aware of the situation and of the disposition of the British ships and the course of the enemy, Admiral Holland signalled his ships in company at 00.15 on the morning of the 24th: 'Prepare for action.' Almost at once the broad battle ensigns of *Hood* and *Prince of Wales* were hoisted to flutter and strain in the wind of their advance.

Throughout that night *Norfolk* and *Suffolk* continued their shadowing of the enemy, always keeping at maximum range of their radar contact. The principal danger to the two cruisers was that Lutjens, knowing he was being followed and that information of his every movement was being transmitted to other British ships, might suddenly turn and destroy them. A tense situation but one of which they were fully aware. Despite this, they maintained their distant pursuit, never losing the fluctuating radar contact with the enemy. By 04.00 visibility had greatly improved, giving a clear range of some ten miles. Wisely Admiral Holland kept radio silence, knowing that to do otherwise would give Lutjens advance information that a British ship or ships were converging on him from the south.

At 05.45 *Bismarck* and *Prinz Eugen* came into view off *Hood*'s starboard bow, and a minute later Holland turned his ships towards the enemy head-on to reduce the range. This, however, reduced their fire-power, for only the two forward turrets of the British ships could engage. Against this, Holland was trying to close the range, knowing the vulnerability of his deck armour plating, and that over ten miles 15-inch shells fired on a parabolic trajectory could plunge down and through the ship's weak deck plating. (Under this distance, the trajectory would follow a more horizontal plane, and *Hood*'s 12-inch side armour plating could take the punishment.) But there was another factor: with *Hood*'s top speed at 28½ knots and *Bismarck*'s at an accredited 31 knots, the former could be outpaced and outmanoeuvred. Hence his determination to get in as close as possible and not to turn to fire broadsides and thereby provide *Bismarck* with a better target.

There now occurred an identification error which was to cost the British ships dearly. Holland signalled *Prince of Wales* to join him in concentrating their fire on the leading ship, *Prinz Eugen*, which

he had mistaken for *Bismarck*. The similarity of the two ships had
deceived him. However, in *Prince of Wales* Captain Leach decided
to disregard Holland's signal, recognizing that the second ship was
*Bismarck*. A second incautious judgement was made by the
decision to operate the two ships as a single unit, forming the attack
only a few hundred yards apart, thus obscuring *Prince of Wales*'s
view of the enemy by *Hood*'s funnel smoke and the pillars of water
from shell splashes around the flagship.

There were no indecisions in the German ships. Both warships
concentrated their fire on *Hood* until Lutjens ordered *Prinz Eugen*
to take *Prince of Wales*.

At 05.52, at a range of nearly fourteen miles, all ships opened
fire. Almost immediately Holland realized his mistake and signalled
*Prince of Wales* to shift target right. *Hood* found the range in the
first three salvoes; in the meantime *Bismarck*'s first salvo fell short
of *Hood* but close, the second astern, the third hit the boat-deck,
starting a fire from ready-use ammunition stored in lockers.

Three minutes later Holland signalled *Prince of Wales* for a turn
to port, to bring the ships on a parallel course and allow full
broadsides on the enemy. But as they began to execute the turn, a
fourth and fifth salvo from *Bismarck* penetrated *Hood*'s armour,
reached a magazine below one of the main turrets and detonated
100 tons of ammunition. Suddenly she exploded, sending an
orange-white fireball a thousand feet high.

At one moment the mighty 41,000-ton *Hood* was there, a
monumental fortress of steel bristling with fire-power, racing into
battle and slowly turning to allow her eight 15-inch guns to bear on
the enemy; the next, in an ear-splitting explosion of spouting flame
and coiling black smoke, she was gone, leaving nothing – nothing,
that is, except the cindered bodies of nearly 1,500 men in a vast
expanding pool of stinking, bubbling, fuel-oil, while debris of
white-hot metal fell from the skies into the ice-cold waters of the
Atlantic, spluttering and spitting as though in protest at the instant
execution. The time was 06.00.

There were only three survivors, Midshipman W. Dundas, Able
Seaman R. Tilburn and Ordinary Seaman A. Briggs. A destroyer
found them, in the last stages of exhaustion, clinging to pieces of
wreckage in a great lake of oil littered with flotsam.

Even the Germans who watched were stilled into shocked silence.
It was just unbelievable that the mighty *Hood* had gone in a
moment of time – an even greater shock to the onlookers in *Prince*

*of Wales*. But there could be no time for pity, for now *Bismarck* and *Prinz Eugen* concentrated their fire on the remaining British ship, which, with her defective guns and a new crew, was hard put to defend herself.

Two minutes later *Prince of Wales* was hit by four 15-inch shells from *Bismarck* and three 8-inch from *Prinz Eugen*. One of the former struck the bridge without exploding, killing everyone there except Captain Leach and a signalman. Despite the setback, she continued to attack both German ships and obtained three hits on *Bismarck*.

Unknown to the British ship, two of her 14-inch shells were to make some contribution to the eventual sinking of the German ship. One shell landed in an oil bunker, producing a serious loss of fuel, and the other flooded one of the boiler-rooms, reducing her speed to 28 knots.

In the event, *Prince of Wales* turned away to the south-east, laying down a heavy smoke-screen to cover her withdrawal. It would have been irresponsible for the damaged British ship to have done otherwise, and the senior officer present, Admiral Wake-Walker in the shadowing cruiser *Norfolk*, ordered Captain Leach to break off the engagement and join him as a covering force. By this means he could keep in touch with *Bismarck*, knowing that Admiral Tovey's force was some 300 miles to the south-east and probably on an interception course with the two German ships.

Although Admiral Lutjens could congratulate himself on having sunk *Hood* and brushed off *Prince of Wales*'s attack, he realized that the damage to his ship had now completely altered the original purpose of the *Rheinübung* mission. The damage to the fuel bunker had made 1,000 tons of oil fuel inaccessible, and as a result of flooding the ship had a slight list to port. His long-range Atlantic raiding cruise now impossible, he set course for St-Nazaire, for repairs at the only one of the Biscay ports with a dry dock capable of accommodating a ship of *Bismarck*'s size. *Prinz Eugen* would stay at sea and would start the convoy-raiding programme as planned.

The news of the loss of *Hood* came as a great shock to Admiral Tovey, as indeed it did to the whole nation, not least to the Admiralty. They responded with all the power of their command. *Bismarck* had to be found and destroyed. But then came heartening evidence of *Bismarck*'s condition. A Sunderland flying-boat reported that the German ship was leaving a trail of oil in her wake, and this was confirmed by the shadowing *Suffolk*.

The news confirmed Tovey's suspicions that *Bismarck* had been more than lightly damaged in the last exchange. If so, would she make for the nearest port, St-Nazaire? It was now time to deploy his forces to cut off all the escape routes the German might use. But this was easier said than done, for the Atlantic area in which *Bismarck* could operate comprised 9 million square miles of ocean. A prodigious task to find just one ship. And Lutjens was a master at escaping the attention of British sea searches. But this time he was at a disadvantage, for the British Commander-in-Chief could make use of his aircraft-carriers, and Lutjens had had no experience in dealing with the power of the Naval Air Arm.

In the event, the British Admiralty drew upon all its resources, and Force H (the battle-cruiser *Renown*, the cruiser *Sheffield*, the aircraft-carrier *Ark Royal* and six destroyers, *Faulkner, Foresight, Forester, Foxhound, Fury* and *Hesperus*, all under the command of Admiral Somerville) was ordered from Gibraltar to cover the area around the Bay of Biscay. The battleship *Ramillies* 400 miles to the south, was ordered to head due north to intercept, in case *Bismarck* should make towards the Azores; the battleship *Revenge* at Halifax, Nova Scotia, was ordered to sail and make an approach from the west, and the cruiser *Edinburgh*, which had just captured the German merchant ship *Lech en route* from South Africa, was diverted to patrol the approach to Brest.

Tovey realized that, unless *Bismarck*'s speed could be further reduced, she could escape or at least get near enough to the French coast to gain the protection of bomber air support. But 400 miles south-east of *Bismarck*'s last known position the battleship *Rodney* under the command of Captain Dalrymple-Hamilton, was stationed in a prime position to intercept her if she should make for St-Nazaire. Anticipating this, he waited. In Tovey's opinion there was only one way to find *Bismarck* and prevent her reaching the French coast – an air strike. He therefore detached the aircraft-carrier *Victorious* to place her within a 100-mile range of the enemy and there mount a torpedo-bomber attack.

At 22.00 nine torpedo-carrying Swordfish, led by Lieutenant-Commander Eugene Esmonde,* set off to find the *Bismarck*. History was in the making, for it was the first time that aircraft from a carrier attacked a battleship.

---

* Lieutenant-Commander Esmonde was killed on 12 February 1942, leading his 825 Squadron of six Swordfish torpedo-carrying planes in an attack against *Scharnhorst, Gneisenau* and *Prinz Eugen* in their Channel dash break-out from Brest. He was later awarded a posthumous VC.

At 23.30 the Swordfish found *Bismarck* after being guided in on their target by *Norfolk*'s radar. The pilots pressed home their attacks with suicidal courage, sometimes closing to within 500 yards before releasing their torpedoes. *Bismarck*, however, had increased her speed to 28 knots and by frantic twisting and turning managed to avoid all the torpedoes except one. This had little effect, for it struck the ship on the most heavily armoured section amidships. Fortunately all the Swordfish managed to return unscathed and land safely on the carrier. It was a magnificent effort which should have had greater success.

The bad luck which seem to have dogged British efforts emerged again. In the early morning of the 25th, *Suffolk* lost contact with the German ship. With Tovey only 100 miles away, *Bismarck* had vanished off the radar screen; consequently he ordered *Victorious* to launch another air search at dawn. Despite the net that Tovey had spread, hoping to cover possible escape routes, it seemed that *Bismarck* might now escape. At this time there were ten convoys *en route* in the Atlantic, which, now denuded of their battleship protection, exposed them to deadly danger; hence the vital importance of finding and destroying the German ship.

Unwittingly Lutjens now betrayed his position. Convinced of the efficiency of British radar and that he could no longer escape detection, he broke wireless silence and sent constant transmissions to Hitler, detailing the victory over the battleships *Hood* and *Prince of Wales*. These messages were easily picked up by the Admiralty in London. But yet again British bad luck persisted. Because of a misunderstanding between the Admiralty, Tovey's destroyer direction-finding apparatus and *King George V*'s navigational charting, *Bismarck*'s position was plotted 200 miles north of her actual position. By this it looked as though she was heading back towards the Denmark Strait. Accordingly at 10.35 Tovey reversed his course and ordered the ships under his command to follow the latest information and head due north. In the meantime Lutjens, unaware of the latest train of events, continued on his course towards the French coast. Several hours later, after a re-calculation of the co-ordinates and a realization that a grave error had been made, Tovey swung his battleship *King George V* around back to the south-east, towards France. By now, however, he had lost time and sea ground and was 150 miles behind *Bismarck*, with fuel stocks running low.

It seemed the odds were all against Tovey. Even the weather continued to favour the enemy, with low cloud and heavy seas making difficulties for the long-range Catalina aircraft of RAF Coastal Command. But then, at 10.30 on the 26th, a Catalina flying-boat piloted by Officer D. Briggs sighted a large warship through the mist. Descending to get a closer look, the plane was immediately rocked by intense anti-aircraft fire. There was no doubt now – *Bismarck* had been found. But the German was only 700 miles from Brest and at her present speed could arrive there on the evening of the 27th.

Despite the concern aboard *Bismarck* that the British had found them, Lutjens tried to lift morale by informing the ship's company that Group West Headquarters in France had assured him that the Luftwaffe was ready to support him by giving cover with bombers as far out as 400 miles, that three destroyers were on their way and that seven U-boats would form a defence screen.

The situation in the British camp was now getting desperate, for the fuel situation had become critical. *Victorious, Prince of Wales, Suffolk* and *Repulse* were so low on oil that they had to return to refuel. So *Bismarck* had to be slowed down, and only a successful torpedo attack by *Ark Royal*'s aircraft could prevent the enemy escaping. Racing in from the west, however, was the Fourth Destroyer Flotilla under Captain P.L. Vian DSO, with the destroyers *Cossack, Maori, Sikh* and *Zulu* and the Polish *Piorun*. Ignoring the Commander-in-Chief's order to join him to form a screen around the flagship, Captain Vian decided that, following the latest sighting, the more important task would be for him to find and attack *Bismarck* himself. He therefore altered course and increased to full speed.

At 13.15 *Sheffield* was detached to try to get a sighting of the enemy, and at 14.50 the first of *Ark Royal*'s striking force was flown off, fourteen Swordfish staggering under the weight of their torpedoes, rocked by the wind and tossed this way and that by the rising and falling deck of the carrier. Barely thirty minutes later their radar detected a ship ahead, and the planes roared down through the cloud to attack. The results were almost disastrous, for immediately they released their torpedoes they discovered to their dismay that it was not *Bismarck* but the cruiser *Sheffield*. At once, Captain Larcom of *Sheffield* increased to full speed, took violent evasive action and managed to avoid being hit. Fortunately, all the torpedoes either missed or exploded harmlessly on hitting the water, due to over-sensitive magnetic detonators, and a terrible tragedy was averted.

The report received by Tovey only added further gloom in the British ships, for it would soon be dusk, with a greater chance of

*Bismarck*'s escaping. It now all depended on two factors: a successful second strike by *Ark Royal*'s aircraft and/or a chance torpedo hit by Captain Vian's destroyers. In *Ark Royal*, frantic preparations were made for the second attack. Magnetic detonators had to be replaced by contact detonators, and this took time.

It was 19.15, in low cloud and poor visibility, before fifteen Swordfish led by Lieutenant-Commander Tim Coode took off from the carrier. Forty-five minutes later they found *Sheffield*, which reported that *Bismarck* was twelve miles ahead and gave them the bearing.

At 20.40 the planes found the enemy ship and immediately dived to the attack. The massive secondary armament of the German's ninety anti-aircraft guns came into full operation, and the British planes were subjected to intense and accurate fire. Despite this, the Swordfish rammed home their attack for half an hour. Two torpedoes hit the ship, the first amidships to explode harmlessly, but the second punched its way into the stern, exploded in the steering compartment and firmly jammed the rudder hard over. Her Achilles heel had been found. As the last of the Swordfish sped away, *Bismarck* was seen to circle twice and then crawl away to the north-west at barely 7 knots, heading straight for the approaching ships of the Home Fleet, relieving Tovey of the task of pursuit.

Aboard *Bismarck* morale had sunk to its lowest depths. It was only a matter of time before the British battleships would find them and, although they would be overwhelmed, they would fight to the last shell. Just after midnight on the 26th congratulations for the sinking of HMS *Hood* poured into the doomed ship, including a special message to Admiral Lutjens – it was his birthday. At 01.53 came a message from Hitler himself: 'To the crew of the battleship *Bismarck*. The whole of Germany is with you. What can still be done will be done. The performance of your duty will strengthen our people in the struggle for their existence.

Adolf Hitler.'

At 07.10 on the 27th Lutjens radioed Group West: 'Send U-boat to save war log.'

It was the last message from *Bismarck*, and the U-boat never arrived.

On the night of the 26th, Captain Vian and his destroyers appeared. All through the remaining hours until 07.00, the destroyers attacked, firing star shells to target their torpedoes. It was impossible to be sure if any hits were scored during those dark hours, but it seems highly likely they were. In the tumult of battle, with the great roar and flash of guns from both sides, it would be difficult for the exhausted *Bismarck*'s gun's crews to know for certain.

With dawn on the 27th came the avengers. With Vian's destroyers settled firmly on the flanks of the German, Sir John Tovey in *King George V* and Captain Dalrymple-Hamilton in *Rodney* appeared over the horizon with their escorts. At 08.45 all three battleships opened fire, with the range at about nine miles. Although the first salvoes from *Bismarck* were uncomfortably close to *Rodney*, the tired guns' crews could not maintain the accuracy of their firing. Soon after 09.00 an avalanche of 14-inch shells from *King George V* and 16-inch from *Rodney* punched into the stricken vessel. An hour later the two British ships moved to within point-blank range of five miles to reduce *Bismarck* to a cataclysm of destruction. What was left of her hull glowed with internal fires as shells and exploding cordite erupted to speed her end. At 10.20 the cruiser *Dorsetshire* arrived to administer the *coup de grâce*. As one of her officers said, 'She [*Bismarck*] was a terrible sight. Her top was blown clear away, flames roaring out in several places and her plates glowing red with heat.'

Yet above the inferno *Bismarck*'s flag still flew in defiance. Battered and torn apart though she was, the great ship would not sink.

By now Admiral Tovey was not only impatient but amazed that any ship could receive so much punishment and yet not go down. Time was running out for the British battleships. Radar had reported that German long-range bombers were approaching, and German U-boats converging on the area. But worse still the fuel situation on both the British capital ships was so critical that Tovey was unsure if he would have sufficient fuel to reach home. In desperation he ordered his ships to go in closer. This they did, *Rodney* firing all her nine 16-inch guns. Then, at a range of only 3,000 yards, she fired her last two torpedoes, scoring a hit. (It was the first occasion in naval history on which a battleship ever torpedoed another.) A further torpedo from *Norfolk* scored a direct hit, but still *Bismarck* would not sink. The time was 10.30.

Although the German ship still floated, it was clear she was finished, and reluctantly, in view of the oil situation, Tovey ordered *Rodney* to follow and set course for Britain. As he left the scene he sent a last signal: if there were any ships with torpedoes they were to fire point-blank into the wallowing hulk.

But Captain Martin of the cruiser *Dorsetshire*, which had just arrived, seeing the two battleships head for home, had already acted. Closing to 3,000 yards he fired two torpedoes into *Bismarck*'s starboard side, then, circling to port, fired another at just over 2,000 yards. Slowly, so very slowly, *Bismarck* rolled over on to her port side and then went down, her flag still flying. The time was 10.40.

The engagement had proved to be one of the greatest sea dramas of all time. The almost unsinkable ship, the fighting spirit of her crew, the incredible punishment endured. Perhaps it was also a lasting testimony to the skilful design of the ship, a honeycomb of watertight cells. She had had seventy-one torpedoes fired at her but had received only ten hits. With *Bismarck*'s steering out of action, was this a tribute to superb evasive action by the enemy or (without detracting from the courage of the Swordfish pilots and destroyers' captains) was it a reflection on torpedo-targeting efficiency?

Despite approaching German long-range bombers and the reported presence of U-boats, the cruiser *Dorsetshire* and the destroyer *Maori* approached to try to rescue those who still clung to debris in the great pool of oil on the surface. The seas were high, making it impossible to launch boats, but life-lines and rope ladders were thrown over and, in a bid to save as many as possible, the British sailors did all they could to haul survivors aboard. In the midst of these efforts, however, the approach of a German submarine demanded that the rescue mission be abandoned, and the two ships, with 113 survivors aboard, steamed away, leaving hundreds of German sailors in the cold waters of the Atlantic. Out of a total of 2,400 men aboard *Bismarck*, only 118 were saved.

The *Bismarck* saga was over, but it had taken eight battleships and battle-cruisers, two aircraft-carriers, eleven cruisers and twenty-one destroyers to find and sink her, with each side losing its greatest warship.

On the morning of 27 May 1941 the Prime Minister announced in the House of Commons, 'This morning, shortly after daylight, the *Bismarck*, virtually at a standstill, far from help, was attacked by British pursuing battleships. I do not know what were the results of the bombardment. It appears, however, that the *Bismarck* was not sunk by gunfire. She will now be dispatched by torpedo.

'It is thought that this is now proceeding ...' Hardly had he sat down than a note was handed to him, and he rose again: 'I ask the indulgence of the House. I have just received news that the *Bismarck* is sunk.'

'The House seemed content,' he wrote later.

The following day he cabled President Roosevelt in Washington: 'I will send you later the inside story of the fighting with the *Bismarck*. She was a terrific ship and a masterpiece of naval construction ...'

It was a worthy tribute to an extraordinary ship that for a time had held at bay the full weight and might of the British Home Fleet. This was the last time in the remaining years of World War II that a German battleship broke out into the great Atlantic Ocean.

# 10   Singapore – the Loss of Repulse and Prince of Wales

*On 10 December 1941, only three days after the attack on Pearl Harbor by Japanese aircraft, which succeeded in sinking most of the American fleet, Japanese troops landed in Malaya and headed towards the British base at Singapore. From there the new battleship* Prince of Wales *and the 25-year-old battle-cruiser* Repulse *sailed north in search of Japanese troop-transports. Failing to find them, they themselves were found by twin-engined bombers based at Saigon. With little cost to themselves, the eighty-four aircraft armed with torpedoes and bombs succeeded in sinking both these great ships.*

On the night of 10 December 1941 the telephone rang at the Prime Minister's bedside at No. 10 Downing Street. It was a call from the Admiralty, the voice that of the First Sea Lord, Admiral of the Fleet Sir Dudley Pound. His voice was constricted, hesitant, a little indistinct. After clearing his throat, the First Sea Lord said 'Prime Minister, I have to report to you that the *Prince of Wales* and the *Repulse* have both been sunk by the Japanese – we think by aircraft – Admiral Tom Phillips is drowned.'

In his memoirs Churchill recorded that, 'In all the war I never received a more direct shock', and later, 'As I turned and twisted in bed, the full horror of the news sank in upon me. There were no British or American capital ships in the Indian Ocean or the Pacific except the American survivors of Pearl Harbor, who were hastening back to California. Over all this vast expanse of waters, Japan was supreme and we everywhere were weak and naked.'

To understand the reasons why these two great warships were operating in and around the Indian Ocean at that period, one has to go back in time briefly and recall the events leading up to this engagement which led to the loss of these valuable capital ships.

Only three days earlier, on the morning of 7 December, there had occurred the infamous and 'never to be forgotten' attack on Pearl Harbor at Hawaii by the Japanese. While peaceful negotiations were still going on between the Japanese ambassador in Washington, Admiral Nomura, and the American secretary of state, Cordell Hull, the Japanese fleet had sailed and been at sea nine days, heading for Pearl Harbor, fully committed to the destruction of the anchored American battle fleet.

On that morning the commander of the Japanese task force, Vice-Admiral Nagumo, approached Hawaii with six aircraft-carriers, *Kaga, Hiryu, Soryu, Shokakau* and *Zuikaku*, with their escorting destroyers and cruisers. Totally unaware of the catastrophe about to overtake them, the Americans went about their Sunday routine in the customary manner, while 200 miles away Nagumo launched 400 fighter bombers and torpedo bombers. At seven o'clock that morning, the enemy planes began their attack on anchored warships, grounded aircraft and installations in and around the harbour.

The surprise was total. Almost every ship within the naval area was hit, including eight battleships. Three of these, *Arizona, California* and *Utah*, were actually sent to the bottom; *Nevada* had to be beached as a burning wreck; *Oklahoma* capsized; *Pennsylvania, West Virginia* and *Tennessee* were seriously damaged; the cruisers *Honolulu, Raleigh* and *Helena* were badly damaged and three destroyers sunk – *Cassin, Downes* and *Shaw*. Out of the aircraft on the ground, nearly 300 were destroyed, and over 3,000 men were killed. For this, the Japanese lost only twenty-eight aircraft. It was, in fact, the most impressive and the fastest single naval victory of the war.

The Japanese, without any declaration had launched an attack on a neutral country. It was this act which brought America into the war at the side of Great Britain. While a jubilant Japan celebrated its 'victory', the wise Admiral Nagumo was quoted as saying, 'We have this day awakened a sleeping giant.' And, as events were to prove later, Japan would pay – and pay dearly.

Meanwhile, just an hour or so before the attack on Pearl Harbor, over 5,000 Japanese had been landed in Malaya, heading for the

British naval base at Singapore. In Britain, the War Cabinet authorized immediate declaration of war upon Japan, and the next day Churchill sent the following letter to the Japanese ambassador:

Sir,
On the evening of December 7th, His Majesty's Government in the United Kingdom learned that Japanese forces without previous warning ... had attempted a landing on the coast of Malaya and bombed Singapore and Hong Kong. In view of these wanton acts of unprovoked aggression ... His Majesty's Ambassador at Tokyo has been instructed to inform the Imperial Japanese Government, in the name of His Majesty's Government in the United Kingdom, that a state of war exists between our two countries. I have the honour to be, with high consideration,

Sir,
Your obedient servant,
Winston Churchill.

Mr Churchill commented, 'Some people did not like this ceremonial style, but after all when you have to kill a man it costs nothing to be polite.'

On the night of 9 December a hastily convened meeting of the War Cabinet was held in order to review the naval situation. The future looked extremely grave, for Britain had lost command of every ocean except the Atlantic. In the Pacific, Australia, New Zealand and the colonial islands were wide open to attack. The only remaining defence in that sphere were the warships *Prince of Wales* and *Repulse*, which at that time were at Singapore. The debate in the Cabinet room centred on the question whether or not to send the two ships across the Pacific to join the remnants of the American fleet. The meeting was adjourned with the intention of discussing the matter the next morning. Only two hours later the issue had been settled. Both ships were at the bottom of the ocean.

The battleship *Prince of Wales*, of 35,000 tons, was a recent addition to the fleet. Launched in 1939, she carried ten 14-inch guns in three turrets and sixteen 5.25-inch. As one of Britain's biggest capital ships she had a complement of 1,500 men. The battle-cruiser *Repulse*, with a displacement of 32,000 tons and a crew of 1,400, carried six 15-inch guns in three turrets and twenty 4-inch. She was a much older ship, of First World War vintage, but completely modernized in the years 1932–9.

When Admiral Sir Tom Phillips, commanding the British Eastern Fleet based at Singapore, received news that the Japanese had launched a major invasion of Malaya, with landings to the north at Singora and Pattani, he sailed on 8 December in his flagship *Prince of Wales*, with *Repulse*, commanded by Captain Tennant, escorted by four destroyers, *Electra, Express, Vampire* and *Tenedos*, with the intention of striking at the troop convoy ships while they were still disembarking. He had made specific requests to the Singapore Air Command to provide fighter and reconnaissance air support for his ships in their daring enterprise. It seems, however, that, due to some confusion in communication, fighter protection failed to arrive. He had received a warning that large Japanese bomber forces were already based at Saigon in French Indo-China, only some 300 miles north of the troop landing-points, but as the weather had deteriorated into rain squalls and low cloud, making it unfavourable for bombing conditions, he pressed on.

On the evening of the 9th, the weather and the visibility improved, and it became apparent that his fleet, Force Z, was being shadowed by enemy reconnaissance. With all hope of surprise gone and the anticipation of bombing attacks likely, Phillips abandoned his enterprise and under cover of darkness turned back, heading for Singapore.

At midnight he received a signal from Singapore that another Japanese landing had been made at Kuantan, on the eastern seaboard of Malaya, only 200 miles north of Singapore. Thinking it unlikely that this force, last spotted by the enemy heading north, would find him so far south by daylight, he accepted the risk and headed his ships towards Kuantan. On nearing the port, a Walrus reconnaissance plane was launched and the destroyer *Express* sent to investigate. They found no sign of the enemy; in fact, it proved to be a false intelligence report. As events turned out, this blunder was to be partially responsible for the loss of these two fine ships.

A Japanese plane then sighted the British force heading south, and early that morning an enemy reconnaissance patrol discovered the ships and reported to base. This was, of course, unknown to the admiral. However, before resuming his southerly course, some time was spent in an attempt to investigate a group of barges which the fleet had passed shortly before dawn. Before finding these boats, however, he received a signal from his forward destroyer, *Tenedos*, on her lone way back to Singapore, that she was being subjected to bombing attacks. It was clear that in a short time *Prince of Wales* and *Repulse* would be discovered. Appreciating the gravity of the situation, Phillips increased speed to 25 knots and ordered crews to action stations.

Just after 11.00 the first wave of enemy aircraft appeared. These were the advance section of eighty-eight planes, twenty-six armed with 500-pound bombs and sixty-two with aerial torpedoes, all escorted by fast Zero fighters with speeds of over 350 m.p.h., which had taken off from Saigon. These planes of the Japanese 22nd Air Flotilla had flown as far south as Singapore without sighting the British ships, and it was only by chance that their course led them straight to their quarry.

With *Prince of Wales* leading, *Repulse* on her starboard quarter and the destroyers *Electra, Vampire* and *Express* in formation ahead, ships' gun crews waited, fingers on triggers. The first wave of nine twin-engined high-level bombers, flying at 17,000 feet, targeted their attack on *Repulse*. Flying through a barrage of anti-aircraft gunfire from the two big ships, impervious to the crash of exploding shells rocketing their machines, they released their nine heavy bombs over the target. Seven fell close to the port side, another to starboard, but the ninth was dead amidships. It tore through the hangar and exploded on the armoured deck below in a flash of flame and splintering steel. Fire began to spread but was soon under control, and the ship's speed was unimpaired.

Minutes later, the Bettys arrived: sixteen torpedo bombers. They appeared first off the starboard bow, speeding on to disappear within a small bank of cloud, and returned in two or three groups, closing in on the flagship's port beam. Every gun from the five ships opened up on the attackers – heavy guns, pom-poms, oerlikons, bofors and 4-inch anti-aircraft, all pouring out a curtain of steel and explosives – but still the planes came on. At 500 feet most released their torpedoes, aimed at *Prince of Wales*, while others flew on with their racks still loaded, targeting on the battle-cruiser.

Captain Tennant, anticipating the lines of foam tracks speeding towards his ship at nearly fifty miles an hour, ordered the ship's rudder to starboard and watched as the torpedoes sped by harmlessly on either side. But the Japanese, liberated from their heavy loads, roared on over the ship, with their air-gunners firing streams of bullets at the ship's defending guns' crews. Many of these were hit, crumpling to the deck in an agony of death.

Flag-Captain Leach, commanding *Prince of Wales*, watched in mounting dismay as the sea came alive with running torpedoes, heading straight for his ship. They were running shallow, their bubbling milky trails lengthening on the surface, six, ten, twelve homing in on the port side, astern, ahead and abeam. Escape was impossible. In desperation the flagship turned hard to port to try to comb the tracks but it was too late. Two of the torpedoes, each with over 600 pounds of high explosives in its warhead, plunged directly into the stern. Two separate explosions lifted the great ship, hurling columns of water high above the stern, followed by the inner cauldron of destruction belching clouds of dense black smoke over the sea. It was a mortal blow, for the explosions had smashed the rudder, jammed both port propellers and torn a huge hole in the ship's hull. Like a huge wounded animal, the battleship heeled over, steaming helplessly to port, out of control, smoke hanging heavily over her bridge and superstructure.

Someone once described the use of explosive projectiles in World War II as 'torpedoes for the letting-in of water' and 'bombs for the letting-in of air'. How true it was now. With most of *Prince of Wales*'s stern blown away, hundreds of tons of water were already rushing in the huge gaping hole, crashing through bulkheads fractured by the explosions, tearing open engine-room watertight doors wrenched and ruptured by the blast. And there she lay, a helpless victim on the sacrificial altar of the ocean.

But where were the British fighters which Admiral Phillips had requested? Both he and Captain Tennant were utterly dismayed by the catastrophe which had befallen them, which in their opinion could have been at least partly offset by the appearance of British air support. Tennant, realizing that *Prince of Wales* was now in no position to contact Singapore, transmitted an emergency signal to base, informing them they were under heavy air attack.

Just after noon that day the Japanese struck again, concentrating on *Repulse*. This time it was a simultaneous co-ordinated attack with a squadron of high-level bombers and another of torpedo bombers. By remarkable anticipation of the fall of bombs and the direction of torpedoes, and by swinging the big battle-cruiser to port or starboard, Tennant managed to escape damage. It was a miracle of survival. All this time, his gunners were pouring thousands of shells into the oncoming aircraft, but still they came on, despite a few of their number being blown apart in the assault.

Even in the heat and thunder of battle, Tennant managed, by signal lamp, to send Admiral Phillips the laconic message, 'Thanks to Providence have so far dodged nineteen torpedoes.'

Fifteen minutes later, with the two ships barely half a mile apart, another attack developed. The first wave of nine torpedo bombers roared in, six targeting *Repulse*, three *Prince of Wales*. This time, however, Providence was not on the side of the old battle-cruiser. Three torpedoes were already homing in, and even while Tennant was successfully combing these tracks, another three planes dropped their torpedoes abeam of his ship. If he swung away to escape these, he would receive the full impact of the torpedoes he was already combing. From one, speeding through the water from the latest three, there was to be no escape. It struck the ship dead centre in a slamming explosion, ripping a great hole in the outer skin of her defensive hull. But it was not a mortal blow, for she had absorbed the impact in her 'blister'. (This novel feature of *Repulse* was an anti-torpedo bulge fitted along and below the water-line, the principle being that a torpedo could explode and expend its energy without damaging the hull proper. In this case it proved successful, for her engine-room was still intact and she could still steam at 25 knots.)

High above them, circling for the kill, were another three or four squadrons of torpedo bombers awaiting their turn. They dived out of the sky from several directions at once, while the gunners of *Repulse* sweated at their guns, pouring a curtain of fire at the diving aircraft. It was impossible to counter all these simultaneous attacks, and soon the sea was again alive with the long, deadly steel projectiles running through the dark waters at incredible speed towards the ship. Despite violent evasive action, there could be no deliverance this time. Four torpedoes hit simultaneously, followed by the roar of explosions, the blast of heat rising to the bridge and the deadly, terrifying noise of ripping, tearing metal. Mortally wounded, *Repulse* came to a shaking stop, listing rapidly.

There was no hope for the vessel, and Captain Tennant, knowing the end was near, broadcast over the loudspeaker system, 'Everybody on deck – prepare to abandon ship.' From escape hatchways and bulkhead doors, through gangways and companionways, those who remained alive came pouring out onto the decks, blowing up their inflatable lifebelts as they ran.

With only minutes to spare before the ship would take her final plunge, Tennant gave the order 'Abandon ship!' By now *Repulse* had listed to 40 degrees, then, rolling slowly further over to 70 degrees, she steadied for a moment. There was no panic among the crew, only hidden fear. Almost resignedly they clung to the high edge of the canted deck, then slid, some uncontrollably, down the ship's side on the slippery coating of weed and oil that clung to the underside. They fell wildly, many injuring themselves on the barnacled steel hull or on the naked keel. But awaiting in the sea there was oil, fuel-oil. For men in the sea, oil is a vicious, iniquitous thing. It burns the eyes, scorches the lungs and tears the stomach in violent outbursts of retching. Few escaped the stinking liquid that lapped obscenely against their faces, spilling into their throats.

At 12.35 the gallant old warship, which had battled with the German High Seas Fleet in the North Sea twenty-five years earlier, slipped silently and quickly below the surface, stern first. As her bows disappeared, a tumult of water leaped upwards, and with it a gush of black fuel-oil that spread over the flattened sea like a cancerous growth. For a moment or more, great eruptions of air burst turbulently to the surface, then gradually, as time passed, the bubbles grew smaller and less frequent, and then there were no more.

Captain Tennant was saved, but not before he had gone down with the ship, which had rolled over on him. He had been drawn down by the suction but miraculously reached the surface still alive, where willing hands hauled him onto a Carley float. By now there were hundreds of men in the sea either swimming to free themselves from the worst of the oil or trying to haul themselves aboard the few Carley floats.

From the bridge of *Prince of Wales*, Phillips just had time to signal the destroyers *Electra* and *Vampire* to pick up *Repulse*'s survivors when the flagship again became the target for another concentrated attack. At the time *Repulse* was being torpedoed, the aircraft which had homed in on *Prince of Wales* had dropped their torpedoes, all dead on target. The battleship was a sitting duck, for her speed had been reduced from the last attack to a mere 15 knots, and with her rudder destroyed she had no way of turning. They struck on the starboard side simultaneously. *Prince of Wales* had been built with a protective belt along her sides of solid steel, fourteen inches thick, running from 100 feet short of the bow to within seventy feet of the stern. This defensive girdle would normally have reduced the impact significantly, but the Japanese had cunningly set the torpedoes to run deep, and within ninety

Magazine of the US destroyer *Shaw* exploding after being hit by Japanese dive-bombers at Pearl Harbor

US ships in Pearl Harbor after attack by Japanese dive-bombers

The moment of impact: Japanese freighter torpedoed by US torpedo bombers. Note wake of torpedo

The Japanese cruiser *Mikuma* on fire after being hit by US bombers

Part of US fleet prior to the Battle of Leyte Gulf

The incendiary bombing of Tokyo by the US Air Force left the city in ruins

Japan's Foreign Minister Shigemitsu signs the treaty of surrender on board the US battleship *Missouri* – 2 September 1945. This brought World War II to its close

seconds they had plunged into the hull below the armour protection. Destruction was complete. The sides of the battleship were ripped open, as with a giant can-opener, allowing the sea to blast its way into and through the tangled wreckage of steel that had once been compartments and bulkheads but were now the devil's scrapyard.

Hardly had the crash and boom of the explosions died away than there came another sound, the familiar engine throb of high-level bombers: nine, closing in from the south, and the battleship was almost stationary. Admiral Phillips and his officers, and the ratings on the upper decks, watched helpless as the nine bombs came wobbling down, growing bigger and bigger, and then they were there, while the world of the *Prince of Wales* erupted into an earthquake of distintegration. The six inches of deck armour plating had prevented a piercing into the ship's bowels but the effect of 500-pound bombs of high explosive and steel shattering into a myriad of shrapnel was devastating. Casualties were frightening.

As the Admiral looked down from the bridge at the carnage below and listened to the sound of the sea pouring through the torn side, he knew his ship was doomed. She settled deeper and deeper into the water. He could no longer hope to save his flagship.

It was just after 13.00 that Phillips' signal led *Express* to come alongside and take off the wounded and all the survivors possible in the estimated remaining ten minutes or so of the ship's survival. Came the order 'Abandon ship!' and those of the 1,500 men aboard still capable jumped or scrambled down nets or ropes onto the deck of the destroyer along the starboard side of the sinking ship. Those who could not reach the rail through the crowd of men simply jumped into the sea from the port side and tried to swim towards the destroyer *Electra*, moving in to the rescue.

Twenty minutes later the flagship rolled tortuously further to port. As she did so, her huge bilge keel rose out of the water under the hull of *Express*, tipping her as the keel rose higher. She was packed with survivors, and it was an alarming moment for her commanding officer, Captain Cartwright. With split-second timing, the telegraphs jangled, the water boiled at *Express*'s stern and quickly she pulled away from the rolling hull. Only seconds later *Prince of Wales* disappeared in a turmoil of oil and huge gushes of water and air, taking with her Admiral Tom Phillips and Flag-Captain John Leach. The losses for the two ships together amounted to 840 killed or missing.

Ironically, overhead four British Buffalo fighter planes arrived from Singapore in time to witness *Prince of Wales* take her final plunge. Too little, too late.

That these two great capital ships were sunk in vain there can be no doubt. They served no political purpose, and if their presence was intended to exercise a vague menace upon hostile calculations, it had failed miserably. The power of Britain's so-called Eastern Fleet was extinguished in a moment of time, before it had achieved the smallest military advantage.

Harsh criticism was levelled at the government for a calamity which, in the opinion of the nation, need never have happened. The report of this lamentable disaster was received in Great Britain with dismay. One newspaper of the day carried the banner headline

PREMIER ACCUSED FOR LOSS OF WARSHIPS

Blunt criticism of the Premier as an advocate and arbiter of strategy, and the assertion that the sending of the *Prince of Wales* and *Repulse* to the Far East without adequate protection was a political decision, was made in the House of Lords yesterday by Lord Chatfield, former Minister for Co-ordination of Defence. The Prime Minister had said on Tuesday, he pointed out – 'That the two ships were sent out as spearpoints.' 'Battleships are not spearpoints, they are not forwards in the game, they are full-backs' said Lord Chatfield. 'Repeated avoidable disasters make a reasonable man wonder whether the strategic machine that guides these decisions is all that it should be.'

The article continued: 'In a Commons debate last night, Commander Southby said – "he could not believe that expert naval officers failed to advise that the *Prince of Wales* and *Repulse* should be accompanied by an aircraft carrier. I have heard it stated" he alleged, "that orders given for an aircraft carrier were countermanded by the Prime Minister himself." '

Another paper carried the headline 'MESSAGE THAT MAY HAVE KILLED OVER 800 SAILORS'. This, of course, referred to the bungled intelligence message that Admiral Phillips received informing him that Japanese troops had landed at Kuantan, which made him diverge from his homeward course to investigate. That report proved to be false. But who had sent it? Certainly not the Japanese, who would hardly have invited resistance to their advance on Singapore. There can be little doubt that the message originated from Singapore headquarters, but no one appears to have accepted responsibility. The time lost on Admiral Phillips' investigation based on the Kuantan report was in no doubt partly responsible for the disaster.

At home, chiefs of staff were deeply concerned about the whole situation and questioned why no fighter aircraft had been sent from Singapore to aid the squadron. But yet again there were no satisfactory answers.

In war, both sides make mistakes, but it begs the question – are wars won by the nation that makes the fewest?

# 11   The Soviet Convoys

Military equipment had to be sent from Britain to the Soviet Union in the Second World War to preserve the Eastern Front, without which the Germans would have been able to turn their full might against the West in an attempt to force a victory. As a consequence, ships were diverted from Britain and sent in convoys to Murmansk in north Russia. The Germans retaliated by building up their naval and air forces in Norway to cut this life-line, even though this meant reducing their attacks on the Atlantic convoys.

The Soviet convoys were identified by the letters PQ when outward bound, loaded, and by QP on their return, empty; from December 1942 onwards, they were identified by the new codes JW and RA respectively. They went as far north as possible to avoid enemy bases. In winter most of the passage was by night, but in the summer it was daylight all the way. Once found, a convoy was attacked continuously – by bombs and torpedoes from the air, as well as by U-boats and surface vessels. The convoy might be aided by the white mist which forms near the ice barrier in summer, but the escorts were as likely to be hindered by sea-temperature variations, forming layers, which their submarine detectors could not penetrate. With this protection available, U-boats could stay surfaced longer than would have been safe in less extreme waters. Despite this, convoys continued to be sailed right round the year, regardless of the disproportionate merchant and naval losses.

In June 1941 Hitler launched a massive attack against the Soviet Union, with the code-name 'Barbarossa'. To the British this seemed a miracle of deliverance, for if instead he had launched an invasion of Britain, the nation would have stood little or no chance of resisting the German war-machine no matter how valiantly it might have fought. 'Barbarossa' provided the Allies with the precious gift of time, time to gain strength, time to re-arm, time to forge weapons with which to fight. The Soviets' defence fell swiftly under the awesome weight of the Nazis' heavy guns and at least a thousand tanks. By November 1941 the German Army was only thirty miles from the gates of Moscow. All the indications were that the Soviet Union would soon be crushed, and if that happened, Hitler would then turn his fury upon Great Britain.

It was clear to Churchill and to the American President Franklin D. Roosevelt that the Allies' salvation lay in supporting the Soviet Union. The Soviet leader, Marshal Stalin, made abundantly clear to the British Prime Minister the desperate situation and the need for weapons with which to repel the Nazi hordes. In reply, the two Allied leaders promised they would send and deliver whatever could be spared to help the Soviet armies and that the United States in particular, with her vast resources, would become the great arsenal of Democracy.

The shortest route was through the Arctic Ocean from Iceland to Murmansk and Archangel, a 2,000-mile voyage exposed to the most violent weather in the world. But the greatest danger was from the enemy, who had established aircraft, surface-craft and submarine bases along the coast of north Norway.

The first of the so-called PQ series of convoys set out from Iceland for the Soviet Union on 28 September 1941, consisting of ten ships loaded with tanks, guns, planes and ammunition, and by the end of the year fifty-three ships had been safely escorted to Murmansk and Archangel without loss. This was largely because the enemy was not fully aware of the importance of the aid provided. The arrival of these ships immediately raised morale among the Soviet defenders, and resistance to the invaders mounted. As the arsenal of weapons, mainly from America, increased, so the size of convoys grew, so now Hitler, aware that one of the obstacles of his eastward advance was the supply of arms to his foe, made a determined effort to halt the flow of war materials by increasing his forces in north Norway. To achieve this, he re-inforced his air squadrons, increased his heavy destroyer and submarine force and moved heavy units of the German fleet further north, ready to move out to attack convoy shipping when called upon.

The latter threat imposed an enormous strain upon the resources of the Home Fleet, such were Britain's commitments in other theatres of war. As a consequence, the escort protection given to convoys was so inadequate as to be almost negligible.

To reach their destination in north Russia, the Royal Navy escorts and their charges had to fight their way through the narrow sea gap between north Norway and the Great Ice Barrier. From 1 March onward, every convoy was subjected to submarine and dive-bombing attacks, and some to assault by enemy destroyers and heavy cruisers. But the greatest threat lay in the presence of the mighty battleship *Tirpitz*, snugly harboured in a fiord at Trondheim from which it would be easy to sail forth and utterly destroy a convoy before slipping back into the safety of one of the Norwegian fiords further north. The situation was of such concern to the Admiralty that the Prime Minister dispatched the following letter to chiefs of staff dated January 1942:

The presence of *Tirpitz* at Trondheim has now been known for three days. The destruction or even the crippling of this ship is the greatest event at sea at the present time. No other target is comparable to it.... If she were only crippled it would be difficult to take her back to Germany. The entire naval situation throughout the world would be altered, and the naval command in the Pacific would be regained.... The whole strategy of the war turns at this period on this ship, which is holding four times the number of British capital ships paralysed, to say nothing of the two new American battleships retained in the Atlantic. I regard the matter as of the highest urgency and importance.

By 1942, the defence of the Russian convoys had been supplemented by the inclusion of escort carriers with Swordfish, Wildcat and Avenger aircraft, which in co-operation with the destroyer escorts took a heavy toll of enemy submarines, and despite the Arctic weather they continued to fly off and land their aircraft in almost impossible conditions. In the convoys of 1944, units of the Fleet Air Arm sank no fewer than eight U-boats and shot down ten enemy aircraft. Of almost equal importance was their inestimable value in preventing enemy aircraft from approaching to launch attacks on the convoys.

It is against this background of the fear of imminent destruction that the story of the Soviet convoys is based, in a storm-ravaged ocean on which convoys of defenceless merchant ships escorted by the Royal Navy defiantly sailed back and forth almost on the enemy's doorstep, daring whatever form of offensive the enemy could mount.

In this brief chronicle of sea war, it is impossible to recount the many battles and the almost commonplace heroic episodes of the Arctic convoy war, but four naval engagements are described (in chapters 12, 13, 15 and 16) which reveal the almost impossible odds that had to be faced and the almost intolerable weather conditions in which the actions had to be fought.

# 12   The Ship That Torpedoed Herself

*In 1942 in the Arctic Ocean there occurred the most bizarre event in naval history, for in March of that year the new cruiser* HMS Trinidad *succeeded in torpedoing herself: the only time in British naval history in which a ship torpedoed herself in battle. It happened not by negligence but by a cruel twist of fate – a chance in a million.*

*That episode and the events preceding and following it are described here by one man who was a survivor of the PQ 13 convoy and of the subsequent massive enemy dive-bombing which six weeks later ended the ship's career. Much has been written of the loss of ships in general terms, but from personal experience the author, who was there, is able graphically to describe the fears and fortunes of the men who physically endured the results of this enemy action.*

At night on 21 March 1942 the brand-new cruiser HMS *Trinidad*, commanded by Captain L.S. Saunders and accompanied by two small destroyers, *Fury* (Lieutenant-Commander C.H. Campbell) and *Eclipse* (Lieutenant-Commander E. Mack), sailed from Seydisfiord in Iceland, escorting the biggest convoy thus far assembled. It bore the reputedly unlucky code number PQ 13 and consisted of nineteen merchant ships bound for Murmansk, laden with tanks, guns, planes, lorries and ammunition. Its route, well north of the Arctic Circle and close to the Great Ice Barrier, offered the greatest distance between it and the German-held bases in northern Norway.

So far all the previous convoys had been largely successful, apart

137

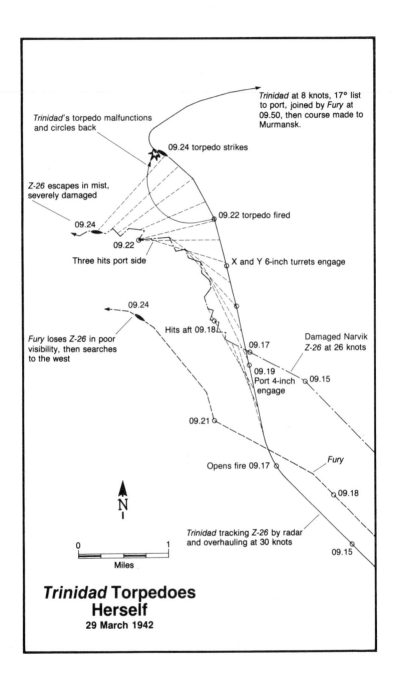

Trinidad at 8 knots, 17° list to port, joined by Fury at 09.50, then course made to Murmansk.

Trinidad's torpedo malfunctions and circles back

09.24 torpedo strikes

Z-26 escapes in mist, severely damaged

09.24

09.22

Three hits port side

09.22 torpedo fired

X and Y 6-inch turrets engage

09.24

Fury loses Z-26 in poor visibility, then searches to the west

Hits aft 09.18

09.17

Damaged Narvik Z-26 at 26 knots

09.19 Port 4-inch engage

09.15

09.21

Opens fire 09.17

Fury

09.18

N

0        1

Miles

Trinidad tracking Z-26 by radar and overhauling at 30 knots

09.15

## *Trinidad* Torpedoes Herself
### 29 March 1942

from the destruction of the destroyer *Matabele* in January, with the loss of almost her entire crew. However, intelligence reports reaching Captain Saunders at the outset of the voyage indicated that PQ 13 was to be the target of concerted action by the Nazi forces in a determined bid to prevent the convoy's reaching its destination.

Only fourteen days earlier there had been other factors which had caused grave disquiet to the First Sea Lord, Admiral of the Fleet Sir Dudley Pound, for at that time it had become apparent that many units of the German fleet were ready for sea to attack convoys. Furthermore, RAF reconnaissance and intelligence were agreed that sailings could be imminent. The Baltic was thought to hold some twenty ships, mostly destroyers with large-calibre guns that could not be treated lightly. The heavy units in this area were the pocket battleship *Scheer*, the heavy cruiser *Hipper*, four light cruisers and the new battleship *Tirpitz*, which was to be the first concern of Admiral Sir John Tovey, Commander-in-Chief, Home Fleet.

At the Admiralty, when PQ 13 sailed, the question arose as to whether the mighty *Tirpitz* would set out into the Arctic to intercept the eastbound convoy. It was a threat which could not be ignored. For Captain Saunders, while there was some comfort in the knowledge that Admiral Tovey would provide a covering force a few hundred miles to the south, it was only his cruiser *Trinidad* and the two escorting destroyers that would be left to face whatever the enemy would throw at them from North Cape, but if *Tirpitz* slipped through Tovey's forces …!

When night turned into inky darkness, *Trinidad*'s latest and most up-to-date radar equipment was able to search for, find and place the convoy just where it should have been. But in the convoy itself there were no such modern aids. Red-eyed look-outs and weary helmsman peered into the blackness. No lights, not even a torch, could be shown. The responsibility of steering even a moderate-sized ship blind in the middle of a fleet grows from initial strain into mental torment as possible disaster is anticipated. Would one hit the stern of the ship ahead, which would not be seen until it was too late? But the first early light of dawn found the convoy still there, though somewhat dishevelled and untidy as the ships shuffled back into position.

Then, with little warning, a raging Arctic gale struck with vicious intensity, and the weather became a greater threat than the enemy.

The sea rose very quickly. Each enormous wave, marble-flecked with translucent whiteness, reared itself up into an awesome mountain of water, seventy to eighty feet high, rushing down upon the ships as though to engulf them. And always there was the wind, screaming like a thousand devils, whipping the crests into a mass of swirling spume. By comparison, deep in the trough between two long waves, the quiet seemed unbelievable. Then followed the long haul, climbing slowly up to another foam-lashed crest, there to re-encounter the unbridled force of the tempest. Spray froze into ice as soon as it hit the steel decks. In the mess decks, things were chaotic. Every article not lashed down or locked away found its way onto the deck, to join the mass of lumber in gangways and compartments, sliding back and forth with every heave of the ship. Later the records showed that *Trinidad* had listed so far over that another one degree would have capsized her and that this was one of the worst storms in the Arctic saga.

The ships of PQ 13 survived, and by the third day the gale eased – but not before it had accomplished what the German Navy failed in, the complete dispersal of the convoy. *Trinidad* was now alone, and the merchantmen were scattered over 200 miles of turbulent seas, each ship a straggler, totally unprotected, an easy target for the enemy. Sixty miles astern of the cruiser, the destroyers *Fury* and *Eclipse* began rounding up whatever ships they could find, and slowly and surely the convoy formed itself into groups, one of nine ships five miles astern of *Trinidad* and another of six, seventy miles ahead to the eastward, two of which lost contact as a result of enemy action and fell astern.

With the improving weather, it was not long before a Blohm & Voss reconnaissance plane discovered the cruiser and settled down to watch and circle at a safe distance. Interception of its transmissions clearly indicated that PQ 13 had been reported to headquarters. Although it was a hopeless gesture, the cruiser's 4-inch anti-aircraft guns opened fire. The plane turned on seeing the flashes and made the signal 'Your shots are falling short.'

Later that day enemy bombers came in droves from their bases at Tromsö, Banak, Bardufoss and Kirkenes. Regardless of the concentrated anti-aircraft fire, the planes came hurtling down through low clouds to release their bombs just above mast height before climbing back into the sky. The attack was relentless, with more and more relief squadrons flying out from the not-too-distant Norwegian coast. It was only by the superb seamanship of Captain

Saunders that the cruiser avoided direct hits, for by taking evasive action and using maximum speed and manoeuvrability to dodge each fall of bombs he was able to race to the nearest patch of snow cloud to hide. Eventually the attacks halted. The two convoy groups were now eastward of Bear Island, with 800 miles to go.

The merchant ships were faring badly. Between the morning of the 28th and the afternoon of the 31st five cargo ships were sunk: SS *Empire Ranger* and SS *Raceland* by dive-bombers; SS *Bateau* by the gunfire of the German destroyer *Z–26*, and SS *Induna* and later SS *Effingham* by torpedoes.

If Lady Luck had in some way been responsible for *Trinidad*'s escape from the Luftwaffe's attack, she now turned her face away. By midnight on the 28th, Captain Saunders received a signal from the Senior British Naval Officer, Murmansk, informing him that a Soviet submarine had reported three large enemy destroyers heading north-west towards the oncoming convoy. They had come from their base at Kirkenes, having been given the position and course by returning aircraft. They then had considerable luck in picking up the SS *Bateau*, a straggling Free French ship, which they immediately sank and whose crew revealed details of the constitution of the convoy and the warships protecting it. *Trinidad* at once collected *Fury* and made a sweep during the night to the south to cover both convoy groups.

The three German destroyers, having swept the area to the north-east without success, turned south-west towards the convoy route, so that, unaware of each other's presence, the two forces were heading directly towards one another. To make matters worse, the weather deteriorated, with heavy black snow clouds drifting at sea-level decreasing the already poor visibility.

In *Trinidad*'s radar office, the duty operator saw an echo on the screen followed by two more approaching rapidly on the port bow. He immediately reported the range and bearing to both the bridge and the transmitting station. It was clear from the tension in the operator's voice that he knew he was on to something. For many, as the captain had foretold, this action would be their first confrontation with the German Navy, and their baptism of fire. Nor would this be a remote, impersonal engagement, firing at an unseen enemy ten or fifteen miles away. As the combined speeds gave a closing rate of 45 knots, it was clear that in a matter of minutes *Trinidad* would be engaging the enemy face to face.

Look-outs on the bridge positions strained their eyes through the sleet and snow, trying to catch the first glimpse of the approaching ships. The advantage of split-second recognition would make all the difference between life and death. In each of the four main turrets, gun crews stood silent, tense and waiting, expectant eyes watching the face of the telephone operator, who, awaiting orders from the transmitting station, would shout the order 'Fire!' A sea battle demands great courage from those whose action stations are deep below decks, unable to see the enemy. They have to operate in an atmosphere of suspense, prepared for catastrophe but praying it will pass them by. At any instant the ship's side might burst inward with ice, water or fire, finishing the deadly work of the explosion.

For both sides the conflict was inevitable: not to destroy was to be destroyed.

At 08.45 the radar office found the range of the echoes to be 10,000 yards, three minutes later 6,000, and at 08.50 it had dropped to 4,000 yards. Until now the British warships had an advantage over the enemy, as the Germans had not realized the full potential of radar for detection and were using it only to plot positions.

As the seconds dragged past and the range further decreased, tension mounted. Until identification was established, Captain Saunders was withholding the order to fire.

Far below, in the bottom of the ship, was the transmitting station, where the complex gunnery predictions were calculated and relayed to the armament. The twenty-one man crew of this compartment were busy plotting the enemy's changing position, having little time to engage in any conversation other than a terse 'Well, this is it boys – Good Luck!'

The function of the transmitting station is, as in other Royal Navy ships, to receive from the radar office and elsewhere such information as range and bearing of the target, then to calculate, among other things, its course and speed. This then has to be converted into training and elevation angles to aim the guns. Even the temperature of the air can alter the flight of the shells, and this and other ballistic information has to be allowed for. Once the computer has evaluated all this data, the directions are relayed to the guns, constantly bringing them up to date in step with the changing situation. In *Trinidad*, these directions took the form of pointers moving on dials, and once the guns were brought into line, bells from the transmitting station would confirm that the armament was on target and that triggers could be pressed. The efficiency of the system was dependent upon the precision with which the men in the transmitting station processed the constantly changing information. The location of this vital link in the armament control was calculated to give the maximum degree of protection to both the computer and its crew. It was placed below an armour-plated deck and in many ships was surrounded by store compartments filled with sacks of flour and other dry provisions. *Trinidad*, however, had been built to a tonnage limitation, so the transmitting station was enclosed on either side by oil-fuel tanks. Knowledge of this did not contribute to a sense of well-being in the occupants of this cell-like space.

Now, in the final moments before the impending action, the excitement of the occasion acted as a stimulant. Fear was forgotten with the realization that the defence and safety of the ship and her crew depended on how quickly and accurately they could produce their calculations, and as the enemy sped closer, turrets were up-dated. On the bridge and in look-out positions, tension was electric.

Suddenly, with the fickleness of this unpredictable Arctic climate, the mist and snow cleared, revealing three of Germany's big Narvik-class destroyers with fire-power almost equal to *Trinidad*'s, heading straight for the British cruiser. These units of the German 8th Destroyer Flotilla were later identified as *Z–24*, *Z–25* and *Z–26*. They were modern, powerful, with a displacement of 2,600 tons (twice the size of their British counterparts), had a complement of 320 and could reach a speed of 38 knots. Racing in at a range of only 1½ miles, they were slightly in echelon from line ahead. In this split second of time – recognition between enemy and enemy, Captain Saunders gave the order 'Open fire!'

The barrage of shell-fire that erupted from the cruiser was mind-shattering. The range was so close that every gun on bearing, from the main 6-inch even to machine-gun batteries, opened fire. *Trinidad* had struck first, and the flight of projectiles hurtling from the 6–inch guns crashed into the leading destroyer, *Z–26*, setting her on fire. Shell-bursts could be seen between the mainmast and funnel, causing a mass of flame and smoke.

Inside the gun turrets of the cruiser, the Royal Marines and other gunnery ratings went to war. The raw crews, despite their hurried training and the earlier despair of the gunnery officer, had risen to the occasion like veterans. No more fumbling or misjudgement: each shell was rammed home with precision, each long sleeve of cordite slipped dexterously into its chamber before the breech slammed shut, followed immediately by the roar of the exploding propellant as the gun fired and recoiled. The acrid smell of cordite fumes belching back into the turret as the breeches were flung open seemed to galvanize the crew into machine-like efficiency. 'Load and fire – load and fire': the orders came faster and faster. Options were none; it was destroy or be destroyed.

The Germans, recovering from their surprise and the ferocity of the assault, began to return fire, and two shells smashed into *Trinidad*'s port side aft just under Y turret.

As the cruiser's shells crashed into and around the leading enemy destroyer, her captain, Commander Georg Ritter von Berger, broke off the engagement and headed north-west into the protection of the swirling snow clouds. With the enemy's command destroyer out of action, *Trinidad*'s gunnery control switched target to the second destroyer. Here again the guns were dead on target, destroying the enemy's forward turret.

Confident that, however much damaged, these three modern destroyers would doubtless mount a torpedo attack, Captain Saunders ordered that his ship be swung hard to starboard. This sudden alteration of course away from the enemy presented the minimum target but at the same time gave the rear turrets of the cruiser the opportunity to maintain a constant barrage of shell-fire.

Even as the turn was completed, two torpedo tracks passed close but harmlessly along the port side. After holding this bearing directly away from the enemy and parallel to the torpedo tracks for two minutes, *Trinidad* again swung hard to starboard. This completed a triangular course, so that she was now heading due north at a speed of 26 knots in order to maintain contact with the enemy. In the decreasing visibility of a snow storm, *Z–24* and *Z–25* had lost contact with their leader, now badly damaged.

On *Trinidad*'s bridge, the sleet and snow had made the use of binoculars impossible, a much clearer view being obtained with the naked eye. A sudden squall brought visibility down to nil but, although nothing could be seen from the bridge, radar picked up a contact at 8,000 yards. This could only be the enemy, so speed was advanced to 30 knots.

Fifteen minutes later the cruiser was overhauling the ship, with the range down to two miles to starboard, still unseen but proceeding on a course parallel to *Trinidad*'s. Captain Saunders now altered course towards the enemy in order to engage him while passing obliquely across his stern. Within minutes the bridge and look-outs clearly saw black smoke in the haze, and then the shape of the enemy ship from which smoke was billowing. The range was down to less than a mile, and without hesitation *Trinidad* opened fire with her forward A and B turret guns, their aim so accurate that all three of the German's after turrets were destroyed. With the range rapidly decreasing, *Z–26* zigzagged desperately to escape further damage. *Trinidad* manoeuvred into a position away to starboard to bring the after turrets also to bear. This allowed the port 4-inch and close-range weapons to open up in an effort to drive the German crews away from their torpedo tubes. Three more direct hits were registered just below the destroyer's bridge but, still defiant, her commander swung his ship to starboard to try to get his forward gun to bear. But only one shell was fired, which proved quite ineffectual.

Saunders' strategy in passing across the enemy's stern had three advantages. It gave the opportunity for all four of *Trinidad*'s turrets to dominate the target; it prevented a torpedo attack, and it denied the German use of his forward turret. Once again the British captain had established and maintained a tactical superiority.

As the pursuit continued numbers of German sailors, supported by life-jackets, were seen in the sea, many already dead. It was presumed that they had either jumped or been blown overboard by the force of the explosions.

If the convoy was to be protected, there was only one course of action: dispatch the enemy as quickly as possible, then swing around to the south-east to seek out and engage the remaining enemy ships. If either or both these destroyers should meet up with the oncoming convoy, now not far distant, they would lose no time in sending as many merchantmen as possible to the bottom, subject to whatever defence the convoy escorts could provide. It seemed incredible that *Z–26* could have suffered so much damage without sinking or blowing up.

In *Trinidad*'s port waist there was a sudden flurry of activity as the torpedo crews swung into action, the drone of the revolving turntable as the tubes trained outboard, their gaping mouths pointing ominously against the white churning wash streaming past from the cruiser's bows. The German ship was now so close that it would be impossible to miss her. The torpedo officer, Lieutenant-Commander Dent, gave the execute order 'Fire one!' Came the familiar click of the tripping lever, the shrouded roar in the explosion chamber, the high-pitched hiss of compressed air and then, with almost startling clarity, the torpedo was on its way, its silver body shining fractionally in the cold air before it plunged into the sea and was gone, streaking towards the stern of the enemy destroyer.

And then something happened – so unique, so bizarre, it almost defied belief, an event hitherto unknown in British naval history. The torpedo began to turn, slowly at first, then more and more as it continued its run. Just short of the German ship it increased its curved course to head back towards the ship that had fired it – *Trinidad*. (Later official analysis speculated that the intensely cold sea water had affected the gyro within the torpedo, which in turn influenced its rudder.) Two hundred yards from the cruiser it broke surface, still travelling at speed, heading straight for the port side. Despite the fact that *Trinidad* was moving at top speed (30 knots) and zigzagging, it was impossible to avoid it.

Horror-stricken, the bridge personnel could only stand transfixed as it neared, knowing that it might well explode in one of the four magazines, which would mean the cruiser's disintegrating in a ball of fire. At that critical moment, when eternity seemed but a second away, Captain Saunders peered over the bridge parapet and casually remarked, 'You know, this looks remarkably like one of ours.' If ever the Royal Navy's reticent appraisal of a perilous situation was demonstrated, it was then.

The lethal steel fish plunged into the port side, tearing away a section of the ship's hull, leaving a gaping hole fifty feet by twenty. The explosion momentarily lifted the ship, and a huge column of black, oily water rose high into the air, covering everyone on that side. The torpedo had exploded in the Royal Marines' mess deck, flooding the forward boiler-room, destroying damage-control headquarters and killing numbers of officers and ratings in the area.

Two decks below, in the transmitting station, the explosion had created more devastation than was at first appreciated. That compartment had been plunged into darkness at once; then, as the ventilation system drew fumes from the seat of the explosion, conditions became alarming. What was not known, however, was that the bulkheads surrounding the TS had been critically weakened and were barely able to support the great pressure exerted on them by thousands of gallons of fuel-oil on the other side. As soon as the supplementary lighting had been switched on, the crew of the TS took up their positions round the computer tables and set about trying to establish contact with the bridge. The long compartment was divided into a small and a large section. In the smaller, Corporal Roger Palmer found that his computer table had been split right across and was useless. Neither here nor in the large section could any contact be made with the bridge.

Reporting to the officer-in-charge, he shouted, 'I am out of communication with the bridge, sir.'

Nat Gould replied, 'You had better come in here.'

Palmer walked through with a seaman and two bandsmen until they were standing by the main computer table, which was immediately adjacent to the foot of the ladder to the access hatch. Turning to the seaman, Nat Gould said, 'Go to the damage control and tell them we need assistance.'

Reaching the top of the ladder, the seaman unlatched the clips and pushed back the heavy armoured cover, only to be swamped by a deluge of oil and water which came pouring through the opening. Clearly the decks above were flooded with oil from ruptured tanks. Climbing a steel-runged ladder and squeezing through a small hatch in a listing ship is difficult enough but to have to do so with the rungs running with slimy black fuel-oil is almost impossible. However, in seconds the seaman was through.

Nat Gould, realizing that in a very short time they could all be trapped, decided to evacuate the compartment. With great courage and dignity he stepped back, placed his hands on the holding-bar of the table and said, 'Abandon TS. It's every man for himself.'

The scramble up the ladder became a struggle for survival. Roger Palmer managed to pull himself up and through the opening, followed by two other bandsmen, Lew Barber and George Lloyd. By the time Lloyd reached the ladder, the oil was up to his waist. It was a feat which would have challenged the strongest men but, whatever the physical ability of these three might have been, it was more than made up for by their will to survive. Gasping and spluttering from the cascade pouring down, they finally emerged in the small space above.

The shock of the explosion had, it seems, also fractured the strong spring which counter-balanced the heavy weight of the steel hatch cover, which normally opened and closed easily and safely. During those moments in which the first four men escaped, the cover stayed open, held in an almost upright position by its own weight. But as the flooding of the ship induced a greater and greater list, the balance became more precarious, causing danger of the cover's falling shut. As the fifth man began to emerge from the hatchway, the cover overbalanced and crashed down on him, breaking his back and firmly wedging his body in the small opening. The frantic efforts of the other men on the ladder to remove him were of no avail. As they struggled, the bulkhead inside the TS collapsed. Tons of fuel-oil surged into the compartment, engulfing the occupants in seconds. Seventeen men died and with them an officer who had sacrificed his chances of survival to allow the men under his command the opportunity to escape.

The four survivors, with oil rising at their feet, managed to scramble out of the second compartment through the next hatch, to find the Royal Marines' deck partly under water and in daylight. The explosion had torn away the ship's side here, and the cruiser was listing to such an alarming degree that sea water was pouring freely in along the waterline. They raced distraught through the mess decks, climbing steel ladders and forcing their way past further clipped-up hatchways and bulkhead doors in an attempt to reach the safety of the upper deck.

Later the three surviving bandsmen met in one of the upper flat spaces. George Lloyd was still being violently sick from the effects of the oil, and Lew Barber just sat, dazed and unseeing. Roger Palmer turned to him and asked, 'Where are the rest of the band?', and was told, 'They are no more, Roger. Only you, George and I are left now.'

The loss of their comrades made a deep and lasting impact on them. The band had worked together as a closely knit unit for over twelve months and, prior to joining *Trinidad*, had travelled regularly every Sunday from their quarters at Heybrook Camp, near Plymouth, to play at the morning service at Wembury church. A memorial plaque to those bandsmen who died is exhibited in the church.

In the forward boiler-room the damage had been just as severe. Following the explosion, a wave of water swept through, carrying Chief Stoker Ellicott and his men to the foot of the escape ladder, where Ellicott and Stoker Petty officer Oakley were badly burned by escaping steam. In darkness, waist-deep in water and with the piercing scream of escaping steam all around them, it was a terrifying experience – until eventually the escape hatch was opened and they made their escape from the rising flood.

*Trinidad*, lying stopped, began to take on an alarming list to port, with the sea flooding freely into the ship through her damaged side. The cruiser was lying to 20 degrees, with seas coming over the upper deck on the damaged side.

A small hole on the starboard side some ten feet square had also been created by the explosion. One of the marines had been blown clear through this hole into the sea but had been carried back again to the ship's side with the next wave, where he clung to a trailing rope. As the ship listed further and further, he had been able to pull himself up the starboard side onto the upper deck, and he was the only man to be saved from that mess deck.

The scene on the upper deck was unreal: men calmly stood waiting with a resigned attitude for whatever might happen next. Around them was the freezing sea, in which no man could survive longer than a few minutes. Below decks were the carnage of dead and dying men and the steady ingress of water. With the ship heeling over, the decks covered in ice and fuel-oil, it needed both strength and dexterity to progress even a few yards.

In an attempt to correct the list, on the instruction of officers parties of men were trying to throw overboard anything moveable from the port side that could not be dragged up to the higher side. Even one of the Walrus aircraft which had been badly damaged was pushed over the side. From the bridge came a call over the loudspeakers for all portable heaters to be taken to the temporary sick-bay to bring some sort of comfort to the badly shocked and wounded. Next, all hands were ordered to take a double tot of rum, and this was a life-saver for many. Frostbite was beginning to take its toll, and it was weeks before those who suffered it fully regained the use of affected limbs. Below decks every attempt was being made to reduce the list to port. Starboard compartments were being intentionally flooded with sea water and fuel-oil pumped overboard from the port tanks.

Then came the good news: the ship was holding. Thanks to the efforts of damage control, the list had been checked. The optimistic forecast was that, given time, the list could be further reduced.

Many of the wounded had been rescued by this time and the most critical cases brought into the wardroom and screened off. When the rum was issued, the master-at-arms, Clifford Avent, asked the ship's doctor if he thought any of these men could take their ration. The doctor, agreeing, added that some were in such a hopeless condition that he doubted if it would make any difference either way. One rating nodded eagerly when asked if he would like a little rum. The master-at-arms raised him gently to allow the liquid to pass into his mouth and a little later he asked for a cigarette. When it had been lit and placed between his lips, he took two long and contented draws, but a moment later his head lolled sideways and he slipped quietly out of this life.

With *Trinidad* critically damaged, virtually helpless and wallowing in a rising sea, it was the escort's turn to become involved in the engagement with the German destroyers. The badly damaged Z–26 had turned south from her escape course northward and was making for home waters.

In the convoy escort destroyer *Eclipse*, Lieutenant-Commander Mack decided it would be safe to rejoin *Trinidad*. When he received the signal that *Trinidad* was engaging the enemy, had damaged a destroyer and was chasing another, some apprehension was felt. This, however, turned to alarm when minutes later a second signal was received reporting that *Trinidad* had been torpedoed. Hearts sank as the crew realized that it was now up to them and the other escort, *Fury*, to defend the convoy against the bigger guns of the predatory German destroyers.

*Eclipse* was not only much smaller than her opponents but carried only two 4.7-inch guns forward, one of which was completely iced up and useless. Sweeping around to the south, she almost at once picked up a radar contact at two miles and closed, thinking it might be a stray merchant ship. She cautiously approached, with her one forward gun loaded and ready to fire. But this was certainly not a merchant vessel. Through the murk, the vague outlines indicated a warship, and the impression given at first by the big gap between the funnels was that this could be *Trinidad*. However, a small reddish ensign flying from a stay, and a clearer look on approach, showed her to be one of the German destroyers. The vessel flashed a recognition signal, perhaps assuming *Eclipse* to be one of her own consorts. All doubts were dispelled when the leading signalman on the bridge shouted, 'German ensign, sir!' They were now within a quarter of a mile of the badly damaged Z–26 and, with recognition established, *Eclipse*'s forward gun opened fire.

As they neared, with the gun's crew slamming shells into the breech and firing at its maximum functional capability, it was seen that the three rear turrets of the enemy ship had been demolished as a result of *Trinidad*'s earlier accurate shelling. One gun, with part of its turret, hung grotesquely over the side, another like a smashed toy pointed skywards, while the third seemed to be jammed sideways aimed downwards to the sea. However, despite much damage, the speed of the ship had not been greatly impaired, and with rapid acceleration she tried to escape into the mist. *Eclipse* was a very lucky ship for if at that moment the big after 5.9-inch guns of Z–26 had been operational, the British destroyer would have been blown out of the water.

Determined not to lose the quarry, *Eclipse* set off in pursuit and soon began to overhaul. The commanding officer of Z–26, realizing he was in a perilous situation, swung his ship around in a half-circle in a desperate effort to allow his forward gun to bear on his pursuer but, not to be denied his victory, Mack clung resolutely to the tail of the destroyer, despite its turning and twisting. He realized that, given the chance, that one forward gun of his adversary would easily destroy his little ship. At times, freak snowstorms brought visibility down to a few yards, and contact was lost, but long oil streaks from the fleeing ship left a trail like a signpost and soon sighting was re-established at a closer range. *Eclipse*'s gun now held the target, and the intensity and accuracy of its shooting began to create havoc on the decks and superstructure of the German vessel.

Driving snow made conditions almost impossible for the gun's crew, but even worse was the effect of ice-cold spray pluming over the bows to fall in a freezing deluge on the forecastle. The British crews on these destroyers, unlike their German counterparts, were not enclosed by turret protection but were partly in the open with any exposed flesh flayed raw by ice particles. Smarting eyes peered through frozen eyelids as they loaded and aimed the gun. Gun-loaders, with frozen hands and frost-bitten fingers, tried frantically to grasp heavy shells which first had to be kicked free of the mantle of ice that encased and impacted them in the shell racks. Because *Eclipse* was low on her stock of fuel, she was top-heavy, exaggerating every roll when the wheel was put hard over to counteract the German's violent alteration of course. Out there on the forecastle, the deck was an ice-rink, making it almost impossible to stand and thereby burdening efforts to feed the gun.

Such was the fierceness of the engagement that German sailors were seen leaping over the side into the icy waters to avoid destruction from exploding shells, although their fate in the sea was even more certain.

'Not to kill is to be killed': the action between *Eclipse* and Z–26 amply demonstrated this precept, for, as distressing as the Germans' plight appeared, *Eclipse*'s crew remembered how one of their sister ships, the destroyer *Matabele* had been torpedoed a few weeks earlier, with only two men saved out of the crew of 200. To allow *Z–26* to continue its attacks on convoys would result in the deaths of many more British sailors. Mack therefore had no alternative but to destroy the enemy.

As shells from *Eclipse* continued to fall on *Z–26*, one must have exploded in the cordite magazine, for there was a powerful blast of fire from amidships. Seconds later, another shell penetrated the boiler-room, and finally *Z–26* slowed and came to a stop. The after part of the ship was almost underwater, with the guns and decks a complete shambles. Approaching with care, *Eclipse* slowly moved up along the starboard side of the vessel. *Z–26*, however, was like a ghost ship, with no sign of its crew. It appears that those who were still aboard were sheltering within the superstructure and bridge, not daring to make a sound. Swinging his ship around, Mack moved down the port side, giving the order 'Torpedo ready.'

Seconds later the whole situation was reversed as two shells came screaming out of the snow-filled sky. Undetected, *Z–24* and *Z–25*, sister-ships of *Z–26*, came racing out of the gloom firing their main armament. Deciding that discretion was the better part of valour, Mack made off at top speed. He conserved his one remaining torpedo in the event he might need it against his new adversaries. Although able to score a direct hit on the leading German ship, *Eclipse* was herself hit by two shells, which, falling among the cordite charges, produced an explosion causing heavy casualties.

Twenty minutes later, after escaping her pursuers, the British ship reached the comparative safety of a group of snow clouds and reduced her onward speed to take stock of her damage. The situation was grim, for the hull had suffered shell penetrations, causing flooding, the funnel and aerials were blown away, and the sick-bay and wardroom were packed with the wounded.

Fatigue and exposure had affected everyone, and double tots of rum were issued to aid recovery and lessen tension. But during that moment of relaxation, action stations were again sounded off, as in the temporary clearance of the snow-storm an enemy U-boat appeared on the surface less than a quarter of a mile distant. Even more dangerous were the streaks of two torpedoes heading straight for the ship. With alarm bells ringing, the crew racing to their action stations and the helm hard over, *Eclipse* just managed to avoid the two long silver missiles streaking through the water, each with 750 pounds of high explosive in the warheads.

With helm hard to port, Mack brought *Eclipse* round to launch a depth-charge attack, for the submarine was already starting a crash dive. He had to make lightning decisions, for time was not on his side if he was to make a kill. For the U–boat commander, however, time and speed were to be his allies if he was to escape destruction – time to be fully submerged and speed to get clear. But Mack also needed speed, for there was always the possibility that he could ram the enemy before he disappeared. On the decks of the racing destroyer men worked frantically to fix depth-charge settings to explode at the correct depth.

But the destroyer was not fast enough to catch the U-boat on the surface: when she arrived, only the swirls and eddies of a record crash dive could be seen. Deck crews now went into action, dropping pattern after pattern of depth-charges, the massive underwater explosions hurling fountains of boiling white water high into the air. But far below, in the depths of the Barents Sea, the enemy was making his escape, and the attack proved fruitless. Dangerously low on fuel reserves and his crew feeling they had had enough war for one day, Mack abandoned the hunt and steered south-east for Murmansk.

An interesting postscript to the sinking of *Z–26* later emerged. Out of the German destroyer's total crew of 320 officers and ratings, 264 were killed in the action. The survivors included the commanding officer, Captain Georg Ritter von Berger, who was killed towards the end of hostilities in 1945. Years later his widow wrote to the author giving her husband's account of the engagement:

As *Z–26* was sinking, the captain, although badly wounded in the face and legs, managed to drag himself off the bridge and arriving at the rail gave the order to abandon ship. The men gave three cheers and jumped over the side into the icy water. As he floated away from the ship he was sure he would never be picked up alive but a life-boat from *Z–24* arrived almost at once and he was carried aboard unconscious. Months later, having recovered from his wounds, he was appointed leader of the destroyer flotilla at Narvik in *Z–32*.

When the Allied invasion of Normandy took place, his ship was sunk in the Channel and, captured by the French, he was imprisoned in the fortress of Gironde Sud. His widow writes: 'In the night, my husband, being a prisoner alone in a house guarded by ragged soldiers, was brought to a lonely place and killed by machine-guns. He was found some days later and buried in a cemetery at Berbuil, Charente Maritime, near Saintes.'

On the wounded *Trinidad*, making her painful way south-east towards the Kola Inlet at a speed of only 4 knots, morale was high. With each mile looked upon as a heaven-sent blessing, optimism heightened, while down below damage-control parties performed something little short of miracles. Mess-deck fires were attacked and dealt with in perilous circumstances – as when flames neared high-explosive compartments. Volumes of black smoke created by burning oil on top of floodwater made things extremely difficult. In some compartments, such was the intensity of flame and smoke that the area was sealed off altogether and allowed to burn itself out.

In time, by a skilful operation of pumping water out from one side and flooding water into the other to counter-balance, the cruiser gradually decreased her list. But it was no time to celebrate, for she was still well over, staggering with every sea, a helpless and perfect target for trailing U-boats or enemy destroyers, and she yet had 150 miles to go to reach the Soviet Union.

Other difficulties had arisen as a result of the torpedoing. The explosion had wrecked the lower steering position, flooding that compartment so that it had to be abandoned. The ship had to be steered instead from the after steering point, which was directly above the rudder itself. Communication with the bridge had also been destroyed, and the only way this could be re-established was by organizing a line of men stretching from the bridge, down to the steering-wheel aft, and passing the helm orders by word of mouth. Slow and cumbersome though it was, it worked and ensured that the ship was moving in the right direction.

Anticipating the arrival of the convoy and its escorts, U-boats had converged around the approaches to the Kola Inlet. That afternoon *Trinidad*'s escorting destroyer *Fury*, sweeping the sea well in advance of the cruiser, sighted a surfaced U-boat and tried to ram her but failed to arrive before the enemy crash-dived. However, the asdic contact betrayed its presence, and *Fury* lost no time in launching a heavy depth-charge attack. This proved successful, for later evidence confirmed that U-boat *585* had been destroyed. In the meantime the surviving ships of PQ 13 struggled on as best they could, in groups of twos or threes or singly. Some, suffering near bomb misses in the earlier attacks, were affected by engine-room and rudder trouble; some, with dislodged cargoes from the effects of the great storm, were listing, and the freighter *Harpalion*, which had been heavily bombed, was limping along several miles astern.

The crews of these ships deserved the highest praise in bringing their cargoes thus far, but they still had to break through the ambush of enemy submarines waiting off the Russian coast.

It was not long before the 5,000-ton cargo vessel *Effingham* took a torpedo in her boiler-room which sank the ship in minutes. Such were the weather conditions that only a few of those who managed to reach the boats in time survived. Meanwhile, the wind rolling up the sea from the north pushed the yawing cruiser from one point of the compass to another. Then came the darkness, giving a measure of protection, for even if the enemy could hear the movements of the ship, it would be difficult to see her. But such was the changeable nature of these latitudes that the wind dropped, the snow clouds vanished, an unnatural calm displaced the turbulent sea and out came the moon. Not a thin, crescented new moon but a huge, full, round moon lighting up the ocean for miles. With the cruiser starkly silhouetted against the brightness of the silver sea inviting disaster, a spirit of despair replaced the buoyant optimism felt earlier.

And then, to set the seal on a grim situation, the engines stopped. Due to the torpedo damage, salt water had been infiltrating the pure water system feeding the boilers, and these had to be shut down. Minutes later *Trinidad* drifted to a standstill. It was dangerous enough to be moving slowly in this moonlit sea but to have to be stopped was a misfortune of the greatest magnitude. The number PQ 13 had certainly lived up to its reputation.

Below decks, in the boiler- and engine-rooms, the crew worked like demons, well aware that a torpedo might come crashing through the fragile hull. On the upper deck, men talked in whispers, haunted by a deep-seated dread, gazing out across the silver-rippled sea. For some time there was only the sound of gentle lapping water against the ship's hull but, as engine parts were disassembled and replaced, there came the clang of hammering echoing across the water, declaring the cruiser's presence. The tension became unbearable, for they were quite helpless, sitting in the sea like a paralysed duck waiting for the big bang. Every U-boat for miles around must have heard the noise: never would they have a better opportunity. Men looked at one another with fear-laden eyes that begged for reassurance or that silently sought answers that could only be inept. For the umpteenth time they checked their inflated lifebelts, ballooning out like capacious bosoms, considering the chances of survival if the torpedo should strike. But their luck held. They were spared the destruction which seemed inescapable.

In the distance, the little escorts raced back and forth, seeking the enemy, daring him to mount an attack. Every minute that passed seemed an eternity. But at last came the blessed sound they had all been waiting for: churning water under the stern. As the propellers turned, the revolutions mounted, and slowly but surely *Trinidad* was on her way. As if with the removal of a melancholy spell, the ship was suddenly alive and full of hope again, moving slowly, but moving.

And so the night passed, with the first light of dawn stealthily emerging from the eastern sky to encourage their southward advance to the coast only twelve miles away. Two hours later they entered the Kola estuary, and *Trinidad* proceeded through the river to anchor opposite *Rosta* and there without delay started negotiations and preparations to enter the Soviet dry dock.

The last of the merchant ships arrived on 1 April, making only fourteen to survive the voyage. It was a sobering thought to the Admiralty that over a quarter of PQ 13 had been destroyed by enemy action. Although *Trinidad* had been critically damaged and *Eclipse* badly mauled, the Germans had lost their large destroyer Z–26, another had been damaged and their U-boat 585 sunk.

The severity and concentration of attacks by German Naval Command on PQ 13 gave a clear indication of the importance they attached to trying to put a stop to supplies reaching the Soviet Union. PQ 13 was the first convoy to be subjected to the strength of this determination and at a time when daylight hours were lengthening. Both the merchant ships and the escorts had the right to be proud of their achievement in bringing the greater part of this convoy through to its destination.

Although Captain Saunders had achieved his purpose, it had been at the cost of the near-destruction of his ship by an incredible stroke of bad luck. Hundreds of torpedoes were fired at the enemy in World War II but *Trinidad*'s was the only one to complete a half circle and return to explode in the ship that fired it.

# 13  The Story of HMS Edinburgh

*This is the story of HMS Edinburgh, a proud and brave ship that would not accept defeat and perished in a blaze of glory. Mortally wounded, defiant to the last, her guns blazed destruction on enemy warships which, although superior in gun power, withdrew in dismay and fear.*

*In 1982 she was remembered again, but for a different reason, for from within her rusting hull a vast fortune in gold bullion was recovered.*

*But* Edinburgh *is to be remembered not as a treasure ship, not for her gold, but much more for her gallantry, not for her fortune but for her fortitude.*

On 8 April 1942 the heavy cruiser HMS *Edinburgh* sailed from Iceland to escort the convoy PQ 14, made up of twenty-three merchant ships bound for Murmansk. Aboard her decks she carried a most unusual cargo, a number of large steel plates, urgently needed for the crippled cruiser HMS *Trinidad*, then lying in dry dock in the Kola Inlet near Murmansk.

*Edinburgh*, a twin of HMS *Belfast*, was a 10,000-ton cruiser and in her role as a fighting ship presented a formidable deterrent to the enemy. Her four triple turrets of 6-inch guns, plus twelve 4-inch, four 3-pounders and sixteen smaller guns to operate in both attack and defence, provided a destructive capability highly significant. In addition, her 21-inch torpedoes, each charged with 750 pounds of explosive in the warhead, lay in triple tubes accommodated on either side of the ship, ready to be launched on their merciless errands.

On this occasion, the cruiser flew the flag of Rear-Admiral Sir Stuart Bonham-Carter KCB, CB, CVO, DSO, commanding the

18th Cruiser Squadron, and had as its commanding officer, Captain Hugh Faulkner (later to become Rear-Admiral Faulkner CB, CBE, DSO).

On Sunday 12 April misfortune struck the whole operation. The cruiser, its escorts and the fleet of merchantmen ran into a thick blanket of fog and subsequently found themselves in a floating ice-field where solid tables of ice crashed into the ships, threatening to engulf them. As a result, hulls became buckled, plates ruptured, causing flooding, keels were crushed and propellers ripped off. To a voyage which had promised well, it was a bad beginning. Later, as the weather cleared, it showed that, of the twenty-three merchant ships which had started the voyage, only eight remained. The rest, badly holed, crushed or slowly sinking, tried to make it back to Iceland. Ironically, the convoy of only eight merchant ships was now being escorted by an impressive fleet of six destroyers, four corvettes, four minesweepers and two rescue trawlers, in addition to the cruiser *Edinburgh*.

On Thursday 16 April, despite the huge protective screen, German U-boats attacked the merchant ships. A furious criss-cross battle developed, with destroyers and corvettes weaving and twisting around the convoy, dropping pattern after pattern of depth-charges around the submerged submarines. Constantly the U-boats were seen to surface, take a quick look and then crash-dive, yet, notwithstanding the concentrated depth-charging, no kills were established. In the meantime the convoy ships had stationed themselves into four columns of two ships each, with the cargo vessel *Empire Howard* carrying 2,000 tons of military stores in the forward column with the commodore, Captain Edward Rees DSO, RD, RNR, aboard and commanded by Captain H. Downie.

Undetected, one U-boat closed in to penetrate the screen of escorts and fired three torpedoes which exploded in the hull of *Empire Howard*. The vessel was quite unable to withstand such an impact. As the explosions tore out the centre of the vessel, she split in two. Within thirty seconds the water was swirling around the bridge. As the ship disappeared beneath him, Captain Downie calmly stepped into the freezing sea, wearing a life-jacket. Through the pall of drifting black smoke all that could be seen was a swirl of black water eddying and bubbling as flotsam from the sunken ship burst to the surface. In the rolling swell, a survivor was carried past him, the commodore, Captain Rees, a smile on his face, calmly trying to smoke a cigar. But as they tried to near one another, a heavy wave carried them apart, and Captain Rees was never seen again. Thus died a brave man who, knowing the inevitability of the situation, faced it with a courage and fortitude shown by few.

As *Empire Howard* disappeared, the trailing anti-submarine trawler *Northern Wave* raced towards the disaster, set on its double task: to attack the submarine with depth-charges and to rescue survivors. However, as *Northern Wave* arrived, there, thrashing about in the sea in the path of the trawler, in a great pool of black oil and debris, were thirty-eight men, waving, shouting and pleading to the little ship to stop and pick them up. The young RNR captain of *Northern Wave* was now faced with a heart-rending decision. The Asdic dome, a submarine-detection device beneath his ship, had been badly damaged by the ice floes at the beginning of the voyage, and he could not confirm his belief that the submarine was beneath him in the middle of the convoy. If he attacked with his depth-charges, he knew that many of those in the sea would be killed outright. If he failed to destroy the U-boat, another ship could be sunk, perhaps two. Reason argued that the killer sub had to be there. He was faced with an almost impossible choice. Should he disregard the existence of the enemy to save the survivors and allow it to escape? His command orders had been clear and precise: 'Attack and destroy. The convoy must be saved.'

Sickened by the decision which he knew he had to make, he gave the order 'Fire depth-charges.' One by one, they erupted from the powered thrower. Moments later the charges exploded, throwing great fountains of water cascading over the dark sea. Few survived; the remainder were killed instantly from the shock waves. As *Northern Wave* approached, many men could be seen in the water, still in life-jackets, who neither waved nor called but who stared at them with unseeing eyes, tossing up and down in the Arctic swell in a macabre dance of death.

Somewhere in the black sea below, the killer U-boat was making its escape with *Northern Waves*'s massive depth-charges exploding all around her. Having dispensed death and destruction, she drew further and further away, surviving, but setting out to seek and find more victims in the savage Arctic war.

The misfortune which had troubled PQ 14 from the start continued to reveal itself, for as the little ship ran on to start rescue operations, engines were stopped and then rung 'full astern' but through an engine failure refused to start again. Down below, superhuman efforts were made to correct the problem and get the propellers moving.

As they drifted through the sea, where some men were still conscious, they approached a raft with six men aboard, and a line was thrown and secured. However, the way was still on the ship, and the raft, still holding, was carried under the stern close to the propeller. With the knowledge that at any moment the engines could be started, with the ship going astern, and the conviction that the blades would hack them to pieces, the order was given to cut them adrift. Ignorant of the reason, the six men stared in disbelief. The relief of such near deliverance turned to agony and tears of rage as *Northern Wave* drifted further and further away. But by now a second rescue trawler, *Lord Middleton*, had arrived and started rescue operations, dragging men aboard barely alive. Almost twenty-five minutes elapsed before *Northern Wave* could get her engines started and return to pick up more survivors.

Eventually the rescue operation was completed and, with no more men to be found, the two trawlers set off to rejoin the distant convoy. Aboard *Northern Wave* and *Lord Middleton*, everything possible was done to revive the survivors, and in an endeavour to restore circulation they were given brandy and whisky. This had the effect of making them sleepy. A few minutes later a signal from the medical officer of one of the escorting destroyers warned the commanding officers of both ships on no account to allow survivors to take spirits. But it was too late. For those luckless men who fell asleep, it was a slumber from which they would never awaken. Although administering spirits would seem the most reasonable thing to do, medical experience has proved that cardiac failure is the result.

From *Empire Howard*'s crew of fifty-four, only eighteen men were rescued, and out of these, nine died aboard the trawlers. And so it was that, with the dead men aboard, a dejected and saddened crew, the asdic-dome non-operational and little or no hope of contacting the U-boat, *Northern Wave* plodded her way eastward to rejoin PQ 14.

On the following day, Saturday 19 April, *Edinburgh* arrived at the Kola Inlet and dropped anchor in the river opposite Vaenga, there to be met by a typical Russian snow-storm, with temperatures many degrees below freezing.

Just before she sailed for home on 28 April, she took aboard a cargo of gold – gold bullion, which in present-day terms would be valued at around £45 million. This was an arrangement between the Soviet government and the Allies as a part-payment on thousands of tons of war supplies for the Soviet armies fighting to hold back the German tide of invasion already on the outskirts of Moscow and Stalingrad. The gold was contained in wooden ammunition boxes, each weighing about a hundredweight, carried to and stored for safety in the bomb-room sited in the bowels of the ship.

There was an atmosphere of apprehension among the crew, for during the loading the red stencilling on the boxes melted in the driving snow and left a trail of scarlet along the decks. It was a bad omen. This, added to the realization that there were thirteen merchant ships in the returning convoy which they had to escort, only increased misgivings.

With *Edinburgh* were six destroyers, *Bulldog, Beagle, Foresight, Forester, Amazon* and *Beverley*, four corvettes, *Oxlip, Saxafrage, Campanula* and *Snowflake*, the armed trawler *Lord Middleton* and two Soviet destroyers. As the QP 11 convoy and its escorts cleared the Kola Inlet, German observers on the tip of the nearby western cape quickly reported its departure to command headquarters in Norway, and from that moment operations were activated to attack and destroy the homeward-bound fleet.

The destroyer escort, commanded by Commander Maxwell Richmond in *Bulldog*, was quite capable of dealing with U-boat attacks, but none of them was sufficiently armed to repel concentrated air attack and far less able to compete with the heavily armed Narvik-class enemy destroyers carrying 6-inch guns. *Edinburgh*, however, would certainly be a match for them, with her radar hunting the sky and the sea, and the Asdic echo-sounding device pinging the depths for lurking U-boats.

Twenty-four hours later, a Junkers 88 reconnaissance aircraft found them. Circling endlessly around the horizon, it watched *Edinburgh* and the convoy and transmitted homing messages to Norway, reporting on the constitution of the convoy, its speed and course. In *Edinburgh*, discovery at such an early stage on its homeward voyage was a matter of concern. It indicated that enemy attacks in one form or another were imminent.

In north Norway, plans were already developing for the destruction of QP 11. Admiral Hubert Schmundt at the German destroyers base of Kirkenes received permission to dispatch three of his Narvik-class destroyers to intercept and attack. These ships were *Hermann Schömann, Z–24* and *Z–25*, all under the command of Captain Schulze-Hinrichs. He also alerted seven of his strategically positioned submarines to converge on the British ships. Although QP 11 was heading due north, Schmundt knew that in a few hours time the convoy would come up against the ice-barrier and have to alter course to the west. With this knowledge, he laid his plans accordingly.

It was not long before *Edinburgh* and the convoy were forced frequently to alter course to avoid icefields and constant sightings of U-boats, which fully occupied the destroyer escorts in dashing around dropping depth-charges. It soon became apparent that this was no position for a cruiser to be in, ambling along at the 6-knot speed of the convoy. Indeed, it was a situation that invited disaster and so, to offset the danger, Admiral Bonham-Carter ordered Captain Faulkner to leave the convoy and to take the cruiser some twenty miles ahead, on a zigzag course to avoid possible torpedoes. After advising *Bulldog* of her intention, *Edinburgh* made off at 20 knots and soon disappeared over the horizon, alone.

The decision to leave the convoy was obviously advisable but, as she sped away, officers of the accompanying destroyers were mystified as to why the cruiser had not detached one of the destroyers to accompany her as a protective anti-submarine consort. In retrospect, it was a decision which proved tactically calamitous. Although for Commander Richmond in the destroyer *Bulldog* there was some consolation in the fact that *Edinburgh* was out ahead protecting the convoy's advance from the threat of enemy destroyers, there was no certainty that a surface attack would be mounted from that direction. It could just as easily come from astern or from the south. With these misgivings, the convoy and its escorts plodded steadily on.

It was at precisely 16.00, while the cruiser was at the termination of her distant patrol, that disaster struck.

Lying across the path of the cruiser, the submerged U-boat 456, commanded by Lieutenant Max Teichert, waited patiently for the approaching ship while his periscope swept the horizon in every direction. Hardly believing his eyes, he could find no destroyer escort in company with the cruiser. Whether he was aware that *Edinburgh* carried a king's ransom in gold bullion is open to speculation, but the sinking of the cruiser would in itself be the plum prize of the Arctic war. Such a chance would surely never happen again.

Controlling his excitement, Teichert carefully plotted the

cruiser's zigzag course until she was well within firing-range. A miss could not be considered, for his stock of torpedoes had been reduced to two. With a last-minute check on course, speed and range, he gave the order 'Fire one!' and seconds later 'Fire two!' As the torpedoes left the tubes, there came the expected shudder, and then the steel fish with their deadly warheads were speeding on their way, targeting on the unsuspecting *Edinburgh*.

On the bridge of the cruiser, the admiral and Captain Faulkner were in the plotting office discussing the situation now they were at the end of their twenty-mile patrol. At that moment the Asdic operator reported a submarine contact and almost immediately confirmed the echo in a voice rising with excitement. The admiral, however, seemed convinced that the echo was an error and, despite the operator's pleading assurance that it was a firm echo and that a U-boat was there, the operator was told to 'disregard' – it was all a mistake. But the young Asdic controller had made no mistake. It was indeed a submarine, and the cruiser, ignoring the clear and earnest warning given seconds earlier, sailed on, blissfully unaware of the two torpedoes streaking towards it. Within the ship all seemed normal; in fact, the pipe 'Non-duty hands to tea' had just sounded. Incredibly no one, not even the duty look-outs, saw the ominous silver wakes of the war-headed steel fish speeding through the dark sea.

Both torpedoes were dead on target. The first, amidships, smashed into the area of the forward boiler-room, destroying every compartment through to the port side, killing everybody in the blast area and flooding nearby compartments under tons of sea water and oil. The second torpedo hit further aft, the explosion tearing off the stern and blowing the steel deck upwards like a piece of cardboard to wrap itself around the triple guns of Y turret, the barrels jutting through the decking. With this great explosion, the rudder and two of the four propeller shafts disappeared altogether. It also had the effect of blasting the lower plates of the ship downward to produce a contorted fin or rudder. Under enormous pressure, tons of sea water poured into the ship, producing a frightening noise of thunder and tearing metal.

In a matter of seconds, proud *Edinburgh* had become a distorted coffin of steel and pulverized bodies, with two enormous holes into which the Arctic Sea now poured. Thus mortally wounded, she drifted to a stop, listing to starboard. Around and above the explosion areas men tripped and stumbled in the darkness, trying to find a way out. All electrical power to gun turrets had been destroyed, and only the forward B turret could be moved at all.

Watching through the periscope of *U-456*, Teichert observed the result of his attack with immense satisfaction, his one regret that he had fired his last torpedo. With only one more he could have applied the final blow. As it was, he could only watch and wait and report the unfolding drama of the crippled cruiser back to Admiral Schmundt in Norway.

Below *Edinburgh*'s decks, conditions were chaotic. In the next few hours many acts of heroism and events of tragedy took place: men imprisoned in compartments hauled to safety just before tons of oil flooded in; stokers and engine-room staff caught in the inescapable blow-out of burst steam pipes in darkness; men trapped alive in compartments already under water, their only link a voice tube to the upper deck as rescue teams tried to reassure them that freedom was near but knowing that their survival was but a chance in a thousand. By now many of the crew had assembled on the flight-deck, stunned but awaiting orders.

The hubbub of speculation ceased as Captain Faulkner hurried towards them. He paused only long enough to tell them that, despite the damage, he had high hopes of getting *Edinburgh* back to Murmansk if all the correct procedures for saving the ship were carried out. As he later stated in a report to the Admiralty, 'The way they responded convinced me that my hopes were shared by all and that the morale of the crew was indeed high.'

As the captain looked aft and saw the twisted remnants of the quarter-deck wrapped around the guns of Y turret, he said quite abruptly, 'The admiral has accepted full responsibility.' That remark and the tone in which it was said left the crew in little doubt that there had been a sharp difference of opinion between him and the admiral from the moment *Edinburgh* had left the convoy, without a consort, up to the time of torpedoing. The question that begged an answer was: would *Edinburgh* have been torpedoed if she had had a destroyer escort?

For Captain Faulkner, the safety of the ship and its crew were his main concern. If the remaining watertight doors and hatches could hold and if the one surviving engine-room could provide enough power to give some forward motion, the chances of returning to Murmansk were good.

During all this time the convoy far to the north had been on its westward course. A signal was received by *Bulldog* reporting that

*Edinburgh* required assistance after being hit by torpedoes. But by now Commander Richmond had his own problems. Enemy submarines were appearing ahead and astern of the convoy, and the accompanying destroyers were dashing around dropping depth-charges in order to keep the enemy submerged. To receive a request for help amidst all this fever of activity was something he could have done without. Though reluctant to spare his escorts, he ordered Commander Salter of the destroyer *Foresight* to take *Forester* and the two Soviet destroyers and speed with all haste to *Edinburgh*'s assistance. It was early evening before they arrived to find that *Edinburgh* had managed to raise enough steam to turn one propeller very slowly.

The big cruiser was in a sorry plight. The first explosion had opened up the hull for over fifty feet, destroying compartments through to the opposite side, with tons of water pouring in through the great hole. Right aft, over sixty feet of compounded wreckage suspended deep in the water and acting as a rudder made her unmanageable.

Valiant efforts were now made to tow *Edinburgh* back to the Kola Inlet, a distance of 250 miles.

It was a correct decision for, unknown to Admiral Bonham-Carter, *U–456* was tailing along at some distance, listening to the feverish activities on the surface to keep the cruiser moving – a movement which was almost negligible, for her forward speed had dropped to 2 knots. And as if that was not bad enough, two discouraging signals arrived. One from the Senior British Naval Officer Murmansk reported that numbers of enemy U-boats were taking up positions between the returning *Edinburgh* and the Kola Inlet. The other, from *Bulldog*, brought the news that they had received a signal from the Admiralty reporting that enemy destroyers had left Kirkenes with the object of intercepting the cruiser or the convoy or both. This depressing news was somewhat offset by a further signal from the SBNO at Murmansk to say that a powerful Soviet tug, in company with four British minesweepers, was on its way.

With enemy destroyers loose in the Arctic and searching for them, it was a race against time. But even with the close support of the minesweepers and the destroyers *Foresight* and *Forester* they would be outmatched and outgunned by the powerful 6-inch guns of the Nazi ships. In the meantime, with the galley out of action, no warmth in the ship and the temperature down to 10 degrees below freezing, the crew huddled together trying to gather some warmth from one another. In groups they waited, anxious and restless, arguing the chances of reaching Murmansk before the enemy found them. From the bridge, Admiral Bonham-Carter and Captain Faulkner peered with cheerless eyes out across the snow-clouded sea, for on their shoulders lay the responsibility of saving the ship, the crew and the vast fortune in gold bullion that lay in the bomb-room. The prospects were not good.

A few hours later *Edinburgh* received a further depressing signal from the Admiralty. It reported that the German pocket battleship *Admiral Scheer* had sailed from Trondheim, Norway, and was heading for the Arctic. The *Scheer* was a sister ship to the renowned *Graf Spee* which had been sunk at Montevideo in 1939. Its impressive armament comprised six 11-inch, eight 6-inch and six 4-inch guns, in addition to many anti-aircraft and smaller guns. If the *Scheer* should intercept *Edinburgh*, it was certain that the British ship would be quickly eliminated.

Meanwhile, about 200 miles to the north-west, the convoy QP 11 edged its way along the boundary of the ice-barrier, protected by the escorts, led by the destroyer *Bulldog*, but at 06.00 on 1 May the first German air torpedo attack of the war in the Arctic took place.

At this time Hitler's planned air offensive against the Soviet convoys had been implemented under the organization of two distinguished Luftwaffe officers – Major Blorden and Colonel Roth. The combined strength of its aircraft amounted to 103 Junkers, eighty-eight long-range bombers, forty-two Heinkel 111 torpedo bombers, fifteen Heinkel 115 torpedo bombers, thirty Stuka dive-bombers and seventy-four long-range reconnaissance aircraft.

Skimming low over the sea, groups of Heinkel 111s attacked in line ahead, forming a wide arc, each carrying two torpedoes. The protective line of escorts opened up with all their anti-aircraft guns, strafing the enemy planes. If this form of attack was intended to instil a sense of panic into Richmond's forces, it was badly misplaced. Out on the flank of the convoy and by far the closest to the Heinkels was the little corvette *Snowflake*. With only her single 4-inch gun and two machine-guns firing at maximum efficiency, she sped on towards the line of attacking aircraft. The accurate shell blasts and concentration of machine-gun fire became so dangerous that the planes were not allowed to drive home their carefully planned attack and in the confusion and near collisions loosed their torpedoes, which ran on targetless to explode among the ice-floes. For over half an hour the attacks were sustained but without success, and with all their torpedoes spent and frustrated in their efforts, the Heinkels returned to Norway.

When Admiral Schmundt received from Teichert the news that *Edinburgh* had been torpedoed and was virtually helpless, he was highly delighted. With no damage to his own forces, the great cruiser had been effaced as a fighting unit and now, badly disabled, she was unable to perform her function as a defending cover for the merchant ships. Against the superior Narvik-class destroyers, the convoy could be considered defenceless – or so he thought! Teichert's report clearly indicated that *Edinburgh* could be attacked at any time, especially at the 2-knot speed she was barely maintaining, whereas the westward-bound convoy far to the north might soon be beyond the range of their attacks.

At 13.00 that day, the enemy destroyers found the convoy and its escorts. Commander Richmond was faced with a difficult problem. Ahead lay masses of drifting ice, necessitating a course south-west. Astern, numbers of U-boats were gathering, looking for an opportunity to close in. Resisting the temptation to go chasing them and thereby weaken the convoy's defence, he tightened the protective screen around the merchant ships and waited. Furthermore, to lessen the choice of directions from which the enemy could attack, he herded the convoy in between the ice floes. This protected the starboard border.

Minutes later from the destroyer *Beverley* came the signal 'Enemy in sight – three destroyers.' Suddenly the German ships opened up with heavy gunfire, and shells started falling in and around the convoy. In a resolute bid to avoid the bombardment, the master of the freighter SS *Briarwood* led the merchantmen through a gap in the ice edge to steam cautiously up through passages between the massive ice floes. It was a hazardous undertaking, for propellers could easily be damaged and vessels rendered helpless. On the other hand, the possibility of torpedoes hitting their targets was greatly reduced.

After dispatching a signal to *Edinburgh* that an attack had been launched by enemy destroyers, *Bulldog* raced across the vanguard of the convoy at full speed, signalling for the destroyers *Amazon, Beverley* and *Beagle* to join her. As the ships sped over the Arctic water, their decks trembling under speed and the guns' crews ready and waiting, the range rapidly shortened. In formation of line ahead, ensigns fluttering wildly in the onward rush, the British ships opened fire.

It was a sea fight in which the ships of the Royal Navy merited the highest praise, for theoretically the British force should have suffered a crippling defeat with their little 4.7-inch guns against the total fire-power of the enemy of twelve 6-inch guns. Richmond was determined that the convoy should be saved. Time after time, the British and German destroyers in line ahead on parallel courses bombarded one another, each side loosing torpedoes at the other. Every time the German destroyers swept around, doubling back on their previous course, *Bulldog* and her consorts turned with them, placing themselves between the convoy and the enemy. Many times the British destroyers were bracketed with 6-inch shells as the Germans tried to find the range, but as each broadside fell to port or starboard, the four ships swung into a new line ahead.

Then, suddenly, *Amazon* was hit with a fury of shells and became enveloped in a sheet of flame and smoke. But still in line she raced on, maintaining her top speed. As the smoke thinned, her commanding officer gazed down on a spectacle of carnage. The forward gun had been ripped away from its mounting, all its crew either dead or wounded. The after gun and the midships 4-inch had also been blasted away, with their crews. The wheelhouse was a shambles, as were the main and auxiliary steering positions. Racing along at nearly 30 knots, *Amazon* was out of control. But now, as *Bulldog* made a sharp turn to regain the previous course, *Amazon* was forced to speed onward. And it was only by astute and skilful manipulation of the engines that her captain managed to bring her back into line of advance. As a fighting ship she was now immobile, but the enemy could not be allowed to know this. In spite of the enormous and grievous damage, *Amazon* continued to maintain her position in line, thus appearing to the enemy as a real threat.

Prevented from breaking through the defence and with shells from the British ships strafing them, the enemy eventually turned away. To give added protection to the convoy, Richmond laid down a thick black smoke-screen between them and the convoy.

A little later the Germans returned, streaking in from the south-east. Without a moment's hesitation, *Bulldog* swept around at speed and headed directly towards them, a millrace of waves streaming back from her knife-like bows. Aggressive in her appearance, to the enemy she seemed clearly committed to their destruction. The sight of the little ship careering towards them, guns blazing, must have struck fear into them, for after impetuously loosing off more torpedoes, they quickly turned away.

Half an hour later, under cover of low cloud sweeping over the ice-covered sea, the enemy returned and again tried to break through. Repeatedly they attacked, six times in all, yet they were repulsed.

By the evening, Schulze-Hinrichs was convinced that Richmond and his forces would rather fight to the death than permit the German forces to break through. Having used up almost two-thirds of their ammunition, Schulze-Hinrichs received orders from Admiral Schmundt to withdraw from the engagement and steam to the south-east to find and destroy the crippled *Edinburgh* barely 200 miles away.

Richmond must have allowed himself a deep sigh of relief as he watched the Narvik-class destroyers sail away. The bluff had paid off. He immediately signalled *Edinburgh* to report that the enemy destroyers had abandoned their attack and were heading towards the cruiser. Savaged and weary but rejoicing in the success of their defence, *Bulldog* and her consorts gathered up the convoy and steered to the west and quiet waters. Later that day *Beverley*'s commanding officer, Lieutenant Price, sent a signal to Commander Richmond: 'I should hate to play poker with you.'

While the battle for the defence of the convoy was going on, *Edinburgh* had made little or no progress towards Murmansk. Although the speed of 2 knots was providing some onward motion, it was only skilful manipulation of the engines that prevented her going round in circles.

When Admiral Bonham-Carter received Richmond's signal that the German destroyers had abandoned the attack on the convoy and were last seen heading in the direction of the cruiser, he set about making plans for the inevitable battle. With only the destroyers *Foresight* and *Forester* to provide protection, he was aware that the cruiser would be almost defenceless against the superior German force. True, the knowledge that the little group of minesweepers was speeding across the Barents Sea from Murmansk provided some comfort, but even if they arrived in time, their puny guns would be hopeless against the enemy.

Throughout that afternoon of 1 May, weary look-outs, red-eyed and sleep-eroded, searched the horizon. Which would arrive first, the enemy or the British minesweepers?

Just after 18.00 a small ship was sighted, approaching from the south-east. On arrival it proved to be a heavy Soviet tug, *Rubin*, and provisions were immediately put in hand to establish a tow wire to *Edinburgh*'s bows. About midnight, with the sun setting low on the horizon but then immediately rising again, the four British minesweepers arrived. These were *Hussar, Harrier, Gossamer* and *Niger*, each armed with only two 4-inch guns.

By 05.30 on 2 May, after careful planning, the tug *Rubin* and the minesweeper *Gossamer* were fully engaged in towing, with the escort of *Foresight* and *Forester* to port and starboard, and *Harrier* and *Niger* acting as a rearguard screen.

To the north, the German destroyers raced south-east at 35 knots to engage the British cruiser. It would not be difficult to find the ship, for Teichert was following and reporting its position. At 06.15 the enemy came upon a long black oil slick and, on the assumption it was from the damaged cruiser, raced on. In the frequent snow showers, visibility varied from two to eight miles. Minutes later the German *Z–25* reported a large ship to starboard, and all three destroyers turned onto the new course. It was indeed the prey they sought – HMS *Edinburgh*.

*Hussar* was the first to see the Germans speeding out of the poor visibility and immediately opened up with her two guns. A new and gallant battle now developed.

As valiantly as *Bulldog* had resisted the enemy's attack, so *Hussar* now accepted the challenge with a similar fortitude and tenacity. But it was short-lived, for eventually, outgunned and straddled by heavy shells, she could do no more than fall back and call for the support of the two British destroyers.

With the first of the gunflashes, *Edinburgh* cast off the tow wires and called on the maximum speed from her one engine-room, 8 knots. This simply resulted in the cruiser's adopting a circuitous course to port, but this seemed far more favourable than being stopped and presenting a sitting-duck target to the enemy. Already shells were falling just short of the cruiser's stern and, with waves creaming back from their slim bows, *Foresight* and *Forester* turned together towards the enemy, guns blazing. The fire-power of the opposing forces now became increasingly one-sided against the twelve 6-inch guns of the Germans.

Meanwhile *Edinburgh*, sluggishly yawing round into the wind, demonstrated that she was still a power to be reckoned with. Although her one and only operational turret could fire manually, with no electrical power it could not be moved to train right or left. As the cruiser slowly yawed around to complete another circle, her 6-inch shells waiting in the guns. She came on target to face the enemy.

At that moment the German destroyer *Hermann Schömann* crossed the line of fire. With his head sticking out through the hatch at the top of the turret, the young gunnery officer Lieutenant R.M. Howe calmly estimated the correct angle and distance and gave the order 'Fire!' The shooting was remarkably accurate. The first salvo landed within a few feet of the German, and in a hopeless bid to escape she tried to turn towards her own smoke-screen, but only seconds later another salvo from *Edinburgh*, her guns spewing tongues of flame and smoke, smashed into the *Hermann Schömann* in a devastating explosion. The heavy shells clawed through the steel hull as if it were paper. Both engine-rooms were destroyed and all control systems rendered useless. Slowly the German ship drifted to a stop. This changed the situation completely, for their original attitude of attack became one of defence. All endeavours were now centred on rescuing the crew of the crippled ship while still keeping up a heavy concentration of gunfire.

It was at this very moment that Admiral Bonham-Carter received from the Admiralty the news that the German pocket battleship *Scheer* had returned to Trondheim.

There followed a wild, erratic fight as the German and British ships, in a hide-and-seek engagement, dashed backwards and forwards among the snow squalls and smoke-screens.

In one of these flurries, Commander Salter of *Foresight* was confronted by the sight of one of the enemy heading straight for him. As she veered to starboard to fire a salvo, a sudden cloud of smoke hid the target, but away on the port beam Lieutenant-Commander Huddart of *Forester* found himself ideally situated to loose his torpedoes and swung to starboard. Then as *Forester* turned, the full violence of the German's superior fire power hit the ship. One shell smashed through the hull, badly damaging the two boiler-rooms, causing many casualties. Another shell landed aft, killing some of the gun's crew, and a third exploded on the forward gun, killing four. From this shell a fragment also hit Lieutenant-Commander Huddart, who was leaning over the bridge, and he was killed instantly. Minutes later, two more shells hit the ship, killing five and injuring another eight. With his commanding officer now dead, Lieutenant Jack Bitmead RN took command and continued the fight.

By now *Forester* was stopped dead in the water barely two miles from the enemy's guns, but *Foresight*, seeing the highly dangerous situation in which her sister-ship was now placed, raced in gallantly to put herself between the crippled ship and the German destroyers. In doing so she invited the concentration of the enemy's fire and was immediately hit by two shells, one aft and the other in the forward boiler-room. The explosions left her with only one gun in action and many casualties. Although the remaining boiler-room was also damaged, there was always the hope of making it operational. But *Foresight* was still literally under the guns of the enemy, and almost fatalistically she awaited the *coup de grâce*. Indeed, the ship was so close to the Germans that there was the possibility of their being boarded and captured.

Below decks, sweating stokers and engineers redoubled their efforts to restart the engines, while on the bridge the crew watched horrified as two torpedo tracks were seen homing in on them. In a state of frozen immobility they waited to hear the explosion which would in all probability kill them, but in that never-to-be forgotten moment, paralysed with fear, the two torpedoes passed under the keel and sped onward towards the circling *Edinburgh*. Seconds later, at the end of their run, one, dead on target, began to splash along the surface. The cruiser, however, completing another of its uncontrolled circuits, was on a collision course with it. The torpedo hit the ship dead centre, and for the third time in three days *Edinburgh* lifted and shook under the concussion of the explosion. Though the enemy was unaware of the bonus they had so undeservedly acquired, for *Edinburgh* this was the final act. The torpedo had punched its way into an area close to the earlier first torpedo, and the ship was almost cut in two.

Despite the hopeless situation, her guns continued to fire. Even the commanding officer of one of the enemy destroyers was reputed to have said at the time, 'Her shooting is remarkably good.' Later accounts revealed that the German ships fired fifteen torpedoes in this encounter.

In the meantime the plight of the two British destroyers was indeed perilous, for it was against them that the fury of the enemy's guns was concentrated. In *Forester*'s badly damaged engine-room, the superhuman efforts of the crew had brought moderate success, and they were now able to raise enough steam to turn the propellers. Without delay *Forester* moved slowly towards her sister-ship *Foresight*. It was only by operating a zigzag course that she avoided receiving direct hits from the straddling enemy fire. But even in her withdrawal she fought back with her one and only after gun and with the eightieth round scored a direct hit on the destroyer *Z–25*, resulting in a brilliant orange flash which must have caused much damage. By now *Z–24*, fully active, had found the range of the crippled *Foresight*, which with only one gun could scarce defend herself. Aware of the parlous situation of her sister-ship, *Forester* gradually increased her speed to 12 knots, closed in and produced a mass of black smoke to screen her from the enemy but in doing so drew upon herself *Z–24*'s fire. Lieutenant Bitmead, by this gallant act, was redeeming his debt to Commander Salter.

While all this was going on, the little minesweepers were trying to defend the stricken cruiser by repeatedly darting forward, shooting at the enemy and behaving, as the Admiralty later reported, 'like young terriers'. In fact, the minesweepers' courageous action amidst the smoke and cloud of battle misled the enemy, who assumed they were destroyers lately arrived to support the British force, and as a result they broke off the action.

With the destroyer *Hermann Schömann* utterly crippled and the *Z–25* damaged, the Germans' main objective now was to secure alongside the *Schömann* and take off survivors. Setting charges, they scuttled the destroyer and set course for Kirkenes, deeply dismayed by the turn of events.

To return to HMS *Edinburgh*, when the torpedo struck, there was a shattering explosion coupled with the sound of rending, tearing metal as the centre of the ship was torn apart and men died. But there was another sound: the noise of tons of sea water flooding in with enormous force. The ship was open from side to side, with the sea rushing through, and the only things holding the vessel together were parts of the upper deck and bits of the remaining hull. Aware that she might break in two, the admiral gave the order 'Abandon ship!' He also signalled the minesweepers to secure alongside, to take off the many wounded and the crew. But in the decks below, other battles were in progress – battles for survival. Decks suddenly ruptured, catapulting men into lower compartments already flooding with oil and in impenetrable darkness. Hatches jammed, imprisoning men who had no hope of escaping.

As Captain Faulkner watched the German destroyers slowly retire southwards, he was reputed to have said, 'I shall never understand why they didn't come in and finish us off. I think they had acknowledged defeat after being so heavily shot at.'

The off-loading of the wounded from the cruiser to the minesweepers *Harrier* on the port side and *Gossamer* on the starboard proved to be a difficult undertaking. The deck of *Harrier* was twelve feet lower than that of *Edinburgh*, and the transfer was increasingly hazardous by the gradual listing of the ship and her rise and fall in the swell. Then followed the transfer of 800 men to the two minesweepers.

At this time the question was asked, 'What do we do about the gold?' It was a question which brought an unprintable answer. Lives were more precious than gold. And there it was left, snug in the bomb-room deep in the bowels of the ship, covered in sea water – 400 gold bars with a present-day total of £45 million. There it would lie undisturbed for forty years, until one day in 1982 a deep-sea diver thrust his hand into the thick silt and lifted out one ingot after another, to establish one of the greatest and most successful deep-sea salvage enterprises in history.

In *Harrier* and *Gossamer* the main fear was of capsizing, and the survivors needed much persuasion to go below and be packed like sardines in the confined spaces. The main thought in everyone's mind was, 'What happens if a torpedo should hit us now?'

Eventually the lines were cast off and the two destroyers and the two minesweepers stood off to watch the cruiser go down. But, almost unbelievably, she refused to sink. After repeated but unsuccessful attempts to send her to the bottom by gunfire and depth-charges, *Foresight* fired her last torpedo. From the bridges and decks of the circling ships the crew watched in breathless despair, knowing that this was the final chapter in the life of a great and proud ship. With almost startling abruptness, the torpedo struck, punching deep into the bowels of the cruiser with a reverberating explosion. Slowly, almost protestingly, she rolled over and, with the bows rising higher and higher, disappeared. From the whirlpool of bubbling, gurgling water came the obscene stench of fuel-oil. As *Edinburgh* disappeared from sight she took with her the bodies of fifty-seven of her crew and five tons of gold bullion. Only a little earlier, *Hermann Schömann* had burrowed into her final resting-place on the sea bed.

After a final examination of the flotsam and jetsam floating above *Edinburgh*'s grave, the destroyers and minesweepers moved off, heading for the Kola Inlet, while to the south the German destroyers *Z–24* and *Z–25* moved steadily on towards Kirkenes.

Both sides had suffered the loss of a ship, each of vital importance to the course of the Arctic war. It had been a bitter naval engagement in which neither side could claim a victory over the other.

Early the following morning the survivors arrived at the Kola Inlet to disembark at Vaenga and Polyarnoe. Shortly after arriving at Murmansk, *Harrier*'s commanding officer, Captain Hinton, was handed the following letter written by the captain of the Soviet tug *Rubin*: 'Dear Sir, Soviet's seaman was witness of heroic battle English seamen with predominance power of enemy. English seamen did observe their sacred duty before Fatherland. We are prouding to staunchness and courage of English seamens – our Allies …' It was a message which pleased and fascinated everyone.

After disembarking, Admiral Bonham-Carter despatched a report to the Commander-in-Chief of the Home Fleet, Admiral Sir John Tovey. Within the context of the letter he said,

> I cannot speak too highly of the behaviour of the Captain, officers and men of *Edinburgh* from the time she was first torpedoed. The coolness, calmness and cheerfulness shown by the Captain was felt right throughout the ship and at no time was there any sign of depression through the intense cold and lack of sleep nor loss of heart despite the knowledge that surface, submarine and air attack was imminent. The way in which *Foresight* and *Forester* went in to attack superior forces and the manner in which they were handled could not have been more gallant …
>
> It is no doubt fully realised how deeply I regret the loss of so fine a cruiser but I hope it will be appreciated that I alone was responsible for the movement of *Edinburgh* and that in no way can any criticism be levelled at Captain Faulkner who I hope will be given another sea command as early as possible.
>
> Rear-Admiral commanding 18th Cruiser-Squadron
> Rear-Admiral Stuart Bonham-Carter

The *Edinburgh* survivors who were landed went ashore with mixed feelings: thankfulness that they were still alive but dismay at the barrenness and desolation of the Russian coast. Many believed that in a matter of days they would be put aboard ships returning to Great Britain. Unhappily this was not correct: in the weeks and months ahead they endured discomfort, freezing cold without adequate protection, and much hunger before returning home.

Unfortunately, many who survived the *Edinburgh* sinking perished in their several efforts to reach Britain.

# 14 Midway

*In the Pacific War it seemed inevitable that the tide of Japanese aggression would overcome American resistance when, in 1942, the USA was forced to defend Hawaii at Midway with only two fully operational and one badly damaged aircraft-carriers and no battleships. This, against a Japanese armada of 200 warships.*

*The Battle of Midway Island was an all-out effort to decide the war quickly and decisively. It was the crucial turning-point, for the Americans won an outright victory, and when it was over, Japanese sea power never again regained the initiative.*

In the annals of American history, one of the greatest naval engagements ever fought was that of the Battle of Midway Island, which took place on 3 June 1942.

The strategic importance of the island can be judged by its geographical position. A mere spot in the great Pacific Ocean of 80 million square miles of sea, it lies about half-way between Japan and the western coast of America and just about a thousand miles west of the United States' important naval base of Pearl Harbor in the Hawaiian islands. These and the fortified outpost of Midway form the apex of the 'Strategic Defensive Triangle', having its base on the Pacific coast between Dutch Harbour in Alaska and the Panama Canal.

To understand the crucial part that this tiny island and the sea around it were called upon to play in the Pacific War, one must consider them in the context of the attack on Pearl Harbor by the Japanese only six months earlier, on 7 December 1941.

Following this catastrophe, America was immediately put on a

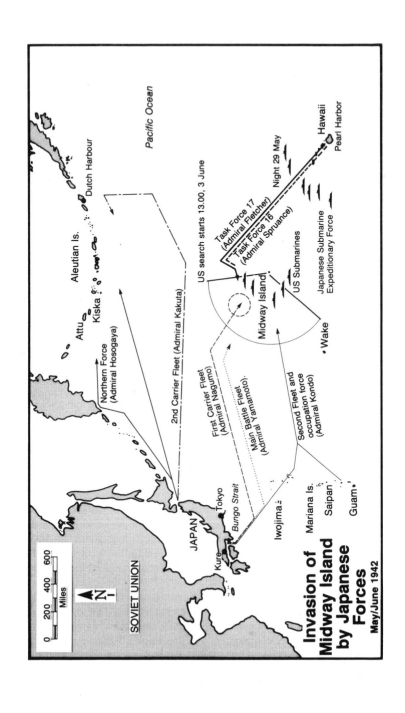

Invasion of
**Midway Island
by Japanese
Forces**
May/June 1942

Pacific Ocean

SOVIET UNION

JAPAN
Tokyo
Bungo Strait
Kure
Iwojima

Mariana Is.
Saipan
Guam

Aleutian Is.
Attu
Kiska
Dutch Harbour

Northern Force
(Admiral Hosogaya)

2nd Carrier Fleet (Admiral Kakuta)

First Carrier Fleet
(Admiral Nagumo)

Main Battle Fleet
(Admiral Yamamoto)

Second Fleet and
occupation force
(Admiral Kondo)

Midway Island

Wake

US search starts 13.00, 3 June

Task Force 17
(Admiral Fletcher)

Task Force 16
(Admiral Spruance)

Night 29 May

Hawaii
Pearl Harbor

US Submarines

Japanese Submarine
Expeditionary Force

N

Miles
0  200  400  600

war footing, with President Roosevelt given full support from the nation. Under such crippling losses, the Navy had to be rebuilt but, amid all the gloom and doom, one piece of good news emerged: the American naval carrier force was not at Pearl Harbor when the strike took place. A significant factor indeed, of which the Japanese Command was acutely aware. Following their success at Honolulu, however, and having gained the initiative, albeit temporarily, the Japanese gained further successes by conquering many of the groups of islands in the Pacific to be used as bases for their drive eastward to the United States.

Stimulated by the victory at Pearl Harbor by so easily penetrating the very heart of the American Defence Triangle, Admiral Yamamoto, Commander-in-Chief of the Japanese Combined Fleet, was convinced that the capture of Midway Island was not only strategically vital but necessary to Japan's survival. His campaign had two objectives: the destruction of the remnants of the American Pacific fleet and the occupation of Midway Island, which could be used as a base for attacking the Hawaiian islands and subsequently the west coast of the United States. By gaining mastery of the Pacific, Japan would be in a powerful position to sue for a negotiated peace on its own terms.

Yamamoto's plan for the final elimination of the American fleet was based on an old and well-tried policy, that of diversion, flank attack and final kill. Part of the Japanese fleet would attack and occupy the Aleutian islands of Kiska and Attu in the north, and while the American fleet was speeding to their defence, the Japanese would bomb and take Midway, which they expected could be occupied with little or no opposition. Then, when the US fleet rushed back to the defence of Midway, Japanese bombers from the newly occupied runways and from their own carrier force would attack the fleet in a concentrated bombing offensive, and so eliminate the last naval resistance. It is doubtful, however, if the United States Commander-in-Chief of the Pacific fleet, Admiral Chester W. Nimitz, would have fallen into such a trap. His astuteness in subsequent engagements proved he was well aware of the duplicity of the Oriental mind.

In the meantime there occurred an event which had a profound psychological effect in two ways. Vice-Admiral Halsey ordered an attack on Tokyo from his carriers *Enterprise* and *Hornet*, which were then only 650 miles away. The sixteen B25 bombers, led by Lieutenant-Colonel Doolittle, although inflicting little physical damage, had a sobering and disturbing effect on the Japanese population, who had been fed on the propaganda that no planes would ever reach the Homeland. The mystery deepened when President Roosevelt jokingly announced that the aircraft had taken off from their base at 'Shangri-la'. Strategists of the Imperial General Staff pored over their maps and came to the mistaken conclusion that the raid must have been launched from Midway Island, but this was over 2,000 miles away! So where was this 'Shangri La'? If, by some extraordinary means, it *was* Midway, it strengthened Yamamoto's argument that it had to be captured.

The bombing of Tokyo also gave a morale-boost to the Americans. It was a 'hit-back' for Pearl Harbor, a first taste of the terrible retribution that was to come.

By early May, the initial plans for the Japanese attack and occupation of Midway had been submitted and approved, followed by the imperial directive. Yamamoto's force was divided into five sections.

1   A northern force under the command of Vice-Admiral Moshiro Hosogaya, with the two carriers *Ryujo* and *Junyo*, eighty-two planes, two cruisers, a screen of destroyers and four transport ships carrying troops to occupy the islands of Attu, Adak and Kiska in the Aleutians, with a secondary objective to intercept any American relief force coming from either direction.

2   A submarine expeditionary force positioning itself in various strategic areas in advance of other groups going into action, the main body strung out in a line between Hawaii and Midway to signal advance information to Yamamoto of the movement of American ships and to attack and destroy as many as possible.

3   The main carrier striking force under the command of Vice-Admiral Chuichi Nagumo, comprising four big carriers, *Akagi, Hiryu, Soryu* and *Kaga*, with 227 planes, two battleships (*Kiriskima* and *Haruna*), three cruisers and eleven destroyers assigned to track and destroy the US fleet.

4   The main fleet under the command of Admiral Isoruku Yamamoto with seven giant battleships, including *Yamato* and *Musashi*, each carrying nine 11-inch guns, one carrier and several cruisers and destroyers. These two battleships were the most superior in the world and designed to outrange the guns of any opponent. They had the amazing displacement of nearly 73,000 tons each and, apart from their 18-inch armament, carried twelve 6-inch, twenty-four 5-inch and 150 anti-aircraft

guns. Their three great turrets were protected by a 24-inch-thick armour plating, a 16-inch side belt and an 8-inch decking. It was considered that the armour belt would stop an 18-inch shell at 20,000 yards and the deck plating a 2,000-pound bomb. The 18-inch guns could fire a shell weighing 1½ tons a distance of twenty-six miles, with a velocity of half a mile per second. Two formidable warships indeed. The Midway occupation force under the command of Admiral Nobutake Kondo was responsible for the capture of the island. His force comprised one carrier, the *Zuiho*, two battleships, eight cruisers, nine destroyers, fifteen troopships carrying 5,000 men, and a number of minesweepers.

Altogether, Yamamoto's armada was made up of 200 ships, including eleven battleships, eight carriers, twenty-two cruisers, sixty-five destroyers and twenty submarines, with a total of 100,000 men.

The element of surprise was to be the keynote for the success of the operation, but in this respect Yamamoto's plan fell apart, for in the meantime American intelligence had intercepted Japanese fleet messages and was able to inform Admiral Nimitz and his staff that the Japanese were amassing a great fleet; its objective – Midway. Such was the weight of information that Nimitz had also most of the details of the planned assault, the ships' disposition and route.

With time running out and to meet the threatened attack, Nimitz had hurriedly to assemble and prepare the resources available, although there wasn't much. He had, in fact, only the carriers *Hornet* and *Enterprise*, a few cruisers and destroyers. In the earlier Coral Sea battle, the carrier *Lexington* had been sunk and the *Yorktown* and *Saratoga* badly damaged, *Yorktown* was urgently recalled from her refuelling base and repair yard in the Friendly Islands and arrived at Pearl Harbor on 27 May with an estimated refit period of at least ninety days. But the Japanese carrier force had already left their home base the day before, heading for Midway. Nimitz needed the *Yorktown*, and needed it badly, and he was not slow in punching home the urgency of the situation and ensuring a crash programme of essential repairs. Ninety days were out of the question, even nine unthinkable. *Yorktown* was ready in three. A special force of over a thousand men had been quickly organized for the 'first aid' repairs, and although the job was crude and rough, she was as sea-fit and battleworthy as she could be in the time at their command.

By 28 May Hosogaya's northern force, Nagumo's carriers, Yamamoto's battleships and the Midway occupation force were all at sea, heading east.

The submarine expeditionary force had left earlier to take up their planned positions around Hawaii to intercept any American ships leaving Pearl Harbor. But with advanced knowledge of the sailing date of the Japanese force and the proposed barrier of Japanese submarines, Nimitz had sailed his carriers *Yorktown* (seventy-five planes), *Enterprise* (seventy-nine) and *Hornet* (seventy-nine) to sea before the submarines arrived. Additionally, he placed his own barrier of submarines on a perimeter arc north-west of Midway. As a consequence, from the time the Japanese submarines arrived on station, their reports to Yamamoto were negative.

By 2 June the American ships were in position some 300 miles north-east of Midway, a little group of twenty-six ships ready to take on the might of the Japanese armada of 200. Nimitz's ships were grouped as two task forces: Task Force 17 comprised the carrier *Yorktown* (commanded by Rear-Admiral Frank Fletcher), two cruisers and six destroyers, and Task Force 16 the carriers *Enterprise* and *Hornet* (commanded by Rear-Admiral Raymond Spruance, who had replaced the ailing Admiral Halsey), six cruisers and nine destroyers. (There were no battleships; what there had been now rested on the mud in Pearl Harbor.) As prepared as they could be, the ships waited, knowing that in a matter of hours the life-and-death struggle for the defence of Midway would begin.

The island of Midway itself has nothing to commend it. Its importance lies in its strategic position as a defence outpost for the United States. Midway is, in fact, an atoll – two tiny islets, crescent-shaped, enclosing a central lagoon, with a narrow channel leading into it and on the western edge an open harbour. One islet, named Sand, is barely two miles long, and the other, Eastern, one mile long. Despite their size, both islands contained their own barracks, power supply, oil tanks, mess halls and runways.

In anticipation of a possible invasion, Admiral Nimitz had paid a surprise visit to Midway in May, inspecting the installations. Defences were improved and its complement of marines and fliers was increased to 3,500 men. In fact, everything that could be done in the time was done. But there was no escaping the fact that the fate of the island depended not on its defences and aircraft but on the two task forces based on its three carriers, patrolling the sea area 300 miles north-east.

Although he accepted the overwhelming superiority of the enemy, Nimitz found one consolatory feature. According to intelligence, the Japanese fleet would divide their forces into five groups, thus dissipating their combined strength. If they had decided to attack in one massive group, Nimitz realized he would have stood no chance.

Yamamoto's campaign opened before dawn on 3 June, when Hosogaya's aircraft took off from the accompanying carriers to bomb the American-held 'Dutch Harbour' east of the Aleutian island chain. But Admiral Nimitz, in command of operations at Pearl Harbor, with his advanced intelligence information was not to be enticed into sending his forces north to intercept the invading force there. He knew that the main Japanese attack would be directed at Midway and would almost certainly approach from the north-west. The weather had deteriorated, and there was no doubt that the enemy would take full advantage of the rain and cloud cover to get as near as possible without being observed. In the meantime Rear-Admiral Fletcher (TF 17) and Rear-Admiral Spruance (TF 16) could only wait until their scout planes could signal the first sightings. Midway Command had also launched a reconnaissance flight comprising twenty-five Catalina flying-boats, with a maximum flight range of 700 miles, covering a westward semi-circle from due north to almost due south, each with its own sector.

At 08.20 one of the Catalinas reported a fleet of ships heading towards Midway from the west and assumed that it was Yamamoto's main body. Nimitz, however, was not convinced, and as the reports built up, he decided that it was not the main battleship or carrier force he was expecting. In this he was right, for the approaching ships were actually Kondo's fleet with troopships and occupation forces. Unwilling to commit Fletcher's task force, Nimitz held his hand while nine B17 planes took off from Midway to attack the convoy. Despite their efforts they did little damage and succeeded in sinking only one of the accompanying tankers. With 700 miles to go back to Midway, tired and frustrated, they then received reports that the island was being attacked by bomber planes.

Meanwhile, 300 miles to the north of Midway, Task Forces 17 and 16 waited anxiously. It was mid-evening, and the Japanese carrier force commanded by Nagumo had not been sighted. As a result, Nimitz directed the two task forces to head south-west towards Midway. During that night of the 3rd and 4th the Japanese and American ships steamed towards one another, Nagumo's carrier force in the van and Yamamoto's battle fleet giving cover from the rear. None of the Japanese admirals had the slightest suspicion of the presence of an opposing task force or even that the Americans had operational carriers in the area.

Long before dawn, Nagumo turned his carriers into the wind and launched his bombers for a strike at Midway. A total of 108 planes took off, comprising thirty-six Zero fighters, thirty-six Val dive-bombers and thirty-six Kate torpedo bombers.

Almost simultaneously with Nagumo's strike force taking off from the carrier *Akagi*, Fletcher launched ten dive-bombers on a hundred-mile search, and Midway sent off sixteen B17s to search for and bomb the carrier force if it could be found.

Nagumo had not committed all his planes: he had kept back half his force in the event of some remote possibility that the Americans could mount a counter-attack. He had already sent up a number of scout planes on an air search with orders to cover all possible sectors and report their findings but, fortunately for the Americans, fate in the form of bad weather and engine problems resulted in the planes' eventually returning without having spotted the oncoming task forces. The pilots' negative reports further convinced Nagumo that he had no surface opposition to contend with, and accordingly he signalled his fleet that he intended to launch a second attack on Midway as soon as the opportunity arose. Overhead, one of the Catalinas from Midway spotted the carrier force through cloud cover and radioed the island and Fletcher that a strike force of Japanese bombers was headed for Midway.

Fletcher now knew exactly where Nagumo's carrier force was and, barely waiting for his returning reconnaissance planes to land, he signalled Spruance with the carriers *Enterprise* and *Hornet* to proceed at speed and attack the Japanese force when found. In response to the advance warning, every plane on Midway was launched, but it was a hopeless undertaking: the defending Midway planes were not only outnumbered but so obsolete that they stood no chance against the new Zero 'Hamp' fighters. Only five of the twenty-seven survived to fight again. Although the runways remained usable, heavy damage was inflicted on installations, fuel tanks and the power station. But the fighting and defensive capability of the island remained intact, and the US gunners shot down a considerable number of Japanese aircraft.

Even as the enemy force circled over the island to fly back to their carriers, the leader signalled that, to eliminate any opposition Kondo's occupation force might encounter, it would be necessary to mount a second strike. Nagumo now had to make a crucial decision. Waiting on the decks of his four carriers were another 108 planes, most armed with torpedoes in the event of an American surface attack, yet his scout planes had seen no US ships or carriers.

Minutes later his mind was made up for him when twelve torpedo planes and B17s from Midway suddenly appeared and attacked the carriers. All the torpedoes missed and no damage was caused, but only three American planes survived the attacks from the defending Zero fighters. It was a tragic ending to a courageous assault, yet it proved to be the effective turning-point in the ensuing battle, for it delayed the launching of the second strike and convinced Nagumo that he must eliminate the probability of further land-based attacks against his carriers. Midway would have to be bombed in a second assault but, as many of his waiting aircraft were armed with torpedoes, he gave the order 'Reload with bombs!' Each plane had to be taken below, its torpedo unloaded and replaced with one 550-pound and two 132-pound bombs, a time-consuming operation.

Even while the torpedo bombers were being lowered, there arrived a frantic message from one of the Japanese scout planes reporting that he had sighted two ships heading south-west. Nagumo demanded more information, but while he waited, further attacks on his ships developed from Midway bombers. Over thirty planes made their assault, but no hits were registered and several planes were shot down. At 08.30 came the message that Nagumo dreaded. His scout planes reported that the approaching enemy ships were escorting an aircraft-carrier believed to be *Yorktown*. It was bad news, for already the planes returning from Midway were circling overhead waiting to land on the carrier's decks. Nearly all were almost out of fuel and if not landed quickly would have to ditch in the sea. After carefully weighing up the situation, the admiral ordered that the carrier decks be cleared and the circling planes brought in.

In a further assessment of the situation it did not appear to be as adverse as he first thought. His four carriers and the escorting battle fleet could easily deal with the small opposing force reported, and he therefore turned *Akagi* and signalled his ships that they, with him, were to proceed at full speed to contact and destroy the enemy. Consequently the re-arming of the planes went into reverse. The bombs now had to be taken off and the aircraft loaded with torpedoes. Such were the confusion and haste that there was no time to lower the bombs and replace them in the magazines, so they were recklessly stacked around the carrier's decks.

In the meantime, over a period of one hour the US carriers *Enterprise, Hornet* and *Yorktown* had launched a total strike force of 152 aircraft. These comprised eighty-five Dauntless dive-bombers, forty-one Devastator torpedo bombers and twenty-six Wildcat fighters.

By 09.30 separate waves of US planes had arrived over the target. They found three of the four carriers, accompanied by six cruisers and ten destroyers. The leader of the first wave radioed back to *Hornet* that the Japanese carrier decks were loaded with aircraft hastily being re-armed and refuelled and that he was about to attack with his torpedo bombers. Unfortunately his protective screen of fighter planes was absent, and although they courageously pressed home their attack, they were immediately shot down by the intensive concentration of anti-aircraft fire from the accompanying cruisers and destroyers. Torpedoes launched by the attackers passed harmlessly by as the carriers adroitly twisted and turned to escape. Five minutes later a second wave of torpedo bombers arrived and strove to break through the curtain of fire. Those that survived were shot out of the sky by the fast Zero fighters protecting the ships. Of the forty torpedo bombers, only six arrived back safely; it had indeed been a suicidal mission but a sacrifice that ironically brought overwhelming victory.

As the Zero fighters were chasing the last of the torpedo bombers at wave-top height, from overhead came the first-wave of Dauntless dive-bombers. They were rugged, tough machines that could take considerable punishment and still survive. At the outbreak of war they were adapted to meet the special needs of tactical warfare, acquiring a larger self-sealing fuel tank, armour plating for the crew and a larger, more powerful engine. Each plane had a maximum speed of 255 m.p.h. at 14,000 feet and a range of nearly 800 miles and carried a bomb load of 500 pounds.

Screaming down from over 20,000 feet with their terrifying whistling sound, the dive-bombers selected their targets. The crowning prize was Nagumo's flagship, the carrier *Akagi*. Led by Lieutenant-Commander McClusky, the first wave pulled out of their dives from a few hundred feet and dropped their bomb loads.

They scored direct hits, and the result was devastating. Amid the flames and the thick black oily smoke rising like a funeral pyre, the bombs that had been left lying on the deck from the careless reloading started to explode. Burning splinters and red-hot metal searing their way into the full tanks of the forty aircraft on deck produced a massive eruption from the spilled gasoline. Primed torpedoes, each carrying a warhead of 750 pounds of high explosive, erupted, ripping open the carrier's deck, allowing roaring flames to gush into the lower hangars and ignite gasoline tanks. The bridge superstructure grew hotter and hotter as creeping flames licked around its base. Charred and burning corpses lay everywhere. Fire-fighters and damage-control personnel ran hither and thither in a wild, hopeless endeavour.

Less than ten minutes earlier, Nagumo, his face wreathed in smiles, had watched as the American torpedo bombers were blown out of the sky, as his famous Zero fighters decimated the few survivors. He had then breathed a sigh of relief as it became clear that neither his carriers nor his cruisers and destroyers had been hit. And then, within seconds of that moment of self-congratulation, the fury of hell had burst out of the skies.

Nagumo, his face now blackened with smoke, and choking with fumes, was reluctantly persuaded by his officers to leave the flagship and save himself. In the meantime, the destroyer *Nowake* had come alongside to give assistance, and it was this vessel that Nagumo boarded, to be taken to the cruiser *Nagara*, to which he transferred his flag.

Although valiant efforts were made by the commanding officer of *Akagi*, Captain Aoki, to save the ship after the admiral had left, the situation became intolerable. Stokers and engine-room staff became trapped below, while intermittent explosions increased the flames until the giant carrier was ablaze from bow to stern. At last Captain Aoki gave the order to abandon ship and, although intent on performing the honoured Japanese tradition of going down with his ship, he was eventually persuaded to save himself and board the waiting *Nowake*.

At the time *Akagi* was being hit by McClusky's dive-bombers, the rest of the squadron burst out of cloud cover and attacked *Akagi*'s sister-ship, *Kaga*. She also had planes on the flight-deck, refuelled and re-armed waiting to take off, thirty in all. Four direct hits were scored on the carrier: one killed everybody on the bridge; another, hitting a gasoline tank, exploded on the flight-deck, setting light to the waiting planes, and soon the whole carrier was a mass of flame. Following a concentrated fire-fighting effort it seemed at first that the fires might be brought under control in time, but then the American submarine *Nautilus* arrived on the scene, and three torpedoes were discharged. The fires increased to such an extent that soon *Kaga* was nothing more than a burning hulk. Soon after came the order 'Abandon ship!' Two mighty explosions ripped the carrier apart and she slowly rolled over and sank, taking more than 800 men with her.

Almost immediately after the simultaneous attacks on *Akagi* and *Kaga*, seventeen dive-bombers from *Yorktown* arrived and launched their attack of the third Japanese carrier, *Soryu*, diving in three waves at two-minute intervals. A total of 3,000 pounds of high-explosive bombs landed on the carrier's flight-deck. Here again, as on *Akagi* and *Kaga*, the bombs carelessly stacked around the decks also blew up, setting fire to waiting aircraft. Within twenty minutes the whole carrier was alight, many of the crew leaping over the side with burning clothes. Below decks, a sudden massive explosion applied the *coup de grâce*. Her commanding officer, Captain Yanagimoto, however, refused to leave the ship and committed hara-kiri on the bridge. At 19.20 the dying carrier settled deep in the water, raised its bows and in minutes was gone.

Only one Japanese carrier now remained undamaged, *Hiryu*, under the command of Rear-Admiral Yamaguchi. This carrier had stayed distant from the other three and had therefore escaped attack. Having received details of the disaster, Yamaguchi decided to attack the American carrier responsible for the débâcle and ordered his most experienced pilot, Lieutenant Kobayashi, to take off, leading sixteen Val dive-bombers and seven Zeros. High over *Yorktown* a Japanese reconnaissance plane transmitted homing signals to Kobayashi's aircraft, directing them to their target.

It was now midday, and while *Yorktown*'s flight-deck crew were preparing to receive their bombers and fighters from the successful attack on the Japanese carriers, radar detected the approaching enemy. All aircraft on deck were immediately airborne and returning bombers signalled away. At the same time, escorting cruisers and destroyers closed in to form a defensive ring around *Yorktown*. These were the cruisers *Astoria* and *Portland* and the destroyers *Hammann, Anderson, Russell, Morris* and *Hughes*. Only twelve Wildcats were able to take off in the time, but these were soon supplemented by several more fighters rushed across from *Hornet*.

Soon after 12.00 the first wave of twenty-three Japanese aircraft arrived. It was instantly followed by a vicious 'do or die' dog-fight in which thirteen of Kobayashi's planes were destroyed by Wildcats, and two more by anti-aircraft fire. But the remaining planes managed to burst through the curtain of fire and score three direct hits on *Yorktown*. The first damaged the boilers, another started a fire that was put out by flooding, and a third put a large hole straight through the flight-deck, destroying communications. To maintain contact, Fletcher transferred his flag to *Astoria*.

While Kobayashi's raid was in progress, *Soryu*'s scout planes that had directed the attacking planes returned to find their home base in flames and had to land on the distant carrier *Hiryu*, there to report to Rear-Admiral Yamaguchi that the Americans had not one carrier but three – *Yorktown*, *Hornet* and *Enterprise*, but that *Yorktown* had been severely damaged in their attack. Yamaguchi therefore concluded that, if *Yorktown* had been made non-operational, it left only two US carriers to contend with. In the event he launched ten torpedo-bombers and six fighters – all he could muster, led by Lieutenant Tomonaga who, with his badly damaged plane, knew he was on a one-way mission. Unknown to him, however, within two hours *Yorktown* was back in business again, making a steady 18 knots.

By 15.00 Tomonaga's force was over the damaged US carrier but, as she appeared to be steaming normally, he assumed that this was a different carrier. He could not believe it was *Yorktown*. Another vicious dog-fight ensued, with the American Wildcat fighters shooting down many of the enemy's planes. A few succeeded in getting through, led by Tomonaga, who, realizing he could never get back, dived onto *Yorktown*'s deck and blew himself up.

The surviving eight planes managed to launch two torpedoes, which scored direct hits on *Yorktown*'s hull. These were the fatal blows and, although still afloat, she was a dying ship.

Even while *Yorktown* was being hit, one of her scout planes, which had earlier taken off on reconnaissance, reported that it had at last found the fourth Japanese carrier, Yamaguchi's *Hiryu*. Fletcher immediately ordered a strike to be launched from *Enterprise* and *Hornet*. A total of forty Dauntless dive-bombers set off from the two carriers.

Preceding them and many miles in advance, some of the remnants of Tomonaga's shell-torn planes were landing on their home carrier, *Hiryu*. There the exhausted crews were told to refuel and re-arm ready to take off again by dusk to make another attack on the US carriers.

While these preparations were being made, the Dauntless dive-bombers arrived overhead. The surprise was complete, for *Hiryu* crew had no radar to warn them. One or two Zeros managed to take off, and the anti-aircraft gunners rushed to their stations. Through the flak the dive-bombers dived to within a few hundred feet of the carrier's decks and released their bombs. Four 500-pound bombs landed square on the flight-deck, mainly among fuel-filled aircraft waiting to take off. Destruction was total. As the aircraft exploded, hundreds of pieces of flaming tailpieces and wings flew across the flight-deck, igniting fuel trucks and bomb-carriers. In only a few minutes *Hiryu* was enveloped in flames and torn apart by repeated explosions. So intense were the fires and so extensive was the damage that the remaining Dauntless planes turned their attention to the accompanying cruisers and destroyers.

The last remaining few of Tomonaga's flagging aircraft, now desperately short of fuel, arrived over the carrier to find it ablaze from end to end. In a last zealous effort they tried to attack the US dive-bombers, despite their rapidly diminishing petrol supply. One by one, as tanks ran dry, the Japanese planes crashed into the sea.

The final hours of *Hiryu* produced a macabre end to the huge carrier. After the order to abandon ship, Admiral Yamaguchi and Captain Kaku lashed themselves to the helm and waited for the final plunge. It came with the scuttling of the ship by an accompanying destroyer which fired two torpedoes into her.

As Admiral Fletcher received the news of *Hiryu*'s destruction, he must have breathed a sigh of satisfaction, for, although *Yorktown* had been mortally wounded, four of the six great Japanese carriers that had launched the attack on Pearl Harbor had been sent to the bottom. The first retributive instalment for that massacre had been paid. In the ensuing Pacific War, worse much worse was to follow, when the Japanese nation would wish that their generals had never started a war against the industrial might of the United States of America, a war they could never hope to win.

Although *Yorktown* somehow managed to stay afloat, even after receiving two torpedoes, Captain Buckmaster gave the order to 'abandon ship' at 15.00 hours in case she might capsize. Valiant attempts were made to keep her afloat, including a salvage party from the accompanying destroyer *Hammann*. Tragically, a Japanese submarine commanded by Commander Yahachi Tanabe slipped through the defending destroyer screen and fired a torpedo into *Hammann* and two more into *Yorktown* before effecting his escape through a heavy depth-charge attack. Soon after 05.00 on 7 June *Yorktown* gently rolled over and sank.

When Yamamoto in his flagship *Yamato* finally received the news that all Nagumo's task force of four carriers had been destroyed, his Oriental inscrutability was sorely tried. His great dream of a Pacific conquest was shattered.

But, however great the setback, Yamamoto was still determined that his campaign to overrun Midway must be accomplished. First, with his armada of battleships, cruisers and destroyers, which were mainly unscathed, it would be necessary to eliminate whatever was left of the American task force in a night engagement. To this end he signalled Hosogaya's Aleutian force to the north and Kondo's fleet to the south to join him. But unknown to him, Fletcher's task force was retiring eastward, determined not to be caught in a night encounter with Yamamoto's battle fleet in which the aircraft could play no part; also Rear-Admiral Nagumo, who had transferred his flag to *Nagara* after *Akagi* had been sunk, was disinclined to share Yamamoto's enthusiasm for a further engagement. Having lost his four carriers and watched helplessly as hundreds of his men were slaughtered, and having barely escaped with his own life, he was in no mood to support what he considered was a rash decision.

And then came the final straw in this saga of the two ingredients of fate and luck. At dawn on 7 June one of the scout planes from the heavy cruiser *Chikuma*, flying through high cloud, sighted the dying *Yorktown*, still adrift, and some distance away the *Enterprise* and *Hornet*. To avoid an encounter with American fighters on patrol, he was forced to take evasive action in the thick cloud. Some minutes later, emerging from cover, he found *Enterprise* and *Hornet* a second time and assumed they were two other carriers. He at once reported sighting five operational carriers. Aboard *Nagara*, Admiral Nagumo was thrown into utter confusion. He was certain that one American carrier had been destroyed, yet here was his scout plane reporting five functional carriers, presumably armed with torpedo bombers, dive-bombers and fighters.

For the dispirited Nagumo, the odds were far too great. It was defeat. He knew it, his officers knew it, and apparently in Tokyo the general staff knew it. He at once dispatched a signal to Admiral

Yamamoto informing him that the enemy's complement of ships now amounted to 'five carriers, six cruisers and fifteen destroyers' and that he was retiring to the north-west. When the admiral and his officers received the message, they were furious. Yamamoto immediately relieved Nagumo of his command and, still intent on his Midway campaign, signalled his northern and southern forces to rendezvous with him as soon as possible to prepare to engage on a decisive night surface action.

But as the night wore on it became increasingly clear that there would be little hope of contacting the American force before dawn. All hope of the advantage of night encounter was therefore abandoned, and with that option gone Yamamoto considered the possibility of an all-out daylight attack on Midway by battleships and cruisers. His combined massive gunpower from all his ships would clear the way for the landing of Kondo's occupation force. This hare-brained scheme, enthusiastically propounded by his operations officer, was immediately shot down by one of Yamamoto's chief advisers, Admiral Ugaki. He was quick to point out that aircraft from Midway plus dive-bombers and torpedo bombers from the US carriers and defending submarines would destroy their fleet long before they could get within striking distance of Midway.

Although the 'save-face' image was dominant among many of the Japanese staff, Yamamoto, after careful consideration, decided to cancel the Midway operation. He ordered all his forces to withdraw and rendezvous for the long voyage back to Japan. The admiral had at last accepted defeat.

By now, however, four heavy cruisers, part of Kondo's occupational force, were only 100 miles from Midway, and when the order to withdraw was received they turned for home. They were spotted by the American submarine *Tambor*, which surfaced to form a better assessment of the situation. As the leading Japanese ship *Kumano* saw the submarine, she immediately signalled for sharp evasive action.

In the panic that ensued, the last ship, *Mogami*, collided with her sister-ship, *Mikuma*. The bows of *Mogami* were badly damaged, and one of *Mikuma*'s oil tanks was ruptured, leaving a tell-tale slick of oil over many miles. Despite the damage, the two ships, with a small destroyer escort, limped their way eastward towards the rendezvous position signalled by Yamamoto. It was not long before twelve bombers from Midway found the ships and subjected them to a devastating attack. The leading US aircraft, hit by an anti-aircraft shell, not only dropped its bomb directly onto the cruiser but smashed into one of *Mikuma*'s turrets. Then more dive-bombers from *Enterprise* arrived, to score repeated hits on the two cruisers. *Mikuma* received the worst of the attacks and minutes later turned over and sank rapidly, with a thousand men aboard her. Although *Mogami* managed to escape, she was so badly damaged that she took no further part in the war for nearly two years.

Six hundred miles to the west, Yamamoto gathered his fleet around him, rendezvoused with his fuel tankers and began the long haul back to Hiroshima Bay, over 2,000 miles away, trying to console himself with the thought that, although he had lost the Battle of Midway, he had not lost the war.

To the east, Fletcher and Spruance decided to call it a day and, with their task forces around *Enterprise* and *Hornet*, their ships running short of fuel and their crews exhausted, they set course for Midway.

The Battle of Midway Island has always been looked upon as the anvil upon which the Japanese sword of power was broken. It also marked the end of the transition period between the old battleship-dominated era and the advent of the aircraft-carrier, which was to affect and motivate the course of future naval warfare. Even the shrewd imperial-minded Yamamoto was forced to retire from the scene of battle without having fired a shot once he had lost his carrier force.

From this point onwards and only six months after Pearl Harbor, the Japanese were forced onto the defensive. Their naval superiority had been broken and some semblance of balance restored between the two powers – though it would take another two to three years and the loss of many thousands of lives to bring Japan to her knees and surrender without condition. Against overwhelming odds the Americans had gained a decisive victory worthy of the best traditions of naval history.

Comparative losses and gains are worth noting. For the loss of one carrier, one destroyer, 180 planes and 300 men, the Americans had destroyed four Japanese carriers, one heavy cruiser and one oil tanker, damaged another heavy cruiser and three destroyers and inflicted losses of 330 aircraft and 3,500 men.

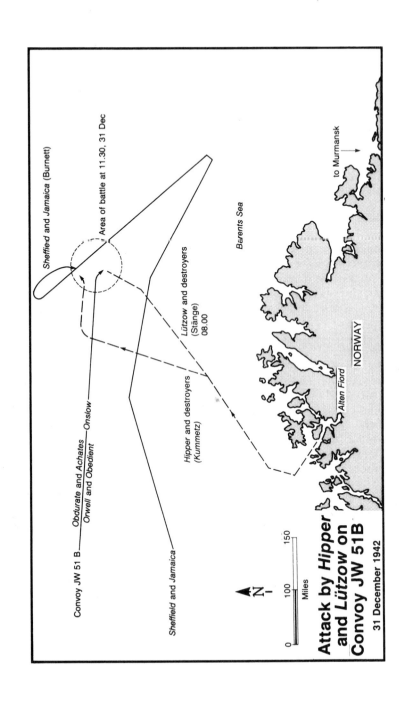

Attack by *Hipper* and *Lützow* on Convoy JW 51B

31 December 1942

Convoy JW 51 B ——— Obdurate and Achates ———— Onslow
Orwell and Obedient

Sheffield and Jamaica (Burnett)

Area of battle at 11.30, 31 Dec

Lützow and destroyers
(Stänge)
08.00

Berents Sea

Hipper and destroyers
(Kummetz)

Sheffield and Jamaica

NORWAY

Alten Fiord

to Murmansk

N

Miles
0    100   150

# 15  Onslow's *Valiant Defence*

*In World War II the 2,000-mile convoy route through the Arctic Ocean from Iceland to Murmansk in north Russia soon became known as 'the Gateway to Hell'. German warships, U-boats, dive-bombers and torpedo bombers could attack at will from their close bases in Norway. But there were other factors which made this voyage a nightmare to be endured. In weather terms it is one of the most tempestuous sea areas in the world, with endless gales, snow, sleet and a sea of frightening waves. Unless a man was rescued from the water quickly, he would be dead in minutes. On the Arctic convoy run no man in his right mind ever undressed; the bulky garments he had to wear would keep him afloat for a few moments.*

*This is the story of a little ship, the destroyer* HMS Onslow, *which, under the command of Captain Robert St Vincent Sherbrooke and in company with its five equally small consorts, in defence of a convoy held off the might of the battleship* Lützow, *the heavy cruiser* Hipper *and six large destroyers. Captain Sherbrooke's gallant action and his outstanding devotion to duty earned him the award of the Victoria Cross.*

In November 1939 Adolf Hitler, in one of his long, vehement speeches to the German masses, declared, 'I shall strike and not capitulate. The fate of the Reich depends on me alone ... I am setting all my achievements on a gamble. I have to choose between victory and destruction. I choose victory ... I shall think only of the victory of my people. I shall shrink from nothing and shall destroy everyone who is opposed to me. There will be no capitulation to the powers outside ...'

It was the speech of a demented man loudly banging a drum proclaiming victory, yet aware of a still, small voice within, warning him that defeat was a possibility.

Less than two years later he lamely remarked to his staff officers, 'If I do not get the oil of Maikop and Grozny [the Caucasus], then I must end this war.'

By the end of 1941 Germany was beginning to feel the effects of a reversal of her fortunes. When Hitler launched 'total war' against the Soviet Union in June 1941, he made a supreme effort to gain a quick verdict in that campaign before the USA and Britain formed an alliance against him. He had gambled on a short war confined to the European conflict, but if, as it now seemed clear, he would have to commit himself to a prolonged struggle against the powers of the USA, Britain and a stubborn Soviet Union, it was essential that he reach and secure the oil of the Caucasus. The simple truth was that Germany was running short of oil to maintain her vast mechanized army, her navy and air force. In the winter battle before Moscow, Soviet resistance had stopped his drive, and he now had to rely on supplies from the Romanian oilfields. But as the campaign grew more bitter and his lines of communication extended, even that source failed to meet his demands.

The Army's needs took precedence, which left the navy in a serious situation. In November 1941 a frustrated Grand Admiral Raeder, Commander-in-Chief of the German Navy, presented Hitler with an updated situation of naval oil resources. The total stocks in hand for both the German and Italian Navies were only 410,000 tons. But even worse was the revelation that, while the monthly requirement for both navies was 200,000 tons, total monthly supplies were only 84,000 tons. Such was the shortage of fuel-oil at this time that Atlantic operations planned for *Tirpitz, Scharnhorst* and *Gneisenau* were postponed. By December Raeder was reported as saying, 'The oil situation is very critical.'

By the spring of 1942 the monthly naval allocation was 61,000 tons, whereas the minimum requirements were 180,000 tons. This reduction caused an intolerable restriction on the mobility of German ships. Even worse news was to follow, for by now the output from the Romanian oilfields was declining. Wear and tear had lowered their yield from $8\frac{1}{2}$ million tons to just over $5\frac{1}{2}$ million, and half of this was needed by Romania herself for her essential economy. It was clear that, if Hitler's armies failed to reach the rich oil fields of the Caucasus, he would not have sufficient supplies to wage naval and air war against the Western Allies on a scale to ensure defeat. As a result, Raeder had to issue orders which restricted naval movements, and throughout 1941 all operations were controlled by the importance of the engagement and where the possibility of a successful result justified the expenditure of fuel.

By the close of 1942 Raeder had become so impatient at seeing his ships swinging idly at their moorings that he made a strong appeal to Hitler to allow his vessels to take offensive action in the Arctic against supplies of war material reaching Murmansk. Expressing his doubts as to the outcome of such an operation, Hitler reluctantly agreed. Raeder, delighted at the prospect of at last proving to the Führer the navy's worth to the nation, set in motion a plan he had already formulated: a concerted strike against the next Soviet convoy travelling east, employing the heavy cruiser *Hipper* and the pocket battleship *Lützow*, with a number of destroyers as escort.

In Britain, after much discussion at the Admiralty, plans were drawn up to sail a large convoy of thirty ships with a strong escort similar to that given to the heavily protected convoy PQ 18. But Admiral Tovey, Commander-in-Chief of the Home Fleet, was against the proposal. He argued that large convoys could easily be split up by the sudden and violent gales which tormented the Barents Sea. Once that happened, the unprotected merchant ships would be scattered over a large area and give the enemy an opportunity to sink these prizes without opposition. After lengthy discussions it was agreed that the convoy should be sailed in two sections, each of about fifteen ships and each escorted by seven destroyers and some smaller escort ships.

This plan was put into operation, and on 15 December the first section of fifteen merchant ships and a tanker bearing the new code number *JW 51A*, accompanied by its destroyer escort, left Iceland for Murmansk, with close cover being provided by the cruisers *Sheffield* and *Jamaica* and two destroyers under the command of Rear-Admiral R.L. Burnett, who carried his flag in *Sheffield*. The commander-in-chief, in the battleship *King George V*, accompanied by the cruiser *Berwick* and three destroyers, set out across the Arctic Sea to provide distant cover in the event of a break-out by any of Germany's capital ships.

The enemy had no knowledge of the convoy's movement, and it had a safe and uneventful voyage. Following Admiralty orders Burnett kept sixty miles to the south of the convoy after passing Bear Island and arrived at the Kola Inlet on 24 December, one day ahead of the convoy.

The other half of the convoy *JW 51B*, which sailed on 22 December, consisted of fourteen ships with an escort of six destroyers, *Onslow* (commanded by Captain Robert St Vincent Sherbrooke, senior officer of the escort force), *Obedient, Orwell, Obdurate, Oribi* and *Achates*, the corvettes *Hyderabad* and *Rhododendron*, the minesweeper *Bramble* and the trawlers *Vizalma* and *Northern Gem*. Following, providing distant cover, was the battleship *Anson*, flying the flag of Vice-Admiral Sir Bruce Fraser, accompanied by the cruiser *Cumberland* and three destroyers.

When the convoy was midway between Bear Island and Jan Mayen Island, a great gale overtook it, and five ships out on the port wing of the column became separated. The gale was of such intensity that it seemed impossible that any man-made structure could survive the weight and ferocity of such seas. Waves became hills of green, relentless water crashing down on the ships as though to engulf them. And with it came the icing, turning masts and superstructures into improbable Christmas trees. Blizzard snowstorms converted the vessels into power-propelled icebergs. Conditions below decks were dreadful, with water pouring down open shafts to saturate everything, and even hardened seamen were sea-sick. In such savage conditions it was not surprising that ships became detached from the main body. In an effort to retrieve the strays, the little minesweeper *Bramble* (Commander H.T. Rust DSO, RN) was dispatched to look for them.

Sherbrooke was not only gravely concerned at the savagery of the gale but more so that the detachment of part of his convoy should have happened at a point at which the enemy would probably mount an attack. Here the passage between the ice barrier to the north, and the enemy air and naval bases in north Norway to the south, was at its narrowest, allowing the convoy little room to manoeuvre. There was another factor which worried Sherbrooke: the guns of his destroyers were icing up, demanding constant and vigorous efforts to keep them operational.

But no gale can last for ever, and by 31 December the storm had moderated to occasional snow showers. With the relief of finding themselves again on an even keel, no sign of the enemy and three of the five strays rejoining, all seemed to be going well.

However, unknown to Sherbrooke, an enemy submarine on patrol had sighted the eastward-bound convoy and reported its movements and constitution to Norway. When this vital information reached the German naval staff, it seemed to Admiral Raeder that this provided the sort of easy success he had looked for, and as a result he issued orders for the sailing of a raiding force of the pocket battleship *Lützow*, of 12,000 tons, and the heavy cruiser *Admiral Hipper*, of 14,000 tons, and six destroyers. While the tactical engagement was to be exercised by Vice-Admiral Kummetz, flying his flag in *Hipper*, he was severely restrained in his strategy by Hitler's inhibiting observations that he was to avoid confrontation with superior forces and that 'caution' was to be the watchword in any naval operation that might ensue.

Having been given the approximate position of the British convoy, Kummetz sailed from Alten Fiord on 30 December with a divided sense of deference to his superiors: to demonstrate his loyalty to the Führer by not placing his ship in danger, and to pacify Grand Admiral Raeder by achieving a substantial victory. Such a conflict was unlikely to provide him with any clear-cut decision he might have to make in the task that lay ahead. In theory, his plan of attack was reasonably simple and strategically sound. *Hipper* and *Lützow* with their destroyers would approach the convoy from two directions. While one would engage the escorts to draw them away from the convoy, the other would move in to attack and destroy the merchant ships.

The powerful armament of the German forces was out of all comparison to the puny defensive gun-power of the British escorts around the convoy. The enemy mounted a total fire-power of six 11-inch, eight 8-inch, thirty-two 5.9-inch, fifteen 5-inch and eighteen 4-inch guns. Against this, all the British force could muster was a total of twenty 4-inch and eight 4.7-inch guns, the latter, dating back to the First World War, mounted on the destroyers *Onslow* and *Achates*. Apart from this overriding superiority, *Hipper* and *Lützow* were protected with hardened steel armour plating four and five inches thick respectively, against which the shells of the British ships would have little effect.

Only an hour or so after Kummetz sailed, he received a signal from German Naval Command which must have made him despondent, especially on the eve of engaging in an operation of

war: 'Contrary to the operational order regarding contact against
the enemy, use caution even against enemy of equal strength
because it is undesirable for the cruisers to take on great risks.' It
provides an insight into the extent to which Hitler's restrictive
policy had affected German Naval Command. It seemed that the
little corporal of World War I had suddenly acquired the
professionalism and expertise of a grand admiral, field marshal and
air force commander all in one fell sweep. As will be seen by later
developments, had Kummetz been given freedom of movement and
the prerogative to use his initiative, he might well have achieved
success, although defeating the puny British escort force would
hardly have constituted a glorious naval victory.

While these events were taking place, Admiral Burnett had sailed
from the Kola Inlet on the 27th with his cruisers *Sheffield* and
*Jamaica*, heading west towards the oncoming convoy, with the
intention of giving it close cover when they rendezvoused. The
intervention of the gale had, however, delayed the arrival of the
convoy, upsetting all pre-arranged calculations. In fact, *JW 51B*
was nearly thirty miles south and fifty miles west of the estimated
rendezvous position. Instead, therefore, of finding himself at the
rear of the convoy as he had planned, Burnett was over thirty miles
north of it. This unforeseeable state of affairs was to have an
important influence on strategic decisions in the naval engagement
about to follow.

In the Arctic at this time of the year there are roughly only two or
three hours of dissipated twilight in the forenoon, but good weather
conditions might give a visibility of between five and ten miles. This
was the time at which Kummetz planned to make his attack. He
had no wish to engage in a night action, for that would be the time
most favourable to the British destroyers to launch torpedo attacks,
and furthermore it would be more difficult to distinguish between
destroyers and merchantmen. In accordance with the plan of
operation, he decided to approach the convoy from well astern as
dawn broke, then race eastwards, his destroyers spread well apart,
and thus overtake it. The original grand strategy would then be
implemented whereby his force would divide and attack from two
directions in the expectation that the British escorts would be
drawn towards whichever of his ships first made contact.

That night *Hipper* and *Lützow* were ordered to open out and be
seventy miles apart at dawn. *Hipper* would be to the north with her
six destroyers, *Lützow* to the south. Just after 07.00 *Hipper*,

steering north-east, passed some twenty miles astern of the convoy and detached the destroyer *Eckholdt* to speed forward to investigate two shadowy shapes, while *Hipper* turned bow on to reduce her own silhouette. When thirty minutes later no report had been received from *Eckholdt*, Kummetz ordered that *Hipper* be steered due east and reduce speed, as there was as yet insufficient light to distinguish the enemy ships clearly. Meanwhile, following orders, *Eckholdt*, with *Beitzen* and *Z–29*, continued to shadow the convoy while the other three destroyers, *Riedel, Z–30* and *Z–31*, moved south to join *Lützow*. Both these groups were heavy units of the destroyer flotilla, each armed with four 5.9-inch guns.

As the first feeble light of dawn penetrated the area, the situation could be summed up as follows:

*JW 51B* steering east, with an escort of five destroyers, two corvettes and a trawler, was in a position about 200 miles north-west of the Kola Inlet; to the north and thirty miles distant was Burnett, with his two cruisers, with little idea of the convoy's position; fifteen miles north-east of the convoy was the little minesweeper *Bramble*, still trying to find the missing ships. None of these groups was aware of the other's position or of the peril that was lurking on the port quarter of the convoy – the battle-cruiser *Hipper* with her destroyers – or that on the starboard quarter, the pocket-battleship *Lützow* and her consorts.

At about 09.00 *Obdurate* and *Hyderabad* sighted two destroyers to the west and, following Sherbrooke's orders to investigate, the unknown ships opened fire with their superior guns at a range of four miles and then retreated. No damage was done, and both British destroyers fell back towards the convoy. Although Sherbrooke had not seen the big German capital ships, he was convinced that a major battle was imminent and, signalling to *Obdurate, Orwell* and *Obedient* to join him, he raced at full speed to the rear of the convoy, its most vulnerable point and its best defensive position against attack.

At 09.33 Kummetz decided to launch his assault, but he now realized that his destroyers were positioned somewhere in the vicinity of the convoy, and in this feeble light it was impossible to distinguish between friend and foe. He dared not open fire for fear of hitting his own ships, and so he had to wait until some form of recognition was established. Minutes later the identity of one ship was determined beyond question, when the British destroyer *Achates* was seen racing along with black smoke pouring from her funnels, laying a thick smoke-screen along the horizon blotting out the line of convoy ships. *Hipper* at once turned to allow all her eight 8-inch guns to fire broadsides but, although there were near-misses, *Achates* escaped damage.

Sherbrooke realized that his destroyers were in a most dangerous position, for *Obdurate* and *Obedient* were some distance away on the further side of the convoy and had had no time to concentrate their forces. The odds were fearful, for he had only *Orwell* with him at the time, and he was well aware that the three German destroyers alone were a formidable foe, with far greater fire-power than anything his own ships could muster. And then, to cap everything, the heavy cruiser *Hipper*, with her big guns and heavily armoured hull, arrived.

Theoretically, in terms of gun-power the German force could annihilate the British escorts, but they had not reckoned on Sherbrooke's defiance, his courage and his shrewdness in defence. Undaunted by this overwhelming superiority, Sherbrooke in *Onslow*, followed by *Orwell*, headed straight for *Hipper* with her two forward guns blazing away at a range of five miles. Assuming that the British destroyer was about to deliver a torpedo attack, *Hipper* turned away.

This sudden deviation and partial retreat endorsed Sherbrooke's conviction that the one thing the battle-cruiser most feared was a torpedo strike. This then was to be Sherbrooke's best attack/defence weapon in the one-sided conflict. *Hipper*, however, had remarkable manoeuvrability, and to ensure a hit on the German, *Onslow* and *Orwell* would have to fire all their torpedoes at once at their greatest speed. Should they miss, Sherbrooke would have shot his bolt and would be at the mercy of the enemy's big guns. The enemy destroyers, however, were nowhere in sight and, fearing that they were at that time speeding around to attack the convoy from a different quarter, he ordered *Obedient* and *Obdurate* to return to their stations while with *Onslow* and *Orwell* he protected the rear of the convoy from the attention of the German cruiser.

At about 10.00 *Hipper* returned to deliver another strike, but knowing the cruiser's weakness, Sherbrooke launched a mock torpedo attack, racing in at full speed, swinging the helm hard over, wheeling away, giving every indication that a spread of torpedoes had been fired. In desperation Kummetz broke off the action and turned northwards. It was the only worthwhile card Sherbrooke held in his hand, bluff, but a bluff that paid off. Kummetz had always dreaded the thought of a torpedo attack, especially in this half-light where the trails were barely visible. And foremost in his mind was that last-minute cautionary signal from Norway: '... it is undesirable for the cruisers to take any great risks.' It was this that governed his tactics from now on. Breaking off the engagement, he laid down a curtain of fire from his after turrets on *Onslow* and sped away, albeit temporarily.

It was not long before *Hipper* returned, delivering occasional lunges at the convoy but being repeatedly frustrated by Sherbrooke's mock torpedo runs. However, to profit constantly from the ruse was another matter, and there was always the possibility that the German might call his bluff.

All this time *Achates* had been racing around the convoy, laying an effective smoke-screen which prevented *Hipper* from spotting the fall of her shots.

It was during this period in the battle that Sherbrooke received a signal from Admiral Burnett, now only some twenty miles away, that his cruisers *Sheffield* and *Jamaica* were racing south at full speed to his assistance. But how desperately Sherbrooke needed their presence, for in the action of speeding round to attack, spray bursting over the forward deck had frozen the two forward guns, rendering them useless. Now, with *Orwell*'s, there were but six operational guns with which to face the enemy.

In the meantime, where was the battleship *Lützow*? Whether by miscalculation or from reluctance to engage in an Arctic battle influenced and dominated by German Naval Command's cautionary signal, (she was almost thirty miles away) the reason is unknown. This at a time when she should have been co-ordinating with *Hipper* to attack the convoy from the south while from the north-west the battle-cruiser was trying to draw the British escorts away from the merchantmen.

Once again *Hipper* returned, firing her main armament, trying to target the convoy ships. But, swinging away to allow her only two guns to bear, *Onslow* opened fire at a range of nearly eight miles and scored three direct hits. Although it did little damage, it was not to Kummetz's liking, and under cover of a smoke-screen he turned *Hipper* away. Minutes later the cruiser re-appeared and swung to port to allow all her 8-inch and most of her 4-inch guns to train on the two British destroyers. Up to this point *Onslow* and *Orwell* had indeed been fortunate, but this inequality in fire power was too much for them.

There was another factor. *Hipper* was now loading her guns with high-explosive charges which even from near-misses were lethal against the thin steel plating of the destroyers. As shells flew over and around *Onslow*, Sherbrooke must have been wondering how much longer he could maintain these thrust-and-parry tactics before his ships were overwhelmed. Soon Burnett's cruisers would arrive, but until these heavily gunned vessels appeared, the protection of the convoy was his responsibility, even though it meant fighting to the death.

And then came disaster, for suddenly *Hipper* found *Onslow*'s range. Four 8-inch shells landed in quick succession, causing immense damage and many casualties. The bombardment obliterated the two forward guns, and a massive sheet of flame enveloped the bridge, splinters of steel slicing through the superstructure. One of the many casualties was Sherbrooke himself: an eye was torn out of its socket to hang down his cheek, and he suffered other facial injuries. Many men would have collapsed under such pain and the loss of so much blood, but not Sherbrooke. From the burned and blackened bridge peppered with shrapnel holes, he continued to direct operations.

Now that *Hipper* had found the range, Sherbrooke realized that the very next salvo would probably obliterate the ship. He immediately ordered *Onslow* to make heavy smoke, turn in a half-circle and hide in the billowing cloud. It was as well he did, for the next flight of shells fell just short of the gallant little ship.

With *Onslow* obscured in the cloud of her protective smokescreen, *Hipper* trained her guns on *Orwell*. As shells fell all around, her commanding officer, Commander Austen, raced back towards the crippled *Onslow* and made further smoke to protect his leader and himself. The situation at this point was nothing less than critical. As his was the only ship effectively positioned to face the German cruiser, should he race out and launch his torpedoes, which might well mean a suicidal mission, or should he maintain his protective screen around *Onslow*? Moments later the choice was taken out of his hands, for *Hipper* was seen to veer away to the east.

Why Kummetz should have abandoned his attack at the very moment when victory was within his grasp is a mystery. *Onslow* as a fighting unit had been rendered useless, and his own gunnery was now so accurate that it was only a matter of time before he could eliminate the remaining escorts and, with *Lützow*, sink the convoy at leisure.

In *Onslow*, Sherbrooke was eventually persuaded to go to his cabin, where the surgeon lieutenant-commander did what he could by the light of a lamp to staunch the blood and ease the pain. Despite his wound, Sherbrooke insisted on maintaining control of his ship and of the general battle situation.

*Onslow* was indeed in a sorry state: her guns were destroyed, all her forecastle area was on fire, shrapnel had punctured the engine and boiler-room, and she was listing to port. So bad were the fire and smoke from the forward deck that the bridge became untenable, and this was followed by news that one of the two boiler-rooms was on fire, with water flooding in through a shell hole. Sherbrooke now ordered Lieutenant-Commander D. Kinloch, the commanding officer of *Obedient*, to take command of the flotilla, and Lieutenant-Commander T. Marchand to take command of *Onslow*. To support him, Kinloch signalled the other two destroyers to join. It was as well he did, for at 10.45 *Hipper* returned to the attack, accompanied by two destroyers. All that Kinloch could do was to copy the tactics Sherbrooke had earlier employed, racing towards the cruiser, pretending to launch torpedoes and turning away into her own smoke-screen.

All this time *Achates* had been racing up and down, faithfully making smoke to cover the convoy, but now she also became the target. In minutes she was hit by a rain of shells. Apart from extensive damage to the boiler-room which reduced her speed, killing forty of her crew, one of the shells demolished the bridge, killing her commanding officer, Lieutenant-Commander A.H. Johns. Although suffering such crippling damage, she bravely tried to continue her smoke-laying assignment to protect the convoy. Her second-in-command, Lieutenant Peyton-Jones, now took command and continued the operation until the engagement was over. But later that day such was the damage received that she capsized and sank, with the loss of sixty of her crew, eighty being saved by the trawler *Northern Gem*.

In the meantime, the three remaining destroyers, *Obedient*, *Orwell* and *Obdurate*, under the direction of Kinloch, continued to harass the German cruiser by repeatedly thrusting forward in mock attacks and firing their little guns in defiance, like small terriers yapping at a growling lion. In these exchanges *Hipper* kept turning away, but in one of the manoeuvres she happened to come upon the little minesweeper *Bramble*, who it will be remembered, was on her own, searching for the missing merchant vessels. *Bramble* stood no chance: *Hipper*, with her heavy guns, moved in and annihilated the little ship.

All this while, *Lützow*, with her three destroyers, had been steadily creeping up on the convoy from the south. Now the corvette *Rhododendron* signalled Kinloch that a capital ship was closing in from that direction. Minutes later *Lützow* began shelling the rear ships of the merchant fleet. For Captain Stänge, the commanding officer of *Lützow*, it was the easiest of targets, for on that side of the convoy there were no destroyers to challenge him. Kinloch must have viewed the situation with despair. The odds were bad enough before, but now he and his two consorts faced not only a cruiser but also a battleship and a total of six destroyers.

The arrival of *Lützow* had coincided with *Hipper*'s temporary absence and, calling upon his sister-ships, Kinloch led the destroyers at full speed across the rear of the convoy to the southern flank and there laid a thick smoke-screen between them and the new enemy, which confused *Lützow*'s targetry. To compound the issue, *Hipper*, with her destroyers, re-appeared and began shelling the convoy from a distance of only four miles. With the convoy on that side now fully exposed, Kinloch led his ships around in a tight half-circle, each with an enormous creaming bow-wave exhibiting that dramatic appearance of attack, to race back through the smoke to defend the northern flank. Hardly had *Hipper* began her bombardment than out of the murk stormed the three little British ships, again adopting Sherbrooke's tactics. But as *Hipper* turned away this time, she straddled *Obdurate* and *Obedient* with shells that caused much damage and many casualties. Despite the southern flank's being left defenceless, *Lützow* amazingly failed to push home her advantage, reporting to *Hipper* that, in the poor winter light, the drifting smoke and intermittent snow showers, it was impossible to distinguish between friend and foe.

To sum up the situation at this point in time: *Onslow* was useless as a fighting unit, *Obedient* and *Obdurate* were badly damaged, and *Achates* had been sunk. Of the five little ships, only *Orwell* remained unscathed.

In all the sea battles of World War II, never had the scales been so heavily balanced in favour of the enemy, but never had so much defiance, so much fortitude and courage been shown by the Royal Navy, placed in such a hopeless situation. However, at that moment, when all seemed lost, when extinction seemed inevitable, deliverance arrived with the approach of Admiral Burnett, his cruisers *Sheffield* and *Jamaica* moving at top speed.

Burnett had assumed that by approaching from the north he would have the advantage of being hidden in the darker horizon. As his ships neared, gun flashes lit up the sky, indicating that the British escorts were fighting a desperate battle to save the convoy. The lighter southern horizon was, however, a mass of smoke and flame, and Burnett could not go charging in without first identifying the enemy. As he advanced, he now had the advantage of spotting the German cruiser against the lighter sky-line before he was seen.

It was in the last of *Hipper*'s evasive actions from the British destroyers that she ran straight into the gunsights of the British cruisers. Burnett's strategy was reaping dividends, for the German was clearly silhouetted. Kummetz on the other hand completely failed to see the looming British ships until *Sheffield* and *Jamaica* opened fire with their 6-inch guns. The German admiral was taken completely by surprise, for it was seen that *Hipper*'s guns were trained to port still firing on the convoy, and before she could adjust to the new situation, four shells from *Sheffield* crashed into the ship. This was a reversal of fortunes and for Kummetz a different kind of war. He was having to take a dose of his own medicine. The grand strategy to annihilate *JW 51B*, which on paper had seemed so easy, was now turning sour. The British shells had caused much damage, flooding one of the boiler-rooms to the extent of putting it out of action and thereby reducing *Hipper*'s speed.

With the range established, *Sheffield* and *Jamaica* opened up with all their forward guns, causing more damage and starting fires in the aircraft hangar. The avenging pursuer had now become the pursued, and in desperation *Hipper* swung away to find refuge in the smoke-screen rapidly being laid down by her own destroyers.

There was much confusion in the engagement that followed, for the battle area erupted into a nebulous hell of shell-fire, smoke and snow clouds, with the British and German ships intermittently appearing and disappearing.

Two of *Hipper*'s accompanying destroyers suddenly appeared out of the murk ahead of the British cruisers. These were *Eckholdt* and *Beitzen*. The former was seen to be broadside on and in an ideal position to fire torpedoes at the leading *Sheffield*. It was a dangerous moment, and Burnett immediately ordered his ship to swing around and steer straight for the German, not only to comb a possible torpedo attack but to ram her. Racing in at almost point-blank range, *Sheffield*'s forward guns poured a devastating hail of shells into the destroyer, which had no chance of replying or even of survival. By the seventh salvo, the ship was a blazing wreck and rapidly sinking, and there was now no need to ram her.

Meanwhile *Beitzen* had become the target for *Jamaica*'s guns but managed to escape destruction by racing away and hiding behind her own smoke-screen. This engagement had created a diversion which allowed *Hipper* to speed off to the west in a desperate effort to escape, with the British cruisers following.

This left Burnett with two options: to go chasing after *Hipper* in the darkness of the Arctic night, with the possibility of a torpedo attack by destroyers, or to return to the undefended convoy. He chose the latter, for this was the primary purpose of convoy defence, to protect the merchant fleet, and he had no means of knowing if other units of the enemy might be preparing an attack.

But the battle of the Barents Sea was over. Kummetz had had enough. Licking his battle wounds, he recalled his destroyers and *Lützow* and set course for Alten Fiord, no doubt wondering if Grand Admiral Raeder and the Führer would consider the engagement an ignominious failure.

On the British side, although Sherbrooke's forces had suffered badly, he and his destroyers had fought off a far superior enemy force and saved the convoy. Despite the overwhelming odds, they had bluffed the German ship throughout the action, and with the arrival of *Sheffield* and *Jamaica* the enemy had been forced to withdraw smarting from the engagement. The outcome was excellently evaluated by Admiral Tovey in his report to the Admiralty: 'That an enemy force of at least one pocket battleship, one heavy cruiser and six destroyers with all the advantage of surprise and concentration, should be held off for four hours by five destroyers and driven from the field by two six-inch cruisers without any loss to the convoy is most creditable and satisfactory.'

One of the most 'satisfactory' results of the engagement was that such was the damage inflicted on *Hipper* she was never again employed in an operational capacity and the enemy had lost one destroyer and had another damaged. There was no doubt that the reason for the British success lay in the time-proven maxim that, 'attack is the best defence', which Sherbrooke had employed with the feeble resources at his command.

In justice to Kummetz, however, his offensive operation was always controlled by the defensive restrictions imposed upon him by German Naval Command under the influence of Hitler. On the other hand, it was not justifiable for Kummetz to blame the failure of his enterprise on the poor weather, as he did, for, after all, the British had had to cope with the same conditions. But there were other factors which contributed to the failure. The behaviour of the German destroyers compared to the courage, resolution and initiative of their British opponents had been deplorable. The apathy and vacillation exhibited by Captain Stänge of *Lützow* in not supporting *Hipper*'s action at the crucial moment had ruined the great plan which on paper had seemed unassailable. Furthermore, Kummetz had failed in his assessment of the battle situation by not knowing when victory was within his grasp.

In Germany, at Hitler's headquarters, the result of the engagement produced exceptional repercussions. At the time when Kummetz was shepherding his disconsolate force back to Norway, an intercepted radio message from a British source claimed that a large German cruiser had been damaged and a destroyer sunk. Such had been Raeder's assurance that his plan could not fail that Hitler had made preparations to claim a great New Year's Day victory. When the result of the action failed to reach him from either Kummetz or Raeder before the receipt of the British transmission, his rage knew no bounds. When the news finally arrived that his ships had failed to interrupt the British convoy, that *Eckholdt* had been sunk and that his ships had scurried back to Norway with damage that would further delay engagements for some time, he was incensed. Later, when Raeder and Hitler met, the latter, who had been brooding on the matter, exploded with one of his most outrageous edicts of the war: 'The fleet was a failure, it had never earned its keep, and as a result of this latest humiliating failure it had had its last chance. All the fleet was to be scrapped and all its guns and armour absorbed into land defence.'

In defence of his fleet Raeder put up a formidable argument. The scrapping of the naval vessels would be a victory gained by the British without firing a shot. But Hitler was adamant and sarcastically pointed out that, whenever the fleet went into battle, it always considered the odds to the point of timidity. This argument amounted to blind stupidity, for it was Hitler himself who had issued strict orders that his ships were not to take unnecessary risks. But it was all to no avail, and as a result Raeder tendered his resignation. Although shaken by the decision of his grand admiral, Hitler accepted and to succeed him selected Admiral Karl Dönitz.

But to return to *Onslow*: on the morning of 1 January the blackened and battered little destroyer, with a list of 14 degrees, slowly crept up the Kola Inlet to Murmansk, where Sherbrooke, badly wounded was transferred to hospital. It was during his convalescence that he was informed that the King had awarded him the Victoria Cross. In reply to the many congratulations from the officers and men of his flotilla he despatched the following signal: 'This award is a tribute to the force in general and I hope will be taken by the next of kin of those who lost their lives as some measure of their country's appreciation.'

# 16  The Destruction of Scharnhorst

*While the heavy battle-cruiser Scharnhorst, of 32,000 tons, remained in Alten Fiord, north Norway, she imposed a constant threat to the Allied convoys operating between Iceland and the north Russian port of Murmansk.*

*As the year 1943 drew to its close, intelligence reports reaching the Admiralty confirmed that Scharnhorst, accompanied by five large Narvik-class destroyers, had sailed north to intercept the east-bound convoy JW 55B.*

*To counter the threat and hopefully trap the German raider, Admiral Sir Bruce Fraser with units of the Home Fleet raced through the wild Arctic seas to intercept.*

*The sea battle that ensued when the two forces met marked the last occasion of a classic surface engagement in the mould of the First World War Battle of Jutland.*

In the early months of 1943 important changes in naval authority in both the British and German commands took place which were to have far-reaching effects on the eventual outcome of the sea war.

On the British side, the Commander-in-Chief, Admiral Sir John Tovey, handed over his command in May to Admiral Sir Bruce Fraser, a man whose tactical skill was outstanding. However, as far as available forces were concerned, he was in no better position than his predecessor. In August also the First Sea Lord, Admiral Sir Dudley Pound, resigned his post owing to ill-health and was succeeded by Admiral Sir Andrew Cunningham, who had commanded with such distinction in the Mediterranean theatre of war.

In the German command, Admiral Karl Dönitz had replaced Admiral Erich Raeder and succeeded where the latter had failed by

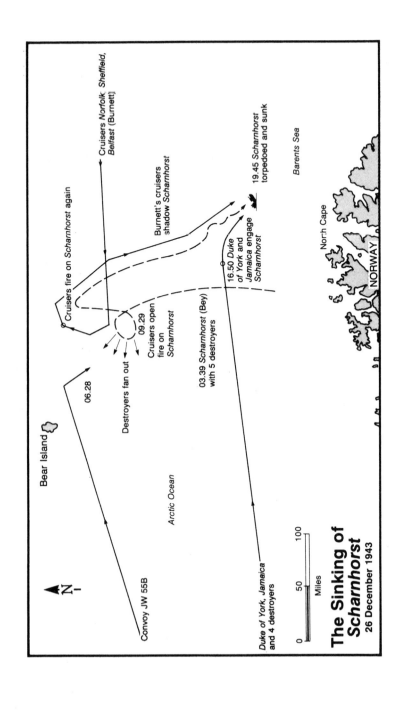

The Sinking of *Scharnhorst*
26 December 1943

N

Bear Island

Convoy JW 55B

Arctic Ocean

06.28

Destroyers fan out

09.29
Cruisers open fire on *Scharnhorst*

Cruisers fire on *Scharnhorst* again

Cruisers *Norfolk, Sheffield, Belfast* (Burnett)

Burnett's cruisers shadow *Scharnhorst*

03.39 *Scharnhorst* (Bey) with 5 destroyers

16.50 *Duke of York* and *Jamaica* engage *Scharnhorst*

19.45 *Scharnhorst* torpedoed and sunk

Barents Sea

North Cape

NORWAY

*Duke of York, Jamaica* and 4 destroyers

Miles
0    50    100

persuading the German Chancellor not to scrap the German fleet as Hitler had threatened. Intelligence reports reaching Admiralty in late March confirmed that the Germans had assembled, in Alten Fiord, northern Norway, a strong battle squadron comprising *Tirpitz*, *Lützow* and *Scharnhorst* – a battleship, pocket battleship and battle-cruiser, with the clear intention of attacking the convoys bound for the Soviet Union, with the coming of the long Arctic daylight hours. Because of this formidable concentration, the Admiralty insisted on the suspension of convoy traffic from Iceland to Murmansk during the summer months.

But there was another factor. The Battle of the Atlantic was reaching its climax, and convoys in this area were pleading for escorts which could be supplied only at the expense of the Arctic convoys. There was every justification for taking this line of action, for during March of that year increased German U-boat activity against the passage of Allied Atlantic convoy supplies had resulted in seventeen merchant ships with their valuable cargoes being sunk in only two days. In substance, Peter had to be robbed to pay Paul.

The temporary suspension of supplies to Murmansk almost created a diplomatic breakdown in Britain's relations with Stalin. It produced such discord that the Soviet Foreign Minister, Molotov, in a meeting with the British ambassador, Sir Stafford Cripps, 'insisted' upon the urgent resumption of the convoys and 'expected' that the British government would take the necessary measures within the next few days. It was this 'demand' that offended Churchill, for, as he stated in his reply to the Soviet leader, the supply of arms to the Soviet Union was not made under any terms of contract or bargain but rather as a declaration of Britain's solemn and earnest resolve. Despite the Soviet leader's reply, couched in the most uncivil terms, Churchill refused to be moved from his decision.

The arrival of the Arctic summer season, when there would be twenty-four hours of daylight, would expose British convoys and their escorts not only to the usual combination of dive-bombing, torpedo-bombing, U-boat and destroyer attacks but now, with German capital ships lurking in Norwegian fiords, ready to pounce, to likely annihilation. As a result, convoy movements would have to wait until November, when, with the arrival of the long Arctic nights, darkness would give some sort of protection. So it was that during the summer of 1943, while the heavy ships of the German Navy swung idly at their moorings, no Allied supplies reached the hard-pressed Soviet armies fighting on the Eastern Front. In the meantime, however, it allowed the Allies to build up massive supplies in the British Isles to mount the invasion of Normandy in June the following year, to relieve pressure on the Soviets.

In keeping with the declared British resolve, the winter convoys of 1943 started on 15 November. The first three, *JW 54A, JW 54B* and *JW 55A* sailed through to Murmansk without interference from the enemy; in fact, the Germans were probably unaware that convoys had been resumed. But by early December British intelligence had learned through decoded radio interception that German Naval Command had received information of convoy movement. It meant that, with units of the German battle squadron concentrated in northern Norway, it would need all the vigilance of the Home Fleet to prevent attacks by these heavy ships. So confident was Admiral Fraser that a raid by at least one of the German battle squadrons was imminent, probably one by *Scharnhorst*, that he rehearsed a number of night exercises in the battleship *Duke of York*, placing the cruiser *Jamaica* in the role of the enemy.

*Scharnhorst* was a battle-cruiser of some repute and considered one of the luckiest of Germany's heavy ships. She had escaped from the Norwegian engagement of 1940 and survived two Atlantic cruises, heavy bombing by the RAF, the Channel Dash and the breaker's yard. She was almost 2½ times larger than *Hipper*, having a displacement of 32,000 tons. Her impressive armament of nine 11-inch, twelve 5.9-inch, fourteen 4-inch and thirty-two anti-aircraft guns, and her complement of 1,800 men, established her as one of the most powerful warships the British might encounter.

At German Naval Command, the news that the Allies had resumed the convoy run to Murmansk stimulated Admiral Dönitz into action. At a meeting with Hitler on 20 December he informed the Führer that it was his intention to sail *Scharnhorst* with destroyers of the battle group in a bid to attack the next eastbound convoy. Hitler's reaction to the news appears to have been one of indifference, which seems odd in the light of his ranting edict twelve months earlier that, '... the fleet was a failure and would be scrapped'. Dönitz's enthusiasm, however, carried the day.

Perhaps it was this buoyant optimism that overruled and blurred the admiral's recollection of *Hipper*'s forlorn escapade twelve months earlier. He must have recognized that *Scharnhorst* would be operating in the same area under similar winter conditions. In the darkness of the Arctic nights British destroyers would have the advantage of delivering torpedo attacks. And there was always the weather, dominated by violent gales, blizzards, paralysing cold and giant seas. The possibility of even locating the convoy by submarine patrol or air reconnaissance in these conditions was severely reduced. And he would not have been unaware of British radar superiority, which could be of the greatest importance in any night engagement.

German Naval Command had developed into an unwieldy line of control between the German Admiralty and its fleet commander. In an important re-shuffle, Dönitz streamlined the chain of command by directing that movement orders should be passed directly from the Commander-in-Chief, Admiral Schniewind, to Vice-Admiral Kummetz, flag officer commanding the battle group at Alten Fiord.

There now occurred another development which was to have a dramatic impact upon the events about to take place. On the eve of the final decision to sail *Scharnhorst*, Kummetz was sent on prolonged sick-leave, and his place was taken by Flag Officer Destroyers, Rear-Admiral Erich Bey. Whether sickness was the real reason for replacing him or whether it was because of his unhappy experience and mishandled judgement when in command of *Hipper* a year earlier, we shall never know.

Bey's wartime sea experience had been occupied solely with the destroyer arm, and although he was a man of courage, his fervent trust that good luck would see him through did not mark him as one of the greatest German admirals of his time.

On 22 December a German reconnaissance aircraft reported a convoy of merchant ships and their escorts just off the Faroe Islands, sailing eastward – which was, in fact, convoy *JW 55B*. When Admiral Schniewind received the information, he brought his battle group to three hours steaming notice and moved his U-boats into position ready to move out for the attack.

*JW 55B* comprised nineteen merchant ships escorted by ten destroyers, *Impulsive, Scourge, Huron, Orwell, Iroquois, Haida, Onslaught, Onslow, Whitehall* and *Wrestler*.

The returning convoy *RA 55A* which sailed from Murmansk on the 23rd consisted of twenty-two empty merchant vessels with an escort of eight destroyers, *Musketeer, Opportune, Virago, Milne, Meteor, Ashanti, Athabascan* and *Matchless*. Close support was given by the 8-inch-gun cruiser *Norfolk* and the 6-inch-gun cruisers

*Sheffield* and *Belfast*, with Rear-Admiral Burnett flying his flag in the latter. To counter and hopefully trap *Scharnhorst* in its expected foray, Admiral Fraser, in the battleship *Duke of York*, with the cruiser *Jamaica* and the destroyers *Savage, Scorpion, Saumarez* and *Stord*, sailed north-eastward trying to shadow the convoy but keeping far enough distant not to betray his presence.

Although German reconnaissance planes had been keeping a constant watch on *JW 55B* during its eastward voyage, it was unaware of the shadowing British battle group some 400 miles to the west. At 14.00 on Christmas Day, Dönitz ordered *Scharnhorst*, escorted by five destroyers, to proceed northward at 25 knots, to intercept and attack.

Dönitz had so much belief in the success of the operation that he claimed, 'The convoy cannot hope to escape.' It proved to a measure of ill-considered confidence. At the last minute the sailing had to be postponed to allow Bey to be transferred from *Tirpitz* to *Scharnhorst* to take command, there to carry his flag, and it was not until 19.00 that day that the battle-cruiser headed out into the Barents Sea. Then, typical of Arctic conditions, the weather worsened, slowing the advance of every ship in that ocean.

It was not at all to Admiral Fraser's liking, for he was well aware that, if a surface attack were to develop, he would be too far away to give it the protection he had so carefully planned. To make matters worse, Burnett's ships were now far to the east, covering the returning convoy *RA 55A*. Fraser was so concerned that he took the unprecedented step – and indeed calculated risk – of breaking radio silence by ordering the escort commander of *JW 55B* to decrease the speed of the convoy for at least three hours while his own force increased speed to 19 knots to lessen the gap. While this measure reduced the distance by 100 miles, his own destroyers over the long haul at that speed were burning more fuel, and this would mean that his action in the battle area might be limited. The continued presence of German reconnaissance planes and shadowing U-boats, by comparison with the apparent undetection of the homeward-bound convoy *RA 55A*, made it obvious which of the two had been selected for attack.

Now came further deterioration in the weather, for the wind from the south-west built up the sea into giant waves which made it increasingly difficult for the lumbering cargo ships and their slow-moving escorts. Even the great 30,000-ton *Duke of York* was tossed around like a cork as the gale increased in fury.

As time passed, it appeared that the enemy had still failed to spot the homeward convoy, and with this seeming advantage Fraser again broke radio silence, directing Burnett to divert his charges further northward and to release four destroyers of the escort force, to speed west to reinforce *JW 55B*. Their joining the eastward-bound convoy brought its defensive strength to fourteen destroyers, a force which, if attacked by German surface ships, would be the type of opposition they feared.

Conditions for radio reception and transmission in the Arctic were uncertain but they had a compensating factor: German radio intelligence apparently failed to detect Fraser's two transmissions. This was indeed fortunate, for if they had been intercepted, Bey would no doubt have been recalled from his mission. As it was, *Duke of York* sped on towards the anticipated battle area, with the enemy totally unaware of her presence at sea.

In reviewing the situation on Christmas Day at command headquarters, while *Scharnhorst* was heading north, Dönitz said, 'A convoy carrying war material for Russia and protected by a cruiser escort that is no match for our battleship, is sailing through an area within easy reach of our battle group. Its position, course and speed are known ... with the superior speed of the German ships it cannot hope to avoid our attack.'

It appeared at first that Bey was to be given considerable latitude in his plan of attack, with discretion to use his own initiative. However, exactly like Kummetz a year earlier, Bey received a qualifying signal from Naval Command stating that a concerted attack would be permissible only if weather conditions and visibility were favourable but to disengage if heavy forces were encountered.

Despite the deteriorating weather *Scharnhorst* raced on, powering her way through the great seas, but it was a far different story for the accompanying destroyers. Their 5.9-inch guns gave them topweight and made them roll dangerously in the heavy swell.

Then, at midnight, fortunately for the British, Bey made his first mistake in a sequence of errors: he broke radio silence by transmitting messages to Group North concerning weather conditions, with further information that destroyer action might be drastically reduced by the intensity of the gale. The unconsoling reply stated that, if destroyer engagement was impossible, *Scharnhorst* would have to pursue the enemy alone. At Ultra Secret's headquarters at Bletchley Park near London, British intelligence's listening service picked up the report, decoded it and immediately passed it to *Duke of York*.

Fraser received the message in the early hours of the morning of the 26th. It was the signal he had been waiting for: 'Admiralty appreciates *Scharnhorst* at sea.' His intuition and logic had been proved correct. The situation in the area of operations at this time could be summed up as follows:

1   *Scharnhorst* was about 100 miles from the convoy, steering north with her five destroyers.
2   Convoy *RA 55A*, westbound, was 200 miles west of Bear Island, moving at 8 knots, its presence unknown to the enemy.
3   Vice-Admiral Burnett's cruisers were 150 miles east of the convoy *JW 55B*, heading west at 18 knots.
4   Convoy *JW 55B*, eastbound, was fifty miles south of Bear Island, being trailed by a U-boat, the latter constantly updating information on the course and speed of the convoy.
5   Admiral Fraser with his battleship force was some 200 miles to the south-west of convoy *JW 55B*, steering east at 25 knots. Speed had been increased after receiving the intercepted message concerning *Scharnhorst*.

Again tempting fortune, Fraser twice more broke radio silence, between 04.00 and 07.00 that morning, first ordering Burnett to report his position and secondly directing the convoy to steer north-east, thereby increasing *Scharnhorst*'s difficulty in finding it and at the same time advancing his own chances of intercepting the battle-cruiser's escape route back to Alten Fiord. But Fraser's luck held, for the enemy again failed to detect the transmission. The Admiral's planned operation was beginning to take shape, for he now knew the exact position of the two convoys with their escorts and in all probability that of the enemy. The trap was set.

Bey, on the other hand, was receiving misleading and outdated reports from German intelligence. One stated that no British support ships had been detected within fifty miles of the eastbound convoy, but that was dated the afternoon of the previous day. He now made his second mistake. At 07.00, assuming that he was not far distant from the convoy, he turned south-west and ordered his destroyers to fan out ahead and investigate. This move brought them against a head-on sea and the fury of the gale. As a result, speed had to be reduced to an insignificant 10 knots, but as a consequence he was dissipating the power of his strike force. He then made a further mistake: without informing his destroyers, at 08.20 Bey suddenly altered course to the north and increased speed. Unwittingly he was on a bearing converging with Burnett's cruisers, and the range fell rapidly.

At 08.40 the inevitable happened: *Belfast*'s radar picked up *Scharnhorst* at a distance of seventeen miles, and the British force, increasing speed, continued to close. It was at 09.20 that *Sheffield* sighted the German at a range of 6½ miles, and three minutes later *Belfast* illuminated the enemy in the Arctic twilight with a burst of starshells.

That morning, at 09.29, the Battle of North Cape began with the 8-inch gun cruiser *Norfolk* scoring direct hits on *Scharnhorst*, destroying her forward radar, causing casualties and starting fires on the lower deck.

Bey had been taken completely by surprise and turned his ship rapidly away to the south-east. His orders were to sink the convoy, not to engage in a gun duel with the British force. With her superior speed, she soon drew ahead of the cruisers and steered north again aiming to reach *JW 55B*. But shrewdly anticipating the move, Burnett headed directly for the convoy to form a defensive screen ten miles ahead of it. Historians have argued that Bey could have held his ground and, with his superior armament, outgunned the British cruisers, but he was now without his destroyers, which were slogging it out some miles to the west. In an attempt to retrieve the situation, he recalled them.

All this while *Duke of York* was steadily closing the gap from the west. The bait to lure *Scharnhorst* was the convoy, with Burnett's cruisers forming the spring of the trap. When by noon Bey had failed to make contact with the British, he repeated his earlier mistake, again depleting his force, ordering his destroyers to re-commence their search for the convoy. By this time they were well to the east and were obliged to turn again and battle their way to the west against the wind and giant seas.

At 12.05 *Belfast* signalled that her radar had picked up the *Scharnhorst* at a distance of fifteen miles, and at 12.20, as *Sheffield* sighted the enemy, all three cruisers opened fire at just over five miles. Once again *Scharnhorst* turned away, which prevented the British destroyers firing their torpedoes at her.

There now followed a gun duel in which *Norfolk* suffered

badly from two direct hits by 11-inch shells. A turret was destroyed, causing many casualties, and the radar was damaged.

*Scharnhorst*'s superior speed was proving its worth, for the British cruisers dropped further and further astern. It became alarmingly clear to Bey that the British had a remarkably efficient radar system. Twice in the dark and the gale they had found him and mounted an attack. He was no doubt reflecting on the earlier cautionary instructions from Naval Command not to take unnecessary risks, and he must have considered the possibility of abandoning the attack on the convoy. At 12.40, with the British cruisers still following him at a distance, he made the firm decision to call off the action and steered south-east for home at 28 knots. He was, however, on a bearing which was to bring him straight into the guns of *Duke of York* and *Jamaica*, converging from the west.

At 13.00 Bey received a transmitted report from the Luftwaffe Group Lofoten to the effect that a reconnaissance plane had located some small ships and one large to the west (this was the *Duke of York* group). Unfortunately for Bey, the repeat omitted any reference to one large ship. If the message had been correctly transmitted, he would almost certainly have assumed that it was a battleship covering force approaching from that direction. He could then have plotted the possible interception point and acted accordingly. But Bey did not appear to have sensed any danger, for he held fixedly on his course towards the quiet waters of the Norwegian fiord. All this time, his destroyers were still doggedly heading west into the storm, searching for *JW 55B*, and they almost succeeded, for at about 13.00 they passed within nine miles of it – without sighting anything. At 14.00 Bey ordered them to 'break off the action'. Captain Johannsen, the flotilla leader, at once queried the signal, asking if it applied only to the attack on the convoy or to the whole operation. Minutes later came the signal 'Return to base.'

It was an order which Bey was bitterly to regret.

Throughout that afternoon, Burnett with his cruisers and the four destroyers settled down to shadow the enemy ship while still maintaining contact with *Duke of York*, providing information on the enemy's course and speed. Unknown to Bey, his ship was surely and steadily moving into the trap which Fraser in his plan of action had rehearsed with *Jamaica*.

At 16.17, while the enemy ship was twenty-two miles away,

she was located by *Duke of York*'s radar, the German still unaware of the British battleship's presence. The net was tightening, and by 16.32 *Duke of York*'s gunnery radar picked up *Scharnhorst* at a range of fourteen miles. Fifteen minutes later the British ship swung around to starboard to allow her turrets to bear and then, with *Belfast*, fired starshells to illuminate the enemy. As the bright falling lights lit up the area and the British ships closed, it could be clearly seen that *Scharnhorst* still had her guns trained fore and aft. The final phase of the Battle of North Cape had begun.

At 16.50 the ten 14-inch guns of *Duke of York* and the twelve 6-inch of *Jamaica* thundered out to inflict much damage on the enemy ship. Bey's immediate reaction was to turn away to port, northward, but he now came under fire from the approaching British cruisers on his left flank and had to turn to starboard again. *Scharnhorst*, after recovering from the initial shock, began to retaliate with shooting which became uncomfortably accurate for the British ships.

Almost imperceptibly Bey's battle-cruiser with her extra speed began to outstrip the British ships, and to Admiral Fraser, closely watching the relative speed on the radar screen, there came the disquieting feeling that, despite the maximum effort given by all those under his command, the enemy might escape. But as *Scharnhorst* gradually increased the distance between herself and her pursuers, so the trajectory of the British battleship's 14-inch shells became steeper, forming a parabola, thus increasing the logical probability that the angle of impact would fall directly on target, causing cataclysmic damage through her armoured decking. Just after 18.00 two of *Scharnhorst*'s turrets were destroyed and her no. 1 boiler-room was so badly damaged that she was forced to reduce speed.

*Scharnhorst* was alone, and Bey was now having to pay the penalty for dismissing his destroyers. As more and more shells hit the battle-cruiser, he dispatched a signal to German Naval Command – 'We shall fight to the last shell.' It was an acceptance of the inevitable. It was now the turn of the British destroyers, and *Savage, Saumarez, Scorpion* and *Stord* came racing in, braving the guns of the enemy to fire torpedoes. In this head-on attack, at least four torpedoes smashed into the hull of the German.

At 19.00 both *Duke of York* and *Jamaica* re-opened fire at a range of only five miles, scoring repeated hits on the stricken ship, causing fires and heavy explosions which soon reduced her to a floating wreck. Closing in, *Jamaica* and *Belfast* each fired three torpedoes, followed by further attacks by the destroyers.

Although *Scharnhorst* fought bravely on, using her smaller guns, by 19.20 such was her list that none of her guns could bear on her attackers, and after one enormous explosion at 19.45 she moved forward, her bows deepening, rolled over and disappeared. Of her complement of almost 2,000, only thirty-six were saved.

In reviewing the engagement, it could be pleaded that, aware of the limitations under which he sailed, the receipt of delayed and incorrect information, and his tragic mistake in the deliberate dispersal of his destroyers, Bey's chances of survival were slim. On the other hand, British strategy under shrewd leadership and by brilliant anticipation, co-operation between battleship, cruisers and destroyers, had gained a decisive victory.

This Battle of North Cape constituted the last time that battleships were engaged in a running fight in the style of the First World War Battle of Jutland without the participation of aircraft, apart from those acting in a reconnaissance role.

# 17  The Allies Take the Offensive

*By the opening of 1944, the Allies on all fronts had gained the initiative, with Hitler's massive war-machine in the Soviet Union being not only stopped in its tracks but driven back. With the opening of the Second Front by the invasion of Normandy in June, Hitler had to withdraw some of his forces from the Soviet Union, which brought greater defeat to his fleeing troops on that front. It was the beginning of the end.*

By December 1943 the German position on the Soviet military front had markedly deteriorated. In January that year the Soviets had launched a massive offensive which forced back the German Sixth Army led by General von Paulus, until they were pinned down in a small area only eight miles long and four miles wide. By the end of that month, von Paulus and his staff were captured, with only 90,000 prisoners, all that remained out of a quarter of a million men. It was a disaster of the first magnitude, and it destroyed Hitler's dreams to conquer the Soviet Union by sheer weight of highly trained armies. As the Soviet offensive grew in power and the bitter winter intensified, so the German armies were forced further and further westward.

All the ground that the Nazis had gained in 1942 had been lost, and they were now 250 miles from Moscow and still retreating. They had suffered terrible losses in men and material, and it was clear that the turning-point had been reached. Heavy bombing by British and American forces on German industrial centres had forced the Luftwaffe into a defensive position, and in North Africa Rommel's so-called invincible army had collapsed, with the capture of a million or more prisoners.

Following the sinking of *Scharnhorst*, Admiral Dönitz was

summoned to Hitler's headquarters to explain the loss of this fine ship. A humiliating experience indeed. A further setback had been the serious damage caused to the great battleship *Tirpitz* when two British midget submarines managed to penetrate the defences at Alten Fiord in Norway and attach four two-ton charges of Amatol to the hull of the ship, which, when exploded, caused massive damage and put her out of action for over six months.

The threat to British convoys was thus diminished but, in a determined efforts to halt further convoys through the Arctic, the number of U-boats on patrol was increased. A desperate move, for by now the Germans were suffering one defeat after another on many fronts.

Following further successes on the Eastern Front, the Soviet armies pushed back their invaders to the borders of Poland and Romania, and the Normandy invasion was imminent. The Second Front opened in June with the invasion of Normandy, much to the delight and relief of the Soviets, who were paying a high price in men in their bid to drive out the enemy. By the end of hostilities the Soviet Union had lost 20 million people in their bid to defeat Hitler.

Knowing the incredible capability of the enemy to repair war damage, the British government decided that a further attempt should be made from the air to destroy *Tirpitz*, and on 12 November 1944 twenty-eight Lancaster bombers launched a raid, each carrying a 12,000-pound blockbuster bomb. Once over the target they set about the destruction of the ship that had imposed such a threat to the Home Fleet and to the convoy route to the Soviet Union. Most of the bombs were on target, scoring direct hits on the mighty battleship, and following one enormous explosion the 43,000-ton *Tirpitz* capsized, her masts resting on the sea bed. In a matter of minutes the pride of the German Navy had been destroyed, having never fired a shot in anger.

Although in the winter of 1944–5 the Germans' tentative move was made to resume attacks on the remaining convoys, the escorts now had the upper hand, resulting in the destruction of several U-boats and many attacking aircraft. By the spring of 1945 the German position was hopeless. However, the excitement and anticipation of pending victory were subdued by the sudden death on 12 April of President Roosevelt.

By 25 April the Soviet armies were on the outskirts of east Berlin, with the Allies poised on the western side. Germany was cut in two, and the Nazi nation doomed. With the ever-increasing sound of nearing bombardment ringing in his ears, Hitler, hiding in his bunker in Berlin, shot himself. Outside in the streets, the so-called glorious Third Reich lay in ruins. In Italy, more than a million troops laid down their arms, and on 2 May 1945 General Montgomery accepted the surrender of over 2½ million men. This was the end.

On 7 May the instrument of total and unconditional surrender was signed, bringing to a close a war which had laid waste vast areas of Europe, destroyed hundreds of cities and towns and been responsible for the annihilation of over 30 million people. That war might have been averted if, in the years of Germany's rise, strong measures had been taken to restrain the Nazis' aggressive policy and to strengthen Britain's forces; the latter would undoubtedly have deterred Hitler from his territorial ambitions and saved the world from a tyranny never surpassed in the dark, lamentable catalogue of human suffering. It was the Roman general Flavius Vegetius who in AD 375 said, 'Let him who desires peace prepare for war.'

Although by the close of hostilities the Allies had disposed of all the German battleships, cruisers and destroyers and sunk 900 of their U-boats, their own losses in ships and men had been most grievous. In the Arctic alone, the cost of maintaining the convoy route to north Russia cost over a hundred merchant ships and nineteen warships, resulting in the deaths of nearly 900 merchant seamen and nearly 2,000 officers and men of the Royal Navy. But Britain had redeemed her promise to the Soviet Union.

In the sea war covering all theatres of combat Britain had lost

     5  battleships
   34  cruisers
    8  aircraft-carriers
 144  destroyers
  77  submarines
  56  sloops
  40  corvettes
  11  frigates
  14  armed merchant cruisers
       and over 2,000 miscellaneous armed vessels

But Britain and her allies had gained the victory and, despite all the blood, sweat and tears, despite the cost, had preserved that priceless gift for which man has striven throughout the ages – FREEDOM. How fitting were Churchill's words in 1942:

What Hitler has done, is to kindle a fire in British hearts here and all over the world, which will glow long after all traces of the conflagration he has caused has been removed. He has lighted a fire which will burn with a steady and consuming flame until the last vestiges of Nazi tyranny have been burnt out of Europe and until the Old World – and the New – can join hands to rebuild the temples of man's freedom and man's honour, upon the foundations, which will not soon or easily be overcome.

These words were prophetic. On 8 May 1945, Churchill was to despatch the following signal to the Fleet.

For the second time since the battle of Trafalgar sea power, relentlessly applied, has preserved and sustained our Nation and Commonwealth and led to the decisive defeat of Germany and her European associates. The Board of Admiralty congratulate all officers and men upon their share in this great victory, confident that the fortitude, skill and tenacity which have made it possible will be displayed with the same distinction and effect in the task yet to be completed in the Far East.

# 18    The Battle of Leyte Gulf

*To return to the last year of World War II, in the Pacific during 1944, the Americans, under the leadership of General MacArthur, engaged the Japanese in a bitter campaign to achieve victory in the Philippines. It involved the rebuilt US naval forces in such a mammoth and decisive battle in Leyte Gulf that it almost destroyed what remained of the imperial Japanese navy.*

Almost 2½ years had passed since the Battle of Midway – years in which the Americans had thrown off the mantle of desperate defence and adopted a resolute offensive role. In that period they had thrust seaward and westward, conquering Japanese-held islands, establishing air and naval bases for the next objective and applying their energies to rebuilding their decimated navy after the attack on Pearl Harbor.

By August 1944 Admiral Chester Nimitz and General Douglas MacArthur, working side by side, although often with differing views, had overrun most of New Guinea and taken the Gilbert, Admiralty, Marshall, Caroline and Solomon Islands, Guam and Saipan, where Vice-Admiral Chuichi Nagumo of Pearl Harbor and Midway battles was killed. Only two months earlier, the Americans had won a victory of epic proportions in the Battle of the Philippine Sea, where the Japanese lost 269 aircraft out of 326 and three aircraft-carriers. Reeling under such defeat, the Japanese were hard put to mount a really effective defence or retaliatory strike. This was due in part to their failure to recognize the importance of the new concept of air power in war.

Admiral Yamamoto had been the primary supporter of air control but with his death the navy gave precedence to its first

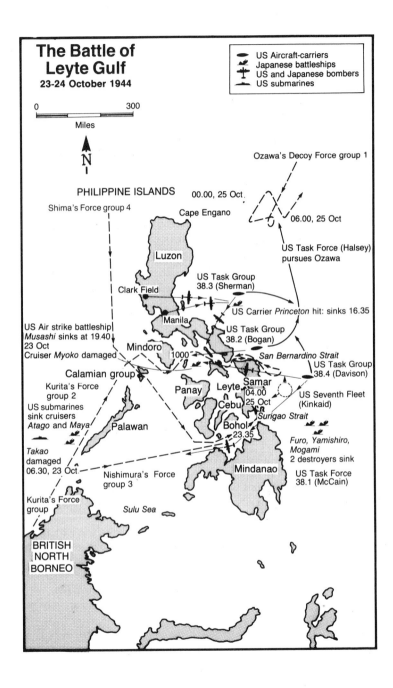

# The Battle of Leyte Gulf
## 23-24 October 1944

US Aircraft-carriers
Japanese battleships
US and Japanese bombers
US submarines

0        300

Miles

N

PHILIPPINE ISLANDS

Ozawa's Decoy Force group 1

00.00, 25 Oct.

Shima's Force group 4

Cape Engano

06.00, 25 Oct

Luzon

US Task Force (Halsey) pursues Ozawa

Clark Field

US Task Group 38.3 (Sherman)

US Carrier *Princeton* hit: sinks 16.35

Manila

US Air strike battleship *Musashi* sinks at 19.40 23 Oct
Cruiser *Myoko* damaged

US Task Group 38.2 (Bogan)

Mindoro

San Bernardino Strait

1000

US Task Group 38.4 (Davison)

Calamian group

Panay

Leyte

Samar

Kurita's Force group 2

US submarines sink cruisers *Atago* and *Maya*

Cebu

04.00 25 Oct

US Seventh Fleet (Kinkaid)

Palawan

Bohol

*Surigao* Strait

*Takao* damaged 06.30, 23 Oct

23.35

*Furo, Yamishiro, Mogami*
2 destroyers sink

Nishimura's Force group 3

Mindanao

US Task Force 38.1 (McCain)

Kurita's Force group

*Sulu Sea*

BRITISH NORTH BORNEO

favour, the battleship. By 1943 the industrial might of the United States had produced another twenty-two aircraft-carriers, while Japan had built only three and had failed to recruit and train sufficient pilots to operate the planes they had. As the quality of the new recruits fell, so the losses increased. During the two years from 1942 to 1944, Japan had suffered the loss of 8,000 planes and an enormous number of pilots. A typical example of this occurred in June 1944 during the re-taking of Saipan, the key Japanese fortress in the Marianas, when nine Japanese carriers with 370 aircraft met fifteen American carriers with over 900 aircraft. This battle became known as 'the Great Marianas Turkey Shoot', for 320 Japanese planes were lost and several battleships, carriers and cruisers sunk. The loss of Saipan was also a psychological blow, for it provided the Americans with a natural bomber base from which to strike against Tokyo, 1,350 miles away.

As the year wore on, MacArthur adopted a new strategy with far-reaching results. His policy of a slogging conquest of one island after another was proving too slow. The alternative was a leap-frogging tactic of annihilating the weakest resistance and bypassing the strongest garrisons, leaving them to wither through lack of supplies.

Immediately after the defeat suffered by the Japanese in the Philippine Sea and the capture of Saipan and Guam, it seemed that a fearless and determined leap across the thousand miles of sea from New Guinea to Leyte in the central Philippines was a reasonable proposition. Yet MacArthur did not altogether approve of taking such a big bite of the apple in one go. He preferred a strike at the island of Mindanao at the southern tip of the Philippines. There were others, however, such as Admiral E.J.King, Commander-in-Chief of the entire United States Fleet, and his operational admiral, C. Nimitz, who stressed the need to bypass the Philippines altogether and make a concerted attack on the island of Formosa (Taiwan), another thousand miles north, nearer Japan itself. This met with the strongest opposition from MacArthur, mainly for two reasons: he argued that failure to recapture the Philippines would dishonour the United States for many years to come, as he had given a promise to the islanders that he would return; he also saw it as an opportunity to eliminate the remainder of the Japanese fleet and thus diminish resistance in the drive to Tokyo. Such was the disagreement between King and MacArthur that President Roosevelt felt compelled to arrange a meeting at

Pearl Harbor where, with their chiefs of staff, some compromise could be reached. Finally it was agreed that Leyte should be the next target, followed by Luzon in the north of the group, action date to be mid-December.

Possession of the Philippines was critical for the Japanese, for the loss of these islands would deny them the resources of the Dutch East Indies, where they controlled vast quantities of oil, rubber and tin. By 1943 Japan was facing an extreme oil shortage, simply because priority had been given to battleships instead of merchant transports to maintain supplies.

It so happened that only one week after the Pearl Harbor meeting Admiral Halsey, Admiral Spruance's successor as commander of the 3rd Fleet, launched a probing raid in the Philippines and discovered that Japanese resistance was weak. Moving north, he attacked Formosa. The Japanese command thought that the big invasion had begun and committed hordes of their aircraft. For the loss of seventy-nine planes and two cruisers damaged, Halsey's force destroyed nearly 600 Japanese aircraft. In the light of this success the date for the invasion of the Philippines at Leyte Gulf was advanced to 20 October.

Following one withdrawal after another from their earlier conquests, the Japanese had foreseen the invasion of the islands even before the Americans had planned their campaign. Gone were the dreams of colonialism – all that remained now was survival. By August Japan had drawn up a number of SHO (victory) plans, aimed at defeating the enemy. The most immediate was SHO 1, dealing with the Philippines, the rest covering the strategic defence of the Homelands from Formosa to the Kuriles.

SHO 1 embraced a complexity of divided forces based on a diversionary tactic. The Japanese fleet was divided into four groups:

Group 1 was the northern force under Vice-Admiral Ozawa, built around the carriers *Zuikaka, Zuiho, Chitose* and *Chiyoda*, with three cruisers and eight destroyers. There were also two battleship carriers with no planes, and only 115 planes on all the four carriers.

Group 2, under Vice-Admiral Kurita, comprised the giant battleships *Yamato* and *Musashi* and the battleships *Nagato, Haruna* and *Kongo*, plus ten cruisers and fifteen destroyers.

Group 3, under Vice-Admiral Nishimura, was made up of battleships *Furo* and *Yamashiro*, a cruiser and four destroyers.

Group 4, under Vice-Admiral Shima, comprised three cruisers and nine destroyers.

The objective, based on surprise, was to eliminate American warships, destroy the troop-landing forces and escape before the US fleet could recover. The necessary ingredient to make this possible was for Ozawa's force to act as live bait by an ostentatious approach from the north to lure Admiral Halsey's 3rd Fleet away from Leyte while the three other Japanese forces penetrated the Philippine archipelago, Kurita sailing around the southern tip of Mindora through the San Bernardino Strait, Nishimura to the north of Mindanao through the Surigao Strait, while Shima from the north-west joined him to support the attack.

American intelligence had failed to learn of Ozawa's decoy plan – something that nearly led to disaster. It was inevitable that Japan would retaliate and, in order to foil any counter-bid, US Naval Command had gathered the most powerful fleet to sail. American Task Force 38 had been organized into four task groups, all deployed on the eastern side of the Philippines, under the overall command of Admiral Halsey. To the north, Task Group 38.3, commanded by Vice-Admiral Sherman, was stationed about a hundred miles off Luzon, comprising the carriers *Princeton, Lexington, Langley* and *Essex*, two battleships, *Indiana* and *Massachusetts*, four cruisers and twelve destroyers.

One hundred and fifty miles south of this and closely guarding the San Bernardino Strait, Task Group 38.2, commanded by Vice-Admiral Bogan, was stationed with four carriers *Independence, Intrepid, Bunker Hill* and *Hancock*, two battleships, *New Jersey* and *Iowa*, three cruisers and fifteen destroyers.

Another 150 miles further south, Task Group 38.4, under Vice-Admiral Davison, with the carriers *Enterprise, San Jacinto, Franklin* and *Balleau Wood*, two battleships, *Alabama* and *Washington*, two cruisers and fifteen destroyers, covered the air space over the Sibuyan Sea and the Surigao Strait.

Task Group 38.1, commanded by Vice-Admiral McCain, had been dispatched south to Ulithi to refuel.

Additional to this, the US 7th Fleet, under the command of Vice-Admiral Kinkaid, positioned itself east of the mouth of the Surigao Strait.

By 17 October, in advance of the invasion, minesweepers had cleared the channels into Leyte Gulf, while the 6th Ranger Infantry Battalion had captured the four small islands adjacent to the gulf.

On the 18th and 19th battleships and cruisers of the 7th Fleet bombarded the beaches and enemy emplacements near the landing-areas, while aircraft from the distant carriers strafed Japanese airfields and defences in the surrounding areas.

By Invasion Day, 20 October, all was ready. That morning the first wave of troops landed on the beaches, followed by General MacArthur himself, proud to proclaim that he had kept his promise to the late president of the Philippines, Manuel Quezon, to return and free the islands. In the next few days nearly 150,000 men and a quarter of a million tons of supplies were landed without interruption. Further inland, American infantry were busy rooting out the 50,000 Japanese who had dug themselves in. In the overall operation, an armada of over a thousand ships had been employed, including carriers, battleships, cruisers, destroyers and tank- and landing-craft.

During this operation, although the Japanese were conspicuous by their absence, their battle groups were in fact already at sea, heading for the central Philippines. Kurita, with his five battleships and escorting cruisers and destroyers, was heading direct for the Sibuyan Sea and the San Bernardino Strait, while splitting away from Nishimura force steaming east across the Sulu Sea towards the Surigao Strait. Meanwhile Shima's force was speeding south to join up with Nishimura for a joint penetration of the US defences, and to the north Ozawa's decoy force moved steadily south towards Halsey's force, hoping to be discovered.

In the early morning of 23 October the US submarines *Darter* and *Dace* made contact with Kurita's ships approaching the Sibuyan Sea. The leading cruiser, Kurita's flagship *Atago*, was hit by two torpedoes and sank within minutes, forcing the admiral to transfer his flag to the giant battleship *Yamato*. Only minutes later another cruiser was sunk and a third so heavily damaged that she could take no further part in the operation. The advance warning made to Halsey by the submarines gave the admiral ample time to deploy his carrier groups nearer the San Bernardino Strait, from where Kurita would be expected to emerge. But Japanese units based at Luzon had already detected the presence of US ships and launched heavy air attacks, particularly on Admiral Sherman's task group to the north. Despite intensive anti-aircraft fire and Wildcat air patrol in which many Japanese planes were destroyed, one enemy plane penetrated the defences and bombed the carrier *Princeton*, which later sank.

However, the Japanese being thus occupied allowed Task Group

38.2 (Bogan) and Task Group 38.4 (Davison) to launch their torpedo and bomber planes against Kurita's fleet without being unduly harassed. Some 250 aircraft took part in the attack, determined to exact revenge for the sinking of *Princeton*. Their targets were the giant battleships *Yamato* and *Musashi*, each mounting 120 anti-aircraft guns. *Musashi* took the main impact of the attacks but, despite being hit by ten torpedoes and six heavy bombs, her 24-inch thick steel turrets, 16-inch side armour and 8-inch deck plating withstood the bombardment. It took another eight torpedoes and ten bombs before she finally capsized and sank, taking over a thousand officers and men with her. Kurita's distress call for air cover from Luzon met with no response, and by the time the attack was over, Kurita had lost eight ships (one battleship, two cruisers and five destroyers). Smarting under the damage inflicted, Kurita pulled his ships westward to regroup. His was still a formidable force, and although there was now little chance of keeping his rendezvous with Nishimura's fleet near Leyte Gulf, he again turned his ships eastward towards the San Bernardino Strait to launch another attack.

To the south, Nishimura's fleet, comprising the battleships *Furo* and *Yamashiro*, the heavy cruiser *Mogami* and four destroyers, headed on towards Leyte Gulf, followed several hours behind by Shima's group of three cruisers and nine destroyers. With no time to wait for Shima's force to catch up with him, Nishimura pressed on with his planned objective, the annihilation of MacArthur's invasion troops on Leyte.

When Nishimura's ships were spotted by American reconnaissance planes in the early morning of the 24th, Admiral Kinkaid, commanding the 7th Fleet, calculated that the enemy would converge on the gulf through the Surigao Strait that night; and he, with Rear-Admiral Oldendorf, set about the deployment of their ships to trap the approaching enemy: and he made his plans accordingly. A fleet of torpedo boats and destroyers was sent through the strait during the night to attack and give advance warning to Kinkaid. As the Japanese ships neared, the US destroyers launched their attacks. It was the first act in a double massacre.

The battleship *Furo* was hit first; burning fiercely and rocked by explosions, she quickly dropped out of line. Then *Yamashiro* received two direct hits, and three of the four destroyers were quickly sunk or disabled. This action left Nishimura with his one damaged battleship, *Yamashiro*, the cruiser *Mogami* and the

surviving destroyer *Shigure*, but still he pressed on. As he turned into
the final section of the strait, he found, blocking his way, five
American battleships waiting silently, like ghosts of the past, most
resurrected from the seabed of Pearl Harbor. But these were no
shadowy, imponderable monuments of the débâcle of December
1941 but tangible, material Nemeses, each of 45,000 tons of avenging steel and hungry guns. Here were the old battleships *California,
Tennessee, West Virginia, Maryland and Mississippi*, most of which
had been sunk to lie on the mud in Pearl Harbor after that attack.
Now, expecting the signal from Oldendorf to open fire, they waited,
guns loaded, ships turned at right-angles to allow full broadsides.

As though committing himself and his ships to self-destruction,
Nishimura came on, taking no evasive action. At 04.00 Oldendorf
gave the order 'Open fire.' At once, devastating broadsides of
14-inch and 16-inch shells from the great battleships blasted the
oncoming Japanese vessels. In the ensuing twenty minutes over 250
14-inch and 16-inch and 3,000 6-inch and 8-inch shells were fired
by the American ships. The result: a holocaust which no ship could
withstand. As the Japanese ships reversed to escape, *Yamishiro* and
*Mogami* were burning fiercely, and minutes later, after being hit by
torpedoes, *Yamishiro* sank quickly, taking Admiral Nishimura and
most of her crew with her.

In the meantime, Admiral Shima, with his three cruisers and nine
destroyers, had entered the Surigao Strait, fully aware of the battle
that raged somewhere ahead, for the flashes of intense gunfire
illuminated the night sky. As he proceeded, he passed the burning
and wrecked hulks of the remnants of Nishimura's fleet and came
upon the shattered *Mogami*, barely moving towards him. In the
confusion that followed, the cruiser *Nachi* collided with *Mogami*,
causing severe damage to her bow. Shima, deciding that discretion
was the better part of valour, withdrew his force, including the
disabled *Mogami*. But Oldendorf had not yet done, and as dawn
appeared, he pursued the enemy through the strait with cruisers
and destroyers and sunk *Mogami* and two more destroyers. Shima's
depleted force, with the only survivor of Nishimura's fleet, the
destroyer *Shigure*, eventually reached the Sulu Sea and escaped.

In this first phase of the Battle of Leyte Gulf, the United States
Navy had won the last naval battle to be fought in a formal line – a
victory made more palatable by the fact that most of the
triumphant ships were those that had been resurrected from the
mud of Pearl Harbor.

Although the American forces had gained a decisive victory over Nishimura's fleet, the rout of Kurita's ships in the San Bernardino Strait had been only partially successful. Matters were made worse by the fact that US pilots had made exaggerated claims, suggesting that Kurita's ships were no longer a force to be reckoned with. Admiral Halsey, accepting this, decided that the greatest threat now stood to the north, where Ozawa's force of four carriers headed south towards him. At that time he had no idea they were 'straw tigers' with few aircraft, intended to lure him away while what was left of the southern forces attacked Leyte. He took the bait – hook, line and sinker – and, having collected the entire 3rd Fleet, raced north, leaving the San Bernardino Strait unprotected.

At this point the misinterpretation of a vital signal almost brought disaster to the Leyte operation. Halsey had signalled to his ships that he proposed to form a small task force to protect the strait, but this, intercepted by Admiral Kinkaid to the south and by Admiral Nimitz overseeing operations at Pearl Harbor, was taken as meaning that he had already done so. In fact, the strait was left virtually unprotected against the heavy battle units led by Kurita, now cautiously navigating his way through. Halsey, heading north, was confident that Kinkaid was maintaining a watchful eye over the area, while Kinkaid for his part was convinced that a guard was already stationed there.

By dawn on the morning of 25 October, Kurita's formidable fleet of four battleships, *Yamato, Nagato, Haruna* and *Kongo*, eight cruisers, *Haguro, Chokai, Kumano, Tone, Suzuya, Atago, Nachi* and *Chikuma*, and eleven destroyers had reached a point a short distance seaward of Leyte Gulf. They were then within range of the American troop anchorages, which were protected only by a light screen of escort carriers under the command of Rear-Admiral Clifton Sprague; an insignificant little force by comparison with the might of Kurita's fleet. Sprague's fleet was made up of six small escort carriers, *Fanshaw Bay, Saint Lo, White Plains, Kitkun Bay, Gambier Bay* and *Kalinin Bay*, and seven destroyers, *Hoel, Johnston, Heermann, Butler, Dennis, Roberts* and *Raymond*, and their escorts. In normal circumstances, a small force such as this, confronted by such a fleet of capital ships, would not have had the slightest chance of survival, but Kurita had no air power to use.

At 06.45, in a heavy rain squall, Sprague's ships were suddenly faced by Kurita's fleet dead ahead. Surprised to find any opposition hindering the onward drive, the flagship *Yamato* opened fire with her 18-inch guns, supported by the cruisers and destroyers. Few actions in naval history can compare with the action that followed, in which a handful of escort carriers challenged a fleet of battleships and heavy cruisers. As the shells splashed around his ships, Sprague turned into the wind, launched the flew planes he had, laid down a smoke-screen and turned away south.

The US planes (Avengers and Wildcats) had frantically been armed with whatever was available – heavy bombs, light bombs, fragmentation bombs, torpedoes and even depth-charges. Amid the smoke and heavy rain that partially hid them, the planes dived down on the enemy ships, causing distraction and confusion. At the same time Sprague's destroyers raced in to within point-blank range before firing their torpedoes. Their courageous action forced *Yamato* to adopt drastic evasive action, thus denying her the advantage of her great guns. During this encounter the cruiser *Kumano* was torpedoed, and soon after the cruiser *Suzuya* was bombed and sunk. In the meantime, Sprague sent urgent signals for help from whatever sources could reach him. Two small escort carrier groups to the south launched their own planes in support, but Kinkaid was virtually out of ammunition, and Halsey, heading north, was much too far away to be of any use. McCain's force, rushing back from its re-fuelling at Ulithi, was still several hundred miles away. Sprague was on his own.

Even though Sprague's pilots eventually ran out of bombs, torpedoes and rockets, they continually dived on the ships below, firing machine-guns, and when this ammunition was used up, they made dry runs across the targets, diverting attention from the troubled escort carriers. But by now the Japanese were finding their targets, and the destroyer *Johnston* was hit by a salvo of shells and sunk. At 09.00 the carrier *Gambier Bay* was set ablaze, and soon after she capsized and sank. Another carrier, *Kalinin Bay*, was hit by a total of fifteen shells.

It was at this point, when Sprague thought that annihilation was inevitable that Kurita, in the rain squalls and the smoke and fire of battle, reached the mistaken conclusion that the escort carriers were big fleet carriers and that the destroyers were cruisers. With two of his own cruisers destroyed and the battleship *Nagato* badly damaged, and fearing the loss of his entire task force, Kurita broke off the action and began to retire, hoping to re-assemble his forces before launching another attack in the gulf. But, as he turned away, US planes from the southern carrier groups arrived in time to sink another two cruisers, *Chokai* and *Chikuma*.

Unfortunately, in the withdrawal, the American ships *Hoel, Saint Lo* and *Roberts* were sunk. These sinkings were brought about by the introduction of the most dreaded weapon of the Pacific War, the kamikaze – suicide – plane. The pilots, sworn to sacrifice their lives for the emperor, deliberately crashed their aircraft, each carrying a 500-pound bomb, onto the deck of US carriers and warships, resulting in sinking the vessel or at least causing incalculable damage.

Now, as Kurita was re-organizing his fleet to strike again, he received the worst possible news. His original orders had been to break through and rendezvous with Nishiruma's force emerging from the Surigao Strait. The report in his hand told him that not only was Nishimura dead but his fleet of battleships, cruisers and destroyers had been virtually wiped out and that Shima's force had withdrawn. Bowing to the inevitable, Kurita gathered his ships and made an ignominious retreat to the west. Again, the greatest naval force Japan had amassed since Midway had been repulsed by a few almost defenceless ships. Once more an action had revealed the vulnerability of capital ships without air protection.

Sprague's frantic calls for help at the beginning of the battle had reached Halsey at a most critical and delicate moment. His powerful 3rd Fleet was about 200 miles east of Cape Engano, the northern tip of Luzon, when he made contact with Ozawa's northern force of four carriers, three cruisers and eight destroyers. By the early morning of the 25th his fleet of over sixty ships, with 700 planes, was in pursuit. Four major strikes were launched with torpedo and bomber planes, resulting in the destruction of all four Japanese carriers and a destroyer. While this was in progress, Halsey began receiving the calls for help from the south. His hesitation to make any move in that direction was, however, decided for him when he received a signal from Admiral Nimitz asking where Task Force 38 was. The inference was clear. In his haste to annihilate Ozawa's force, he had failed to ensure that a sufficiently strong force remained to cover the San Bernardino Strait against the possible return of Kurita. Late that morning, after dispatching a group of cruisers and destroyers in pursuit of Ozawa's crippled fleet, he reluctantly turned south. But it was far too late to catch Kurita now, and although Halsey's force managed to sink two cruisers and two destroyers, the remainder of Ozawa's ships escaped.

Thus ended the Battle of Leyte Gulf, ironically fought away from that area of water. For the loss to the Americans of three light carriers and three destroyers, Japanese losses were three battleships, four carriers, ten cruisers and ten destroyers, and many warships were so badly damaged that they ceased to be a threat in what remained of the Pacific War. The Americans controlled the seas with a massive fleet ready to accept whatever action the Japanese might deliver. The navy of the Rising Sun was beaten and fleeing; now only remnants of their once massive fleet remained. Only the kamikazes were left, supplied from a volunteer source of raw recruits whose lack of flying-skills would prove no obstacle to the ultimate objective.

# 19   The Eclipse of Japan

*The war in the Pacific, which had begun in December 1941, was now drawing to its close, with the Japanese paying the bill in full for the attack on Pearl Harbor. By July 1945 their navy had been virtually destroyed, their great ships lying on the sea bed of the Pacific Ocean. With the dropping of the atom bombs on Hiroshima and Nagasaki, the Land of the Rising Sun surrendered unconditionally, bringing to a close the greatest war in the world's history.*

Despite the Japanese defeat at Leyte, the war was not yet over. The Japanese, who still possessed many of the Pacific islands, stubbornly resisted attempts to dislodge them.

In January 1945 the Americans began the long, hard road to Tokyo. By 5 January American submarines had sunk most of Japan's deep-water merchant shipping, with the result that that month no oil reached the mainland to feed Japan's war-machine. Despite great cost to their troops, the Americans re-occupied the island of Iwo Jima on 19 February, inflicting on the Japanese the loss of all 23,000 of their defenders. Next came Okinawa, defended by 100,000 troops. It took three months before the island was in American hands, such was the stubborn resistance set up by the fanatical Japanese. The cost to the Americans was terrifying: 40,000 casualties, including 12,000 dead, 750 planes destroyed and thirty-five ships sunk. The price to the Japanese was 135,000 killed and 8,000 aircraft destroyed. Apart from the stubborn defence of the island, one reply from the enemy was the impact of its suicide planes, the kamikazes, who deliberately crashed their planes on American warships, causing grievous damage and loss. In three main attacks, over 1,400 suicide planes were involved, resulting by the end of June in the sinking of twenty American vessels.

This campaign gave the Allies a bitter foretaste of what they could expect if they tried to invade the Japanese mainland. It was estimated by the US joint chiefs of staff that, if this was undertaken, the total potential cost could be a million American lives. A way had therefore to be found to force the Japanese into surrender without the planned invasion taking place.

In the meantime, the American air force, its B29 Super-Fortresses now based at Okinawa and the Marianas, made a decisive contribution to the eventual surrender of Japan. On the night of 9 March Major-General Curtis E. LeMay, commander of 21st Bomber Command, mounted a massive raid on Tokyo with a force of over 300 B29s, carrying 2,000 tons of fire bombs. Its three-hour attack was concentrated on downtown Tokyo, a sprawling area of wooden frame buildings. The effect was devastating, for long before the last aircraft had departed, that part of the city was a volcano of crimson flames and swirling yellow gases, with over a quarter of a million buildings destroyed. The number of people killed in this raid – 85,000 – was greater than those to be killed in the atomic bomb drop on Hiroshima in August.

The following day, 310 B29s took off, their target Nagayo, Japan's third-largest city, where 1,800 tons of incendiary bombs were dropped, causing widespread destruction and casualties. On 14 March a similar raid was carried out on Osaka, another congested and inflammable city, destroying nine square miles of factories, steelworks and docks. Two days later a raid was targeted on the port of Kobe. In these last two raids alone, 7,000 people died, 20,000 were injured and 200,000 homes destroyed.

By the end of July the American fleet, with its aircraft-carriers, was able to bomb the remainder of the Japanese fleet, immobile through lack of oil and anchored in home waters.

In strikes including the battle for Okinawa, the Americans destroyed the huge battleship *Yamato*, the cruiser *Yahagi*, the battleships *Haruna, Ise* and *Hyuga*, and the cruisers *Aoba, Oyodo*, and *Tone*, with many destroyers. The Japanese Navy no longer existed. Pearl Harbor had been avenged and the words of the man who had led that raid in 1941, Admiral Nagumo, 'We have this day awakened a sleeping giant', had been proved true.

The destruction of their cities was causing deep concern to the

Japanese cabinet, who now faced a dawning realization that defeat was inevitable. The imperial household wanted to terminate the war, and attempts were made to negotiate a face-saving peace with the then neutral Soviet Union. This ended in failure, due to the immovable stance adopted by the Japanese minister of war, General Anami, who was determined to prosecute the war to the bitter end.

Although the champions of US strategic bombing were still hoping that the effects of this form of attack would force the Japanese into unconditional surrender, the option was fading as peace-feelers collapsed. Alternative ways had to be considered to reach this ultimate objective with the minimum loss of American lives, and as a result, after much heart-searching, it was decided to drop the atomic bomb to precipitate the end of the war.

On 26 July 1945 President Roosevelt issued an ultimatum to Japan for unconditional surrender, the alternative to be utter destruction. The terms were rejected and, despite millions of leaflet warnings dropped on their cities, there was no further response.

As a result, on 6 August the first atomic bomb fell on Hiroshima, resulting in the incineration of 61,000 people, followed by a second, on 9 August, on Nagasaki, killing 35,000. The next day the Japanese Government agreed to accept the ultimatum.

The Allied fleets entered the Bay of Tokyo, and on 2 September the formal surrender was signed on board the United States battleship *Missouri*, in the presence of General MacArthur, almost six years to the day since war had been declared between Great Britain and Germany.

The last chapter in this brief saga of World War II cannot close without a special tribute to the United States and to its president, Franklin D. Roosevelt. The Americans bore the full weight of Japanese aggression in the Pacific which threatened the western flank of the United States – aggression which cost the lives of hundreds of thousands of servicemen and women and which at Pearl Harbor almost destroyed the whole American fleet. Despite this, the president, sharing the agony of Britain's lone fight against what appeared to be its impending destruction, devised Lend Lease aid to send planes and tanks and guns with which Britain was able to stand and fight. It was in those dark days of 1941 that he dispatched to Mr Churchill a letter in his own handwriting quoting the famous lines of Longfellow:

Sail on, O ship of State,
Sail on, O Union strong and great!
Humanity with all its fears,
With all the hopes of future years,
Is hanging breathless on thy fate.

# Bibliography

Becker, Cajus, *Hitler's Naval War* (Macdonald & Jane, 1974)
Busch, Fritz-Otto, *Sinking of the Scharnhorst* (Futura, 1974)
Campbell, Ian, *The Kola Run* (Futura, 1975)
Churchill, Winston, *The Second World War* (Cassell, 1949)
Costello, John, *The Pacific War* (Collins, 1981)
Dove, Patrick, *I Was Graf Spee's Prisoner* (Cherry Tree Books, 1940)
Drake, Millington, *Drama of the Graf Spee* (Peter Davies, 1964)
Grenfell, Russell, *The Bismarck Episode* (Faber & Faber, 1948)
Humble, Richard, *Hitler's High Seas Fleet* (Pan/Ballantine, 1972)
Lund and Ludlam, *PQ 17: Convoy to Hell* (New English Library, 1973)
Macintyre, Donald, *Battle for the Mediterranean* (Batsford, 1964; Pan, 1970)
Newton, D. and Hampshire, A., *Taranto* (W. Kimber, 1959)
Pack, S.W.C., *Battle of Matapan* (Ian Allan, 1972)
Pope, Dudley, *73 North* (Weidenfeld & Nicholson, 1958)
Roskill, Captain, *HMS Warspite* (Futura, 1975)
Schofield, Brian, *The Russian Convoys* (Batsford, 1964; Pan, 1971)
Smith, Ure, *Encyclopedia of Sea Warfare* (Salamander, 1975)
Strabolgi, Lord, *Battle of the River Plate* (Hutchinson, 1940)
Taylor, J.C., *German Warships of World War II* (Ian Allan, 1966)
Wheeler, H., *People's History of the Second World War* (Odhams Press, 1941)
Winton, John, *Find, Fix and Strike* (Batsford, 1982)

# *Index*